Robert Hovda

Edited by John F. Baldovin s.j.

Robert Hovda

The Amen Corner

A PUEBLO BOOK

The Liturgical Press Collegeville, Minnesota

A Pueblo Book published by The Liturgical Press.

Design by Frank Kacmarcik.

Library of Congress Cataloging-in-Publication Data

Hovda, Robert W.
    Robert Hovda : ''the amen corner'' / Robert W. Hovda ; edited by John F. Baldovin.
        p.   cm.
    ''A Pueblo Book.''
    ISBN 0-8146-6150-5
    1. Catholic Church—Liturgy.   I. Baldovin, John Francis.
II. Title.
BX1970.H75   1994
264'.02 — dc20

94-7254
CIP

Contents

Liturgical Presiding/Ministry

Liturgy, Justice, and Peace

Liturgy and the Arts

Preface

In 1983 the editors of *Worship* asked Robert Hovda, a veteran of the liturgical movement, to contribute a monthly column on liturgy. Some forty-seven essays, entitled "The Amen Corner," were the result. Several years ago I started asking Bob to collect a number of these gems into a book to serve a wider public. He would always respond with characteristic gruffness that the pieces were not good enough, too disconnected, too time-bound, and so forth. It was a great sadness for the Church and particularly for the movement toward liturgical renewal when Robert Hovda died suddenly on 5 February 1992. Not long afterward, it seemed to me that Bob had been too modest about the value of the pieces reprinted here and so I proposed that they be collected in one volume. Fr Michael Naughton O.S.B. of The Liturgical Press was kind enough to agree.

I have entitled this collection *Robert Hovda: "The Amen Corner."* These pages include thirty-one of his "Amen Corners" from *Worship,* including his valuable contribution to the aesthetics of the liturgy in "The Vesting of Liturgical Ministers," and, as a kind of epilogue, a fitting tribute to his life and work in his own words, his response to the North American Academy of Liturgy's Berakah Award for 1982.

These essays reveal Robert Hovda as a master pastoral liturgist. To him the phrase "pastoral liturgist" was similar to "institutional church." As he liked to repeat about the latter — "there ain't no other kind." For him, no one could truly be engaged in the serious study of liturgy without becoming passionate about what it means for the life of the church and the individual Christian today — indeed for the life of the world. In these pages you will see that Hovda never loses sight of a powerful vision of a society blessed by gospel peace and justice and powered by the living church, alive particularly in the liturgy, that "primary and indispensable source." In fact, more than a collection of disparate pieces on various facets of the liturgy, these essays show a marvelous coherence in what we could call a "liturgical ecclesiology," with a vibrant worshiping assembly at its center.

Moreover, not only what Hovda has written makes these essays worth reprinting and (for many I hope) re-reading, but how he has expressed it. Let one example — from "The Vesting of Liturgical Ministers" — suffice:

"Good liturgical celebration, like a parable, takes us by the hair of our heads, lifts us momentarily out of the cesspool of injustice we call home, puts us in the promised and challenging reign of God, where we are treated like we have never been treated anywhere else . . . where we are bowed to and sprinkled and censed and kissed and touched and where we share equally among all a holy food and drink."

I have always found Hovda's style both refreshing and stimulating. He can be inspiring, sensible, caustic, sardonic, gentle, critical, visionary, lyrical, wise — often all within the same piece! He is certainly never dull. You will find a good deal of repetition here — of ideas and phrases — but always in matters that bear repetition like Hovda's unrelenting criticism of the liturgical "star syndrome," the cancer in our life of worship that leads us to pay more attention to our ministers than to God and the world as God would have it.

I am very grateful to Michael Naughton for his encouragement in making these essays available, as well as to James Connor S.J., Elizabeth Kostelac and the staff of the Woodstock Theological Center (Washington, D.C.) for their editorial help.

I have certainly learned more about liturgy — and about honesty and integrity in the service of the Gospel — from Robert Hovda than I could possibly include in this brief introduction. A few months after he died he was to have given a speech entitled "The Liturgical Renewal Can Be Renewed." To hear him was to be excited by that vision of hope and confidence in the God of our forebears, the God of Jesus Christ.

I hope that you will enjoy the same experience.

John F. Baldovin S.J.

Introduction: Apologia for a New Column*

At a lunch in the dining room of The Metropolitan Museum of Art
during the January meeting of the North American Academy of
Liturgy, the editors of *Worship* asked me to undertake the task of
writing a regular column, to appear in all issues except the NAAL
one in July. Given the awesome setting, the friendly company,
and the latter's freedom from illusions about me, I had to take the
request seriously. Besides, The Liturgical Conference had given me
ample opportunity to develop a taste for writing during the years
I worked on its staff, 1965–1978. . . .

The witness of lifelong experience leaves no doubt in my mind
about my gifts for provocation, whether or not it supports the
more desirable talent for refreshment. And my feelings as a grateful alumnus of St John's University and Seminary and as a benefi-
ciary of *Orate Fratres/Worship* and the monks responsible for it are
a strong encouragement.

I chose the name, "The Amen Corner," for several reasons
(which indicate my concerns in approaching this task). "Amen"
continues to be, as it has been from the ancient roots of our tradition, one of the most important words in our liturgical vocabulary.
It suggests no mere passive acquiescence but, rather, like "Right
on!" and "You said it!" and "Sing it again, sister!," an active, responsible, even enthusiastic joining in a deed that *needs* our participation. In liturgy, this translates as a summoning of one's full
baptismal dignity and responsibility to transform the texts and
movements of the tradition into the here-and-now symbolic action
of the whole assembly — in other words, to create liturgy.

*Worship, March 1983

Looking for a way to use that word, I found "The Amen Corner" in a dictionary I use (abridged), defined as: "1. U.S. a place in a church, usually at one side of the pulpit, once occupied by those worshipers who led the responsive amens during the service. 2. any special place in a church occupied by zealous worshipers." Any implication of a rift between ministers and "worshipers," or a return to the former division of the worship space into sanctuary, choir and nave, must be, of course, rejected. We recognize again now that presider and other ministers are, first of all, part of the assembly and can function properly only as such, as the assembly's voice and hands and body for specific ritual acts that require our amen quite as much as anything they say or do. And we are again aware that the worship space is one, with all of us together as liturgy's subject, and not a series of spaces implying various degrees of involvement.

Apart from that minor problem (probably created by our clericalist guts), the name seemed a good one. Although a bit strange to Catholic ears, its Protestant flavor can be welcomed as one of the graces of that movement, in a magazine as devoted to Christian ecumenism and to the reunion of the churches as *Worship* has proved itself to be. We are well past the stage and time when most of the differences among ecclesial families seemed only divisive and alienating. Now, happily, we are less concerned with an ecclesiastical culture than with a gospel that comes to every climate and every culture as a seed and eschews, like the incarnation, nothing but sin. We know now, although we have not yet done it, that we can join hands in reunion, respecting our variety as enrichment. And, where our focus is the central one of public worship, the commonness of our problems is infinitely more impressive than any peculiar ones we do not share.

If, in choosing that name, I seem to be presuming on the territory of "laypeople," I should explain at the outset why I think otherwise. In my opinion, the word "lay" and all its compounds no longer have a useful or helpful place in the ecclesial lexicon, and indeed are thoroughly retrogressive in their contemporary implications. The church needs and rightly uses special names for specific functions, services, ministries. For its members without such roles, the designations "Christian" and "believer" and the like seem to me adequate. Whatever its noble origins, the term "lay" conjures up visions of crowded waiting rooms in doctors' offices and sounds much like "consumer," "patient," "client." Those visions and sounds are totally opposed to scriptural, conciliar and sacramental notions of church membership.

My thirty-three plus years as a Roman Catholic presbyter, far from alienating me from the major part of the Christian assembly, have made me increasingly critical of the vestiges of clericalism in our language and other customs. And fourteen years on the staff of The Liturgical Conference offered me the opportunity to participate in Sunday Mass without any specific role of leadership almost as often as I presided and to have my eyes opened to the realities of not only "The Amen Corner" but also the less "zealous" areas (if indeed they can be locally identified). So, while clericalism, like sexism and racism and classism, sticks to the insides of a person with remarkable tenacity, my bent and experience make it less likely to be a major impediment in this column's effort to represent the general body of reform-minded church people.

"The Amen Corner" is not abstract, has a firm location in the concrete gathering of believers on Sunday. So this column intends to deal with concrete issues and attitudes experienced and observable in those gatherings, those assemblies. The name connotes a highly appropriate emphasis on the local, flesh-and-blood assembly (whether it is called parish or something else), rather than on "the church" as universal reality. In my youth, we spoke and thought always of "the church" and almost never, except as buildings, of "the churches" that make up, in their relations and joined hands, "the church." The church we thought and talked about was universal and abstract, and therefore was as beautiful and flawless as our minds wished to make it.

One of the reasons why conciliar reform and renewal has been so unsettling for many Catholics is the Second Vatican Council's insistence (from first to last) that the local parish is not merely an indifferent tap on that universal keg, but the real locus of church, where church "is at," its sine qua non. Being part of such a local church, its worship, its mission, its common commitment and mutual support, is the only way one can be part of "the church," and belong to Christ. There are sisters and brothers in faith who have never grasped that elementary truth, flitting from service station to service station on the local level — for a "good liturgy" here, "good preaching" there, "good music" somewhere else, maintaining some kind of imaginary universal church membership card. And, of course, never finding what they seek, because what they seek is what only their settling down in one, particular, local faith community can create. A "good" experience of liturgical celebration on Sunday depends far more on that kind of personal-communal identification than on its (nevertheless important) artistic and ministerial components.

"The Amen Corner," also, is a living group of people. While it is grateful for the rich tradition that has brought us the structures of our rites, their marvelous rhythms and alternations, fruit of the experience of countless generations, it will not tolerate any implication that liturgy belongs to the past. Liturgical celebration requires an assembly of living believers and is always a current, present deed — not only here but *now*. The writer of this column is not a liturgiologist, a scholar, an expert in the roots, the history and development of the rites. All of us need those experts very much indeed, as we have seen in the work of sifting out the tradition and setting it in order that has been going on since the Second Vatican Council.

But to bring the symbollic actions outlined in the liturgical books to life as the worship of a contemporary church is to enter a pastoral area that is singularly devoid of experts. Scholars, as such, in the field, tell us how people in former times and places celebrated common prayer in a way that was meaningful for them (or customary), restoring clear lines of development, warning us of distortions, pitfalls, blind alleys. But they do not specify solutions for our experience today. Their science is limited to the foundation work: enabling us to appreciate our inheritance and to discern the difference between a healthy growth and irrelevant accretions or malignant tumors.

Public worship is a work of our own corporate being as church in our own time and in our own place, guided and modified, of course, by our desire and will to maintain close ties and relations with all other local churches. There are people who can help us in making these inherited structures live and pulse with our spirit and blood, because they are artists, or because they have uncommonly sensitive antennas for such work, or because they have considerable experience in commitment to liturgical planning or leadership. But they (and we who must search them out) are without the helpful signposts of degrees or credentials. In the end, only the experience of the concrete church proves the helpfulness of our adaptations and their congruity with the gospel and the signs of the times.

So this column will be full of opinions. They will be sober opinions, opinions which have been developed after hearing many responsible sources and which have been scrutinized carefully in the light of both the good news and the present time — but opinions nonetheless. They invite consideration, critical attention and debate. All of which, it seems to me, puts us on the right track for serving churches that are in the process of rediscovering themselves as unfinished, pilgrim entities.

"ENDURING PERMANENT DISSATISFACTION"

That is the notion of church that will underlie everything written in these pages: that unfinished, pilgrim entity, full of debate, controversy and turmoil. There is an aphorism that has nourished me from my youth (whose author I cannot remember): "To be a Christian, a member of the church, is to have the courage to endure a permanent state of dissatisfaction." The church is the only institution in the world, I think, that makes this principle its raison d'être, its constant intention, because it is always under the loving judgment of the living God (not as a momentary posture, but as its very being and life). And this is strangely comforting. Because this is what it means to be a human, too, a contingent creature in process of growth and evolution. The church is not only a community of sinners, but also a sinful community.

If the church were viewed as a finished product, who could endure it? You could no more stand it than you could stand yourself, if you viewed yourself in that way. This doesn't mean we can't be happy. But it does mean that if anyone expects the church to be a haven of agreement, free of tension, turmoil, controversy, that person is looking in the wrong place. Like each of its members, the whole pilgrim community is riddled with tension and conflict — appropriate to travelers struggling along the way, trying to realize the reign of God in the midst of overpowering and unlikely circumstances.

There is not now — and there never has been — anything idyllic about the church or life in the church. We are a gang of wayfarers who have been given a faith vision, a biblical word, a sacramental and symbolic deed (all of them showing the same kind of growth and development from their beginnings), which offer an insight into God's purposes, but whose revelatory gifts we bear in earthen vessels. The enemy of those gifts is always just as much inside me and inside the church as the gifts themselves are. If I can't stand the heat of that tension and conflict, that turmoil and controversy, that permanent state of dissatisfaction, then I'd better get out of that particular kitchen. In that case, the kind of peace I am looking for is not Jesus' kind, is a kind of peace I will never find in the faith community of the biblical covenant, in either Judaism or church. That kind of peace is the kind you get when you trade your critical freedom in for a lesser kind, a more manageable kind of god — a dictator, a frozen ideology, any closed interpretation of reality.

The community of the word of God is always besieged by the word it proclaims. The community of the sacramental symbols of the Lord is always besieged by the symbolic acts it celebrates. The community that shares the vision of faith is always under siege by that same vision. And this restlessness, this tension, this conflict between our natural adjustment to the world as it is, on the one hand, and our faith-word-sacrament-signs-of-times rattling at the chains of the status quo, prophetic crying out and radical rejection, on the other — all this is not only appropriate to church. It is its necessity, its nature, its mission, its reason for existence.

We are not always sufficiently appreciative of this messiness. Sometimes we are even silly enough to agree with the *New York Times'* Roman correspondent who hailed the new code of canon law as the end of an era that began when Pope John decided to call the Second Vatican Council. The media are such obstinately stupid reporters of church life and events! Better remember what a recent pope, of increasingly happy memory, said about that same codification of custom: that the purpose of the new code was to relieve the church of a certain dominance which law had achieved during stagnant periods and to restore the social prescriptions we call the code again to their modest place as one small aspect of ecclesial life.

No, the church is a motley, straggling band of wayfarers in process. And our reform is never-ending. The biblical God is never captured — only worshiped. And the liberation and solidarity of the human family, which mark God's reign, keep "a-inchin' us along," as the gospel song exults.

LITURGY IN GENERAL

1

The Saving Evangelism
of Our Symbol Language*

The late Gerald Vann used to say that the church speaks and
communicates in two ways: in the language of symbol and in the
language of dogma. It seems to me that the former includes all of
liturgy, scriptural word and story as well as sacramental action in
general. The latter, for my purposes here, includes not only those
rare definitions of dogma and doctrinal statements or formulae,
but also the catechisms of our recent past, papal and other episcopal speeches and writings, and other official and semiofficial at-
tempts at codifying the present belief of the faith community.
Even in his time, Vann lamented that so many believers drift
away because they have absorbed only the second way, only the
language of dogma.

I think this is a legitimate and thought-provoking distinction,
even though all words are symbols. Language is symbolic, and,
above all, the language we use in speaking of the divine and the
transcendent is highly symbolic. Our problem is that when we are
dealing with scriptural story, homiletic proclamation, sacramental
action, we find it easier to understand that our communication is
symbolic, aweful, worshipful; but when we get a doctrinal statement or verbal formula in our hands, we seem so often to lose
that fear and reverence and begin to act in a possessive, self-
confident, imperialistic way. An English writer put it this way:
"The Gospel of charity is obviously violated and obscured by un-
charitable evangelism. Any method of evangelism which brow-
beats rather than elicits, which is self-asserting and not

*Worship, November 1984

self-effacing, which has vulgarity and ostentation where there should be awe and simplicity, which seeks 'popularity' and 'success' at all costs and not the stark grandeur of truth, will cause many to stumble, and we shall be guilty of a great offence.''[1]

Brain-oriented speech (the language of dogma, at least as we frequently use it) is so much more limited by the language, the speaker, the time, the place, the whole cultural situation, than is the person-oriented communication of symbol. The effort to be precise in "capturing" a truth — a truth which is one aspect of the revelation of a way of life that is still unfolding, still in process — tends in the absence of a profound sense of mystery to bring out grasping, self-centered, possessive qualities in all of us. It is a great temptation, and the conviction that one is doing God's will can make us blind to it.

Nothing turns people away from the gospel and the church as much as a clerical caste which appears to have assumed possession of both. Popes and other bishops, in their desire to serve, need an even stronger sense of human limits than most of us. When we are part of a culture that is bent on domination and exploitation, we tend to use even our formulas about the divine and the mysterious in a domineering and swaggering way. We see it in the papers, the other mass media, literature and the theatre — that is the way the church is perceived in our time. It has been especially evident during the political campaign which will be over by the time this column is published. The slightest acquaintance with church history would remind those media that popes and bishops are quite as frail as the rest of us. But the media are as ignorant of that as they are of Scripture and sacrament, of our primary and indispensable symbol language. Any public statement becomes, by virtue of the power of the media, "the teaching of the church."

Whereas, as Vann also said, the language of symbol may be temporarily forgotten, or may be shuffled off to the periphery of consciousness in a certain kind of culture (like our own), but it is never lost, it does not cease to exist. And it is still powerful, even when we are unconscious of it. In traditional imagery, it affects

[1] E. J. Tinsley, "The Incarnation and Art," in *The Church and the Arts,* ed. Frank Glendenning (London: SCM 1960) 22.

the "heart" of the human being rather than merely the "head." It involves not merely receiving information, getting an idea, but living something out — in the story, in the symbol, in the sacrament. When the Bible speaks of "hearing they did not hear or understand," it is because the heart did not come to the aid of the head. Since the biblical covenant invites us to a way of life, and not just to a series of propositions, the language of symbol is its favorite as well as its most adequate communication. . . .

All who regard the Sunday assembly with its symbolic communication in biblical story and shared holy food and drink as our primary and indispensable sources of formation, gospel truth and growth in faith — we are blessed far beyond our desserts. We can take in stride even the brittle, harsh and absolutist rhetoric of some of our leaders and place such self-assertion in the context of a sinful yet worshiping community. We are involved in the communication of the gospel at its most basic level, a level which precedes and is fundamental to all theologizing and all administration.

When the covenant people of early Judaism, our ancestors in faith, compiled the stories of creation that were eventually committed to writing as part of Torah, at the beginning of Genesis, they were clearly of the opinion that the chief moral problem with which humanity contends is our desire, our need, our determination to be god, to be the "boss," the master. Their faith and hope and love toward a partly revealed and partly hidden Holy One, who had called them from darkness into the light, to do justice, to seek peace, to overthrow all powers that threaten the dominion or reign of God — all this had convinced them that the most contrary thing in human experience is the human person's native resistance to that dominion. By some deep urge of our individuality, we resent dependence, mortality and human limits. Idolatry always begins here.

We are blessed to be working with that way of teaching which is consciously and intentionally worship, and which therefore minimizes most effectively our native tendency to self-idolatry. The church teaches best of all in symbol language, Bible stories, the action of eating and drinking in common around the holy table (Christ), the environment and arts that shape our worship. These simply will not permit us to delude ourselves into thinking we are gods. In awe before mystery we accept them as God's gifts, and gifts so reverent towards us creatures and so discreet that they reach deep inside through all our faculties to move our hearts.

They show us how to love but they do not force us . . . ever. The parables of Jesus are one example. Jesus does not give us an answer to memorize. Jesus tells a story and invites us to imagine that we are its characters, and then to imagine how we would act under the same circumstances. Enabling us to make a free decision, using our consciences as responsible adults. No answers, 1, 2, 3 — only the spirit and the power and the motive to make a right decision. Liturgy is the environment that makes possible in this world an experience of its destiny and call to be the new Jerusalem, the holy city. Our communication in such symbols is so deep that it forms us from inside out, rather than vice versa. From a change of heart, rather than from coercion or authority or applied answers. The liturgy is indeed the primary and indispensable source of the true Christian spirit.

It is the classic depth and universality of the symbol language of liturgy that saves us from superficial distortions and traps. It is this "environment" that is the context and the interpretation of all of our dogmatic, doctrinal, discursive speech. It is not the latter that interprets the former, but the contrary. If we have a deep unity on this symbolic biblical and sacramental level, then we can trust each other to grow up and make a variety of contributions (including a number of mistakes) to our common seeking of ways to realize the reign of God. Faith's vision of the goal does not supply a vision of the means necessary to get there, except that means must be consonant with the goal, must be means of love — so varied efforts and ways are of the essence of the enterprise. But if we have lost that deep and classic oneness, then we have to substitute a superficial party line and a sectarian passion for literal conformity. As William F. Lynch once wrote: "[There is an] instinctive drive in the human soul toward ritual. This drive toward common movement and ritual existence is one of the most powerful movements in the soul of the human creature. If it is choked off and denied on the deepest and religious levels of existence, as indeed it has been, it will concentrate the whole of itself on the most superficial levels of life, the immediately social, and will end in becoming an absolute, a parody of itself and of its own dignity. Whereas, if we were really united at the bedrock of our natures, most of the pressures toward the kind of conformism we really hate would be enormously lessened."[2]

Gustavo Gutiérrez, author of the twentieth-century classic *A Theology of Liberation . . .* , addressed a preaching conference at Riverside Church in New York two years ago. He talked about the conditions for finding a way to talk about God in our current world scene. Echoing the scriptural refrains, "I will destroy the intelligence of the intelligent," "I thank you, Father, for hiding these things from the learned and the clever and revealing them to the little ones," Gutiérrez reminded us of the prophets' and of Jesus' experience with those in the faith community who believe they *know,* those who fancy themselves the private owners of the knowledge of God. He spoke of the profound mystery of the biblical God and of how, if our words are to be worth anything at all, they have to be preceded by much silence — by a conscious effort to place ourselves before the ultimate Ground of being, doing reverence before that which gives meaning to the totality of life, with contemplation, awe, wonder, prayer. With that kind of primary experience, he said, we might dare utter some words.

Gutiérrez' conditions for cogent speech about God in our time are precisely the conditions constructed by the church's symbol language. Like the prophet Elijah, we who see our primary faith-font, in that way of teaching, in that kind of communication, let the blustering winds, the violent earthquakes, the fires of condemnation pass by unheeded, so that we can experience God in the "tiny, whispering sound" (1 Kings 19:12).

The "drifting away" from the church (and therefore from the gospel, unless one is satisfied with a parasitic way of life) on which Vann was commenting twenty-five years ago has now assumed the proportions of a mass movement. Those among us with roles of leadership in the church have a special responsibility to heed this sign of the times and to realize that we are alienating sensitive seekers from a Way which is not ours, a Way which belongs to covenant, Law, prophets, Messiah.

Popularity, either in the church or out of it, is not the measure. The Bible is full of the appeal of false prophets. Human beings

[2] *Christ and Apollo: The Dimensions of the Literary Imagination* (New York: New American Library, Mentor-Omega Books 1963) 175.

like to believe that there is a nice clear answer for every question and that somebody else has it even if I don't. Until we relate to God quite intently, we rather like browbeating, self-assertion, vulgarity and ostentation. Love is much on our lips but it has yet to penetrate to the level of our convictions and desires. When somebody comes along who speaks positively, confidently (especially if he or she provides a sanction for the hatred, suspicion, or prejudice we feel in any case), we swallow it hook, line and sinker, whether that person is an astrologer, a palm or tarot-card reader, a general, a president, or an ecclesiastic. Our history affirms the mysterious, unquenchable appeal of dictators.

It doesn't do at all to pretend that this sort of thing never happens in the church and in its life. It seems to my reading that that is what Jesus was struggling with so frequently in the faith community of his own Judaism. The difference may be subtle, but it is critical, between those leaders who call people to worship and to obey the Holy One who is beyond us all, and those leaders who (no doubt with the best of intentions) act as if they know in detail God's design for everyone, as if they are privately privy to the divine will. Jesus did not condemn their roles or offices in the faith community, for the faith community needs roles and offices of leadership. But Jesus did condemn their pretensions, even when they were well-meant. Jesus invites us all to assume a common stance before God, that of daughters and sons, sisters and brothers, sinners all.

The word of God in the living tradition of Judaism and Christianity must never be confused with the literal word of modern usage. The word in our tradition is image and wonder and deed, and was among us not primarily in drawn characters but primarily in our flesh. An evangelism which is too much influenced by a cerebral and pragmatic culture and which therefore wrenches ''the teaching of the church'' from its symbolic context in its primary and indispensable sources and isolates it in the literal and arid atmosphere of statements, propositions and information — such an ''evangelism'' is a diminishment of the gospel so severe as to be a distortion.

2

Celebrating Sacraments "For the Life of the World"*

That title doesn't sound quite right to many of us. Not because it
isn't right, but because our understanding of the relation between
the church and the rest of the world got bent out of shape somewhere along the line. The title is right, absolutely right . . . and
orthodox (to use a noble word that has suffered some trivialization
again in recent years). But that bent shape of ours began to imagine (and then insist on) a dichotomy between church and world.
We tried to make them entirely separate and distinct realities, although we must have known all along that the church has nowhere else to exist except as part of God's world. All is God's.
And the world is God's long before Judaism and church are born
— in the time that God created.

So there can be no merely ecclesiastical interpretation of the biblical covenant and message, and there can be no "Amen," no acceptance of the word of God at all, unless it is spoken by a faith
community that is vitally, intentionally, committedly part of the
world, belonging to the world, living in and for the rest of the
world. Judaism and church do not exist for themselves, although
we frequently act as if we do.

Because so much of our discussion of liturgy and sacraments is
produced by clergy, and because clergy are particularly susceptible
to the temptation of that "bent shape," that ghetto isolation of
church from the rest of the world which we are supposed to be
serving, it might clear the air a bit to think about the sacraments
from the viewpoint of some of the old basic journalistic, "secular"
questions: who? what? when? where? why? That clerical suscepti-

*Worship, January 1988

bility is not a fault as much as it is an almost inevitable by-product of their full-time and permanent service in the church and the phenomenon called "clericalism," which has evolved a whole set of expectations and requirements tending to separate and isolate the clergy from the rest of the church. It is shared by the communities of men and women in vows and by many other full-time church "professionals."

Who Celebrates Sacraments? The only possible answer to that "who?" is "the baptized and presently committed faith community, the Sunday assembly, the church." Both worship (including sacraments) and mission are the whole church's work, service, ministry in and for the world. As the body of Christ, the entire faith community (concrete in every Christian's local church — that is, Sunday assembly) is the basic minister. All individual and group particular services in that ministering community are specialized, auxiliary, and dependent on the ministry of the whole, because none of us individually is the whole Christ. The body needs many part-time and full-time servants, skills, talents, energies, voices, hands, feet, and so on, to do the body's work with good grace and maximum effect. The point here is the whole church's need and the whole church's work.

Once we grasp that basic ministry of the whole church, both for worship and for work, then we can begin to understand and have a proper regard for all the specialized ministries the church needs. The trouble is that our clericalism has so distorted those roles that the understanding we seek keeps slipping out of our grasp. Our feelings about baptism and the initiation process are underdeveloped. Our feelings about ordination and the vows are vastly overblown and inflated. Our language betrays the inversion. "They" are the church. "We" are "their clients," "their patients," "their consumers." No. The sacraments are liturgies which all the baptized celebrate as Christ's body (in a particular place and time), and in that celebration as in the rest of our life as church we employ specialized ministers for the many tasks which require given talents, training, commissioning or ordaining. We are a community of different gifts — none of us passive, none of us capable of doing everything that needs to be done.

So the clergy do not "bring the sacraments to us." Our celebration of the sacraments needs them and other specialized ministers for the sake of right order, relating this celebration to those of the other local churches, appropriate leadership, embodying our solidarity in Christ. When we act in concert with the leadership of these specialized ministries, then, that is what we must see: ourselves, our embodiment — not an outsider, not a stranger, not an enemy. His or her voice is our common voice. His or her hands are our common hands. That is why they are the voice and hands of Christ . . . because we are Christ's body.

Our recovered (at least in parishes that are alive) initiatory process is the agent and sign of a recovery from the ills described. It will take time and so is an indication of the faith community's primary agenda from now on — an experience for old-timers as well as for newcomers: an experience of leaving behind a way of life that was supported by the status quo in order to embrace and be embraced by a community offering a new way of life, a new orientation, and the mutual support that such a conversion requires. No one will desire, no one will need to celebrate sacraments (those images of heaven, of God's reign of justice and peace, of the liberation and reconciliation that faith sees as God's design for the world) unless that person deeply feels that humanity is made for something better than we have thus far achieved in our institutions and our culture. Only one who feels the pain of oppression and division is going to be drawn to the biblical message, the gospel, the sacraments.

What Is It That We Do in Celebrating Sacraments? We speak often of sacraments as if they were things, objects. They are not. Sacraments are deeds, symbolic actions of a faith community. "All this you were allowed to see that you might know the Lord is God and there is no other" (Dt 4:35). First of all, then, when we do sacraments we worship God, whose sole dominion we celebrate. We reduce all other powers and allegiances to creature size. And we thereby create the atmosphere, the environment of humility and mystery and awe in which believers live their lives — a humility on our part that should make us supremely conscious of our commonness and equality as daughters and sons of God.

When we celebrate sacraments we also "play kingdom." We act out the reign of God, the reign of justice and peace, for it is toward that end that we must move ourselves and our world. The realization of our liberation and our reconciliation in God is the sacramental and liturgical scene. We step out of the status quo with its oppression and division and into the design of God which gives our lives meaning and purpose. So that the business of the whole world is this evolution toward freedom and oneness. In worship we have no blueprints for how we pursue these gifts here and now. God leaves that to our ingenuity and our imaginations. In worship we have something more important — the vision of what we are aiming at. And the aim, right here and now, is everything.

In that kingdom play we also are nourished by our "primary and indispensable source," the liturgy. For in the liturgy the Bible and the sacraments or other symbolic actions are joined to form us at the fonts of God's revelation. All of us are interpreters of those sources, and the church recognizes varying degrees of authority among us interpreters. But all of us depend commonly on the sources. There are no private avenues. In a mass media age, with its capsule headlines and its star syndrome, it is especially difficult to immerse ourselves in the sources, the liturgy, and resist the quick fix.

In addition to all this, celebrating sacraments touches the times of our lives, not with recipes but with vision. We can figure out recipes appropriate to the signs of the times here and now, if we have the vision. If we don't have the vision (if we never grow up and become adults), no recipe means anything. The water bath, chrismation, the Lord's Supper, absolution for penitents, anointing for sick persons, blessing the unions of lovers, ordaining pastoral ministers, farewell to dead sisters and brothers — these rites which we celebrate can integrate the scattered pieces of our lives in a universe of faith-meaning.

When Do We Celebrate Sacraments? "In the midst of the local church at its principal gathering, in the Sunday assembly." For the faith community gathered is the prime symbol of Christ and the primary agent of Christ's action. I know that this is hard for us to accept, but it is fundamental. One does not like to make fun of genuine sentiment, but it can give rise to extremely counterproductive habits. For example: when a person or a family is about to celebrate a special anniversary at a Mass, or a wedding, or a baptism, or a funeral, it is only rarely the regular worshiping community, the local church involved, that is the first consideration. No, we fly in some wandering cleric because he is an uncle or a nephew or a friend or otherwise sentimentally involved. Airports all over the land are full of clerics with little black bags ready to preside at sacramental celebrations anywhere, at a moment's notice.

Yet it is the basic gathering of the local church, the Sunday assembly, which is the normal minister and context of sacramental celebration. We seek the appropriate faith community, *with* its normal bishop/priest presider. We know well that that cannot always be the case, but we also know that it can be the case far more often than it is. We have to speak not only about where we are right now but also about where we are going. Having the right aim is what the here and now are all about. Eucharist, of course, is its raison d'être every Sunday. The greatest of all the Sunday assemblies, the Easter Vigil is the normal scene for the sacraments of initiation: baptism, confirmation, eucharist. Infant baptisms no longer need be done in haste, but can be scheduled if not for Easter at least for a major festal celebration, allowing time for parental instruction first. The eucharist is again being understood as the primary sacrament of reconciliation, with penance as a secondary one. Countless parishes are finding it helpful to schedule public anointings of sick persons able to get to the assembly on one or two Sundays of the year. And the more one thinks about it, the less reason there seems to be to deny the possibility of ordination, funeral or marriage also in connection with that gathering, as long as it does not preempt the entire service and is a modest part of it. And even when the Sunday assembly is clearly impossible, some gathering of the local church for any sacramental celebration is critical.

Where Are Sacraments Celebrated? Where else but in the world and "for the life of the world"? Celebrating a sacrament or any other liturgy is God-centered not because God needs liturgy but because we need God-centeredness. Like the church which is their minister, the sacraments exist for all people, to give life, hope, vision. To activate imagination. They are terrestrial realities, on the earth and for the earth, in humanity and for humanity. But we keep wanting to make ecclesiastical playthings out of them, confining them to a little church ghetto. One of the problems in celebrating is this alienation of church from the rest of the world and its consequent narcissism. A church that pretends to exist for its own sake is a travesty and a tragedy. How many parish schedules look as if they were designed to consume all the time of all their members, instead of being designed to inspire those members to live elsewhere and to get busy about inching the world toward the reign of God.

It is against the ways and the other institutions of our world here and now that the sacraments have to rub, so that we can begin to see how to change things — to make our competitive scrambling more like the shared supper of the Lord. We must not be an island for those afraid of the mainland, nor a retreat for those tired of living, nor a Disneyland for those who want only to be amused. In those scenes, the sacraments have no meaning at all.

Why Celebrate the Sacraments? More than words, more than language, more than even the poetic language of the Bible, celebrating sacraments involves a comprehensive, bodily, symbolic communication uniquely capable of touching and quickening human beings. We are complex creatures and the word needs the deed as much as the deed needs the word. The symbolic texts of the Bible and the symbolic acts or deeds of the sacraments and other liturgies together constitute a source that offers life to all of our many levels and gifts.

So we have to confess that those miserable strains in and around our tradition which have promoted the idea that God's grace can reach only humans who have stripped themselves of everything but their brains are serious enemies of God and of faith. To be at home in the world and in one's body, comfortable with what we are, grateful not only for mind but also for imagination, fantasy, memory and all the sense faculties which our capitalistic, rationalistic, pragmatic culture diminishes or tries to hide — this is the kind of spirit and attitude we need for celebrating sacraments. To celebrate a sacrament is not merely to say the words associated with the rite, but it is rather to act out the rite, to perform a choreography. The power of sacramental action is the whole experience.

Let the symbolic action, whether bathing or supping or anointing or laying on of hands or any of the participating sounds, smells, textures, sights, tastes be unabridged and full, unexplained because they explain themselves. The sacraments are as earthy as we are, as our world is, that's why! "Your kingdom come. Your will be done on earth as in heaven."

Our placing ourselves and our imaginations at the Lord's Table, in the holy city, the new creation of God's reign, is altogether for the sake of transforming us and our world. God reveals in symbolic word and deed what the liberated and reconciled community of humanity must become, asks us to grow up into the fullness of Christ by permitting us to act it out in rite. To do this, God gathers us together first. Together. No more Sunday Masses than the one or two or three necessary to accommodate the number of members in the local church. Several assemblies are really several local churches.

And in this gathering a variety of ministries and distinction of roles proves that reconciliation is not a matter of uniformity, nor of the tyranny of the majority. The celebrating assembly gathers us together in the conviction of our solidarity without erasing human differences. It teaches us to value our variety, to be enriched by each other's different gifts, to become more human and complete by empathy with those unlike ourselves. So we need male and female, old and young, handicapped and "normal," black and white and brown and red and yellow, all temperaments, all cultural and ethnic values, all sexual orientations — there is no given in the human condition that cannot be reconciled in this ministry of reconciliation.

The Liturgical Conference has long served the churches in this country as a voice relatively free of the ghetto isolation I discussed in the introduction to these questions. In *Liturgy*, the Conference's journal, Volume 6, Number 4, Virginia Sloyan writes "from the pew" about the Sunday assembly experience: "Convincing us that we exercise a crucial role in the liturgical celebration, that we in effect *are* the celebration, cannot be achieved by verbal persuasion. . . . We can sense very clearly when our role is crucial to an endeavor, whether it be the liturgy or anything else; we know when we enjoy and find meaning in assuming a particular role; and at some point we decide if we want to give ourselves to the event in question. . . .

"And Sunday after Sunday, we nourish a hope, faint and often unfulfilled, that our worship will take us to places of beauty and meaning we do not normally inhabit, places we have helped to create, places we will return from, refreshed and whole. 'Where there is no vision,' Proverbs reminds us, 'the people perish' (29:18). We come to this setting to hear the sacred story and pray the great prayer with sisters and brothers, hoping to feel enlarged, expansive, full of praise, better than we are, knowing this is the way God sees us in Christ Jesus.

"We cannot be trained to listen creatively, respond enthusiastically, offer warmhearted peace greetings, or form images that will delight and challenge throughout the week, any more than a child can be trained to express exhilaration at finding a beautifully wrapped package under the Christmas tree, only to learn that it conceals socks and underwear. The utilitarian has little interest for the child and no place in the liturgy. . . .

"Perhaps if we find out what this mystery we celebrate is really about, we will have second thoughts about engaging in it. But I don't think so. We are not nearly so frightened about the implications of living the gospel as we are at the prospect of lives without meaning and liturgies without life" (pp. 14, 17, 19).

3

Beware of "Liturgists" and All Specialists!*

Actually, any member of a community of biblical faith, Jewish or Christian, is a liturgist, since the basic meaning of the term is simply one who acts ritually in worship. And liturgy is the symbolic action of a faith community, in which that corporate entity, including all its members, is the doer. Liturgy is the symbolic action communicating, nurturing, expressing the faith of the community, the church. Just as social action (another aspect we have managed to isolate as a specialty) is the same community's work of undertaking the mission which that faith entails: creating in social structures and in the life of the world that reign of God which we have played, acted out, celebrated in the symbols of our rites.

Here, however, I am using the term "liturgist" in the popular sense in which it is ordinarily employed: a liturgist is one who has a regular role of special responsibility for or leadership in liturgical celebration, while the term "liturgiologist" is reserved for scholars whose research, writing, teaching open up the history and development of liturgical tradition or concentrate on certain aspects of the rites. Needless to say, all believers are immensely indebted to both groups of specialists, and should be grateful for and appreciative of their great contributions to our nascent liturgical renewal.

But my intention in this column is to continue the train of thought begun in the last issue. If you remember, the point of those comments was the difference, the tremendous difference it makes, whether a believer chooses to live cooped up in an ecclesiastical "world," a total culture, a detached "spiritual option," or whether that believer makes God's world (the only world there is) a real home, of which his or her church is a part, and for

*Worship, March 1984

which his or her church offers inspiration, worship, support, nourishment, and vision of what must come to be. To be consumed by an ecclesiastical system or to be fed by and in the church for life in the world — that is the question.

It might seem at first glance that such a train of thought is less germane to the purposes of a column on liturgical renewal than are some of the topics discussed in earlier issues. I hope, however, that on second thought you will agree with me that no specific ritual question is or can be more germane to our concerns here than this apparently abstract one. And no conditioner of our values, our interests, attitudes, undertakings, is more concrete and pervasive than the "place" we have decided to occupy . . . the "place" one chooses to be the focus of one's commitments and contributions as a part of the human enterprise.

So the title word "beware" should be taken quite literally: be wary, be cautious, be careful (in addition of course, to being grateful for and appreciative of specialists). Specializations are as natural as any corollary of human limits. As one gets older and wiser, it becomes more and more evident that you can't make a significant contribution in any particular area of human life unless you concentrate on it — to the neglect of concentration on other areas. Specializations are the seed of human progress. We owe our breakthroughs and our advances to them.

However, if they are too self-contained, too isolated from the broad and common needs of human survival and progress, they cannot function for our good. To benefit from specializations, society seems to require a strong sense of solidarity, some kind of basic familial or corporate ethos. In an ideology of individualism, specializations seem to lead to fragmentation and irresponsibility. The lack of a corrective social atmosphere, ethos, corporate spirit leaves them to themselves. There is no common area (where all specialists are first of all human beings) of responsibility and commitment to the economic-political-cultural life of humanity to elicit and employ the various contributions of our specializations.

A church that is vital, strong, united on deep rather than superficial levels, will contest and counter that cultural disintegration. The Christian church may be such again in time, if it achieves a reunion with diversity and if our reforming spirit does not lag. Although there are already some signs that they are beginning to regain that capacity, the churches generally are still to be counted among the groups more influenced by than influencing the culture they share.

Perhaps we see the effects of isolated specializations more clearly in the broad cultural scene than in our ecclesial life. They are a principal reason for what seems to me a terribly depressing political scene in our country (and, I am sure, in others as well). Campaigns are without issues, because issues belong to the various and highly complex specializations. Scientists can unleash the power of the atom, but they cannot share a common human responsibility for the way we use that power. Bishops of the church, it is widely said, are not "competent" to prepare a pastoral letter on the great moral issues of war and peace. Preachers are supposed to avoid "politics" and relate the good news only to the private lives of believers. Not only the medical profession but a frightening number of other work-segments of society protest that the technical complexity of their fields precludes any common human judgment or critique.

We hide in our corners and leave the economic system that governs all of our lives to the economists, and the political system (originally calculated to increase the sharing of responsibility) to the politicians. As a result, none of us seems to be prepared to assume the obligations of a citizen in a democracy. And the ship of state has at its helm not the candidate of a party or movement with a broad program addressing the felt and common needs of all the people but whatever television personality captures the public fancy. The reason, in part at least, is that we identify and define ourselves solely in terms of our particular specialty, and recoil in horror from the responsibility of creating a society that integrates all specializations and enables each to make a utilized contribution to the common good.

Don't we suffer from much the same sickness and abdication of human responsibility in the church? We are clergy or musicians, social actionists or ecologists, writers or religious, architects or liturgiologists, artists or engineers, consultants or commission members, and so on. That's all right, and even good, if we don't get stuck on that relatively superficial level of skill and in that pigeonhole, if we maintain a foothold in the human scene, with some common human interests and commitments.

As far as it goes, as I said above, that kind of particularity and specialization is necessary. But it doesn't go far enough. It stops short of both incarnation and epiphany, of both full humanity and human communication. We say that so-and-so is "into" computers or "into" liturgy, as if to explain or exhaust the purposes of a life, a person! And I think we should be just as dismayed by people who are "into" liturgy in this way as we are by people who are "into" computers in this way. Because this way is no way to live. Aptitudes, skills, talents, training (all great gifts from which society should be able to reap a common benefit) become retreats from life, excuses to absent oneself from the human task, alibis for non-communication, narcissistic indulgences.

We are aware that the church scene, even in its most dismal periods, has been sometimes graced and sometimes cursed by little islands of care and concern for public worship, participation, liturgical environment and the arts that serve symbolic action. There has always been a parish here or a parish there which, by virtue of some priest or other staff person, or some particularly motivated and bold member, has acquired a reputation for dignity and sincerity in public worship, for good preaching, for enthusiastic participation and a variety of ministries, for exceptional music, for attention to the visual arts. That island or oasis phenomenon is a grace when it is part of an ecclesial awakening to gospel values and mission, a curse when pursued as "our" self-conscious specialization, distinguishing us from hoi polloi — and usually a mixture of both. The islands are more numerous now, but it would be hard to prove that we have moved beyond that stage. Most of the examples we can cite, even now, are those of specialists who are "into" this or that, with mixed results.

Society in general has cause to fear and to attempt to repair the disintegration of specializations-gone-mad. Christian believers possess additional and powerful motives for rejecting the isolation and protectionism of specialists and realizing a common sense of responsibility for and participation in the economic-political-cultural life both of humanity and of the church. We are now in an advantageous position for that realization, for our time is one of broad and basic reform. No longer is a living and direct contact with our scriptural and sacramental sources the privilege of a specialized elite in the church. Now, in the Sunday assembly, all baptized

Christians share the same gifts in the same way. And those sources permit no retreat from common human responsibilities.

The mysteries of incarnation and epiphany, especially, alert Christians to humanity's role in the coming of Christ in glory, the coming of God's reign. Incarnation implies an enthusiastic worldliness, and epiphany a passion for communicating, for sharing, for manifesting. First of all, the serious believer and believing community become part of the human race in desire and intent, recovering what David Steindl-Rast calls the basic religious experience: the experience of belonging, of being at home in God's world and saying honestly and wholeheartedly, "I belong." And then they communicate, manifest the reign of God through that belonging and with that belonging and in that belonging.

Those of us whose specialization is liturgical celebration are equipped for an important contribution to this integrating task. Liturgy assumes and aids the integration of both person and community. Not only sacrament, where the communication more obviously is not merely verbal and rational, but also the word of God proclaimed and preached deal with us as whole beings (senses, emotions, imaginings, memories, ideas, reasoning, all brought together). Neither source is satisfied with a merely cerebral approach, nor with any single group of specialists. And the assembly that breaks the bread of word and sacrament is ecclesial, called to be *common*, out of every specialization, lifestyle, sex, class, color, condition.

So there is nothing precious, elitist, or luxurious about what we "liturgists" seek, at best. We seek to communicate, to proclaim the symbolic word and celebrate the symbolic act wholly and completely, involving every level of each complex human being and all the members of an equally complex corporate entity called church. Integration and reconciliation are a sine qua non of liturgy. What is at stake in the concerns of our "specialty" is not merely an articulate theology of worship or a cultivated aesthetic sense (although they are important, too). What is at stake is the Christian revelation, in which the saving mysteries of cross and tomb depend upon incarnation and epiphany, depend upon a common human presence and a common human mission.

Like the good news itself, and like the title of one of the books of a hero of my youth (Eric Gill), *It all goes together*. Every cause (specialty), every genuine aspect and facet of church renewal is related to what we seek. So we "liturgists" will be true to our concerns only by supporting all of the other renewal efforts in the church (as continuing and ceaseless): reform in our self-understanding as church; reform in liturgical practice; reform in economy, property and budgeting; reform in moral and doctrinal teaching; reform in qualifications, training and lifestyle of ministries; reform in administration and organization; reform in sense of mission and in political and economic (and military) responsibility; and all the rest.

The massive indifference and sometimes hostility we meet, whether we are specializing in one area or another, are not merely problems of different theologies or of different tastes. They are faith problems, exacerbated by a culture in which specializations are not complemented by a sufficiently strong social corrective. This appeal — not to get disoriented by isolating our own specializations — is analogous to the cultural situation in our society. It is natural that women, the unemployed, blacks and other minorities of color, gays and lesbians, those chronically suffering substandard conditions in housing, food, clothing and education, should concentrate on their own hurts and on the seeking of justice for themselves. That's natural. Wouldn't one hope, however, that their common suffering would make these groups more sensitive to injustice in every area? would make for solidarity, not for jealousy and infighting?

In the same way, the uphill nature of any renewal effort in the history of the church should make us natural allies of all the other genuine and gospel-oriented reform efforts going on. To cease being human and become merely specialists, to be isolated or set against each other by the forces that resist change — this is what we must avoid. And this is why we must be wary of *any* specialization, including our own.

4

Historical Studies and
Contemporary Worship*

Language always hangs loosely on the frame of existence, and
people of faith should possess an exceptionally keen awareness of
the fact. It seems to me, however, that one can accept that fact
and still lodge a legitimate complaint occasionally. And I would
like to lodge a small complaint in this column, at least for purposes of discussion. I fear that the phrase "pastoral liturgy" is
misleading many.

"Pastoral liturgy" is one of those phrases (like the distressingly
popular "institutional church") whose currency has the effect of
obfuscating rather than clarifying. Any and every liturgy in any
and every liturgical tradition is pastoral. Yet students of liturgy
who are committed to a pastoral ministry in today's church frequently appear to be in anguish because they say they cannot find
in liturgical degree programs the "pastoral liturgy" courses they
are looking for.

Instinctively one wants to sympathize with them, because their
perception of the sad state of Sunday celebration in most American parishes is quite accurate and cries out for pastoral attention.
Their concerns, basically, are those we should all share. Thank
God for every student seeking to serve the church who recognizes
the priority of the Sunday assembly and the necessity of realizing
in that assembly a vibrant and awesome experience for all. That
kind of commitment to today's church will never underestimate
the Sunday communal event, even though it is also aware that its
formative and inspirational character depends not only on the

*Worship, March 1986

authenticity, intelligibility, beauty and vitality of the rite but also on the degree to which the assembly's faith has been expressed by service to the world of which it is a part. The work of becoming comfortable with symbolic communication, with the opening up of the shriveled and desiccated symbols of our liturgical tradition; the work of developing a taste and a thirst for the excellences of professional music leadership as well as for the environmental and visual gifts of first-rate architects and artists; and the work of cultivating a consuming desire to *communicate* through the proclaiming and preaching of the word and the ministering involved in the supper — all this work which should be at the head of the pastoral minister's agenda is still trying to get its foot inside our door in these still early, infant days of renewal.

But when one hears the suggestion or implication that courses in "pastoral liturgy" are the answer, one should stop and think very carefully. My experience does not correspond to that kind of "solution." And when this anguish of sharp young types has been expressed, I wish now that I had replied in this manner: "Why are you looking for them? Why not get your teeth into the tradition, deeply enough to taste and savor, to acquire a foundation, and then trust yourself and the community you serve to make the applications? Experts, liturgiologists can help us experience, feel, live the tradition in the context of a previous time and place, but there are no experts in the contemporary application. This latter effort is our work, current, immediate, ongoing, without the analysis one gains from distance. In this work there are only people like ourselves, and we must do our best and share our efforts and submit it all to a judgment that only time and experience can make. To prejudice the search, the effort, the imagination by a precipitate packaging and dispensing of weakly based or insufficiently tried recipes and techniques is a radical disservice to the tradition and the church. Liturgy is never contrived or invented. It grows, slowly, and its refiner is Christ in the baptized, the *sensus ecclesiae*. A variety of efforts solidly based in the living tradition, efforts to clothe the tried and refined ritual structures with our living flesh and blood — that variety is what we need now, so that the church can in its slow time reject the idiosyncracies and the less useful and embrace into its common patterns of worship all that illumines and vitalizes."

Of course, I could never have given that answer to the question without having it written on my cuff, but something like that would, I think, be the most helpful response any queried sage (old-timer) could give. Instead of that, I am afraid we sometimes assume the validity of the quest and the question, and institute a search for "pastoral liturgy" courses that is apt to settle for lightweight "biblical" commentary, the kind of secondary and tertiary doctrinal interpretation which the mass media call "the teaching of the church," historical bits and pieces devoid of the depth that brings a people and an age to life, and an exposure to the "arts" designed to satisfy only a tin ear and a bleary eye.

Let me repeat. We need a *today* commitment in every student for the presbyterate or other pastoral ministry. When pastoral ministry degenerates into a caretaking operation, or a secure status, or an ecclesiastical success ladder, or a mere sinecure for persons whose real vocations lie elsewhere, we are in a bad way. It is not that ministry itself, but the studies that best prepare us for it, which are my concern here. And I propose no "answers" but only some reflections about those studies.

I suspect some liturgiologists have delved so deeply, particularly, and even exclusively into a certain period of history and the church's ritual structures and life of the time that they never emerge into the daylight of today's problems in today's church. If that is their life and work it does not make much sense to ordain or commission them for pastoral ministry. And a student for pastoral ministry clearly does not want that kind of exclusive concentration or specialization. But to say that such specialization has nothing to teach one preparing for pastoral ministry is seriously to misunderstand the nature of the subject we are dealing with. That kind of liturgiologist (or a similarly "out of it" biblical scholar, cultural anthropologist, church or art historian, etc.), who seems uninterested in today, may so illumine the era and area of his or her expertise as to enable the tradition to impinge on our contemporary experience in truly marvelous ways. Not that many scholars and researchers are such cave-dwellers or so narrow — but it can happen. And even one who fits that caricature can be a source of great insight, more relevant to contemporary problems than some "pastoral liturgy" people whose "relevance," like waterskis, keeps them on the surface of the liturgical sea, skimming, getting wet only by accident. Getting wet in liturgy, in its biblical and sacramental roots and development, is the *basis* for a helpful pastoral adaptation today.

And I don't say this abstractly but from my own experience of thirty-seven years active in the priesthood, presiding in the Sunday assembly and writing and speaking all the while about the importance of its quality and experience. One would think that my lack of academic credentials, of any formal graduate program in liturgical studies, would make me particularly susceptible to a "pastoral liturgy" mindset. But despite that serious omission, I had a lot of help from the academic and scholarly arena: through seminary at St John's Abbey in Minnesota with teachers like Godfrey Diekmann and Paschal Botz, a few courses from Johannes Quasten later on, The Liturgical Conference's Liturgical Weeks, reading and lectures and other serious liturgy meetings, and the benefit of all that came to me during fourteen years working for The Liturgical Conference. The list of those to whom I am indebted is long and rich.

It has occurred to me with regularity during these years (and at first with some surprise) that the most provocative, eye-opening, helpful experiences of my life and ministry which were gained from that long list of wonderful people have been, not the popular, pastoral interpretations, but the kind of narrow and deep historical scholarship and research that some with a shortsighted "pastoral" concern wish to escape. The lectures, literature and conversations which seem to me to have been most enriching and stimulating have been, not those attempting to be contemporary and pastoral, but rather those attempting either to immerse you in the liturgy of another time and place or to draw from such a liturgy basic conclusions about principles of rite.

If you are fortunate enough to find and gain those insights into our roots and our development, then continuing the life and growth in our time is up to you. If one is conscious of the Sunday assembly and its liturgy as our regular experience of primary sources (Bible and sacrament) and as a living tradition (never static, finished, completed), then it seems to me that pastoral ministers cannot avoid leading by careful trial and error out of the experience of their own and others' faith communities. On a pilgrimage we have the rich experience of a Judaic and Christian liturgical tradition, but no maps or charts to direct our steps today. We have ritual structures refined and developed by the loving use of our spiritual forebears. Academic work can open all that to us, illuminating us with past experience, discoveries, mistakes. But academic work that calls itself "pastoral liturgy" must be acutely aware of its limitations and its brashness.

Right now we are in the early stages of a comprehensive reform effort, designed by a council of the church to get us back on the pilgrim path of never-ending renewal. And we are in a moment of one of those reactions against repentance and change with which human history is prodigal. So there is even less ecclesial support for progress than under the church's ordinary plodding circumstances. This is another cogent reason why the student for pastoral ministry, with a contemporary commitment and therefore willing to be the goad, gadfly, prodder, agitator we need, is best advised to study the roots, to feel and attach oneself to the roots, and to sort out the story of the tradition's development, so that growth can happen organically (in the only way liturgical celebration can develop).

Specialization is always a double-edged sword, so all human functions, vocations, responses to a call of one sort or another have reason to be modest. To perform a function well, to be true to a vocation, to answer a call of conscience and community with the verve and energy it merits — this, frequently if not generally, means to specialize, particularize, concentrate to such an extent that other important things get short shrift or neglect. To particularize and concentrate to the greatest effect requires both a conviction of the importance and human need of the pursuit in question and a narrowing of one's field of vision. The paradox is evident in the experience of anyone who is captured by a function, vocation, call. Whether the thing we have a talent for doing, the thing that needs to be done, is in the arts, the sciences, the trades, the crafts, the service vocations of church or public or private enterprise, or elsewhere, it demands an attention which does not permit one to be "well-rounded." None of us can be or do all things, even all necessary things. A sense of solidarity with the rest of the church and the rest of the human race, whose members supply the things one cannot be or do, is what permits our specialization — and what requires it.

This is no great insight, admittedly. But paying some attention to it, reflecting on it, can be helpful. One of my previous essays in this space appealed for the solidarity just mentioned ("Beware of 'Liturgists' and All Specialists!" see above, pp. 25–30). In this essay my point is that such solidarity is productive of progress and growth only to the extent that all of us are grateful for, eager for and respectful toward others whose talents, specializations and works are different from our own. Studies in preparation for a truly contemporary ministry in this area need depth and penetration into our history more than anything else. Academic studies equip us for our work, not by pretending to do it for us, but by communicating the most thorough knowledge of and feel for our liturgical past and sources that are possible.

There are analogies. It's a bit like the difference between the moral theology that was taught yesterday and that of today. The prefabricated answers, the lists of DOs and DON'Ts so popular during a period when interpreters seemed enough and sources seemed unimportant, when pilgrim adventure was displaced by good housekeeping, belong to yesterday. Now great leaps in all of our sciences, technologies, and in human experience generally have reduced the value of past conclusions and have demanded the formation-in-depth of adult consciences capable of making decisions and choices in the light of faith, free from the *domination* (not from the inevitable and modest influence) of mores, social pressures, human passions and past interpretations.

When he was asked how one might become a church musician, Archbishop Weakland of Milwaukee is reported to have said, "First, become a musician." I think the kind of reflection I have been trying to encourage in this column goes beyond what students in programs of liturgical studies can most profitably seek. All of us in jobs, functions, offices of leadership in the churches are challenged by this same reflection to look carefully at the priorities of the local faith community and see whether they reveal the conviction that the Sunday assembly is its crucial heart and center.

This primary job of bishops, pastors and other pastoral ministers is not fulfilled by the articulation of theory or doctrine: "The liturgy is source and summit, etc." It requires the hard and unrewarding work of being goads, gadflies, stingers of consciences (including our own). It requires the scrapping of old budgets and the creation of new ones which reflect this priority. It requires stringent (and relevant) qualifications for ministry. It requires a rigorous search for competence and excellence in every role of leadership in the Sunday assembly. Theory is not the point. I am not writing about believing in some corner of our minds that the Sunday assembly, word and sacrament, is the heart and center of the church's life. I am discussing an experience, rare in our parishes and among our people — an experience of such beauty, truth and goodness in covenant, Law, prophets, Christ and gospel that we will no longer tolerate that event being a kind of ecclesiastical Major Bowes Amateur Hour. That event demands competence and excellence for the sake of *communicating* in the symbol language of rite.

5

"What Happened . . . ?"*

A recent letter from a professor/writer/editor included an aside: "I still haven't read a convincing analysis of what happened to 'our' hopes for good liturgy; with 'victory' at the Council . . . I expected something better than we got. . . .''

A "convincing analysis" is beyond the scope of this column. I think almost all of us who were identified with what was called "The Liturgical Movement" in preconciliar times have voiced the same complaint and owe it some reflection. That reflection is not easy, and it cannot be done by merely studying liturgical practice, for conciliar reform is not only basic (liturgy) but also comprehensive, touching every aspect of Christian life. Liturgy is related to all those other strands, and influence is mutual. We are summoned not only to a different "church-view" but also to a different "world-view." The complaint is justified. If we do not aim high, we make no progress at all. But for the sake of our own faith and hope, we need to remember Newman's hymn: "I do not ask to see the distant scene; one step is enough for me."

A healthy and even wonderful process is afoot these last twenty-five years. These first, halting steps are not merely gratifying; they reveal, in the infancy of recovery, more and more about the sickness that has affected our ecclesial life and they demand more time for remedy than we had earlier imagined.

Perhaps the question should be "What didn't happen?" Or, as I prefer and hope, "What has not yet happened?" For we have not yet reached a consensus among the churches in communion with the Roman church about the basics of the process/pilgrimage. Consensus at the Council was a stunning gift of the Spirit which

*Worship, January 1989

should have been much more widely distributed. What has not yet happened is a general appreciation and possession by all the churches (including their leadership) of that vision and consensus. It was due to the light that biblical, early church and other studies in the last century had thrown on our sources, expanding awareness of our Jewish and Christian tradition. Add to this light a pastoral experience that found this new knowledge in happy correspondence with felt contemporary needs and the signs of our times, together with preparatory and postconciliar commissions that did not disdain pastoral experience, and you have the makings of a real rejuvenation — not a return to the past, but the emergence of formerly hazy building blocks which in our further building we ignore at our peril.

After a long interruption in the movement/pilgrim self-awareness of the covenant people, during which a large part of that people established itself as a "perfect society," with institutions appropriate to its presumably finished and adequate embodiment of faith's vision (like Jesus, "the reign of God" incarnate, instead of *a sign* pointing to the reign of God), it is not difficult to understand why such an effort at rejuvenation is traumatic, especially for a Vatican, once servant, now master, whose administrative interests are for tidiness and order.

The inspired gift of the Council and the leadership evident there were clearly destined for tough times. Most of the faithful were unprepared. Even those of us who expected "something better than we got" were nevertheless still expecting something to be *given*. Much of the three-year leadership of the bishops during the Council did not survive the return trip home; the "experts" (to whom we owe so much) dispersed, and there were blank looks on the faces of the many who, having thought they had "the faith" well in hand, were being invited to resume the interrupted pilgrim trail.

The invitation was not merely to an unfamiliar liturgical *engagement*, although that had a first place appropriate to our "primary and indispensable" biblical/sacramental source. The invitation was to a total reappraisal of discipleship, beginning with a recovered initiation process as the agenda of the basic church, the Sunday assembly. Elements include the rescue of baptism and baptismal commitment from the shadows of the clericalism that had become "the church"; emphasis on the local and primary churches as well as the familiar stress on their communion; an adult rather than a rote morality; a witness or mission that is always countercultural because its vision is the liberation-reconciliation, justice-peace of the reign of God; a God who commands *today*, not merely the after-life; and so on.

The shock of this kind of comprehensive, strong biblical and traditional appeal for the activation of faculties which had grown stiff and resistant to change could not have been unexpected. There was really no RSVP attached to the appeal — just a confidence that change is possible. Those who were waiting, hoping, praying for it needed no RSVP. For many, however, the Council quickly became another group of ecclesiastical documents, whose dynamite was discreetly reduced to cap-gun proportions with the gradual release of "changes" in bits and pieces. It could have been otherwise only if we had possessed the kind of church structures which will be developed when and if and as renewal progresses.

However, the pops of the cap gun have not been without effect. Only in the most deeply rutted dioceses, parishes and religious societies do we now find the kind of ghetto or "cultural Catholic" dominance which was formerly widespread. Reform and renewal efforts are inevitably sometimes clumsy and mistakes are made. That's the way life is. And the new life spreading through the churches finds crevices for its expression even in this present reactionary moment.

In this brief space I can cite only a few examples of good seeds being planted and cultivated in these early decades of what the Council implied would be a continuing reform. We see the gradual adoption by a constantly increasing proportion of parishes of the most important of our postconciliar liturgical developments: the Rite of Christian Initiation of Adults, with its catechumenate, its eventual total parish involvement, its rescue of the liturgical year. As we realize that this is not another "program," but rather the living out of the very nature of the church, there is every reason to believe, despite our idols of individualism and competition, that we will thereby recover a corporate sense of being one body with Christ as head, of deep relation with the rest of the faith community, and indeed with the rest of the world — an indispensable basis of liturgical celebration.

Nothing is more inimical to the kind of Sunday assembly we

now desire than the lack of solidarity, the obvious way we gather as lone consumers in a vast spiritual enterprise, and with the notion that any local outlet will do as a dispensary. The amazing thing is not that our liturgical life is frequently repulsive, but that it survives at all in such a scene.

Some of us have experienced the fortunate parishes here and there where initiation has been the agenda for several years and where the first effects begin to show. Clericalism fades (not fast enough, but it fades) and the community begins to see and feel and talk and act as *church* rather than as consumers, clients, patients, "laypeople." Liberation and reconciliation, the marks of the reign of God and the purposes of God's creation, become interiorized and we see the liturgy as *our* celebration of those gifts of God *which we need*. Until we realize our own and our sisters' and brothers' oppression (idols, powers) and division (prejudices, discrimination), it is not surprising that we bring little spirit to the liturgy's "acting out of the reign of God." But when we feel the purpose of our lives is justice and peace, we have something animating to bring to our worship. As long as the accursed polls reveal the political and economic attitudes of most believers to be roughly indistinguishable from those of our society's voting majority, we have no right to expect liturgy to be anything but perfunctory.

Another reason, I think, why it takes so long, so very long, to see the fruits of what we've been about this last quarter century is our cultural indisposition to contemplation and therefore to the language of symbol, the language of liturgy. We have long ago lopped off the "significando" from the "causant" of liturgy or sacrament. We tend to think that the words, the texts, *are* the liturgy, and the rest is mere decoration. Our efficiency and pragmatism and pseudo-scientism and capitalism are impatient with anything that defies questions like "What's it worth?" and "What'll it do?" The symbol language of Bible and sacrament, of liturgy, requires a total human opening up (body, senses, imagination, memory, as well as reason) and attention. Its communication is deeper, more comprehensive and more universal than our twentieth-century vernaculars. Our words do not explain it. It explains our words, comes to their aid, supplies what their limitations lack.

Evidences that we sense this cultural handicap are mounting and suggest better times ahead: recognizable bread, broken and shared from a common plate, wine shared by all drinking from common cups, in the eucharist; immersion in baptism; more parishes hiring professional music leadership; more emphasis on beauty/awe/reverence awakening us to transcendence to balance the new and also important hospitality; and concern for ministerial style and competence. The rites of liturgy, done fully and richly and without hurry, image the reign of God in ways deeply felt and deeply formative.

Even seminaries finally suspect that they are not as helpful in these struggles as they should be, perhaps because they belong to academe, a world which in the West has tended to overrate intellectual abstraction, alienate theology from its pastoral origins, and diminish if not discredit every human faculty except the rational. Twenty-five years after the Council, we are still not producing *pastors*, presbyters who have aptitude and training for faith-community building as well as its liturgical climax: presiding in the Sunday assembly. Awareness of the problem is growing, and the basic ecclesiological reforms under way imply and promise ministerial reforms to follow. An encouraging number of the latter are now being widely discussed and actively sought: the substitution of qualifications for ordained ministry which have something to do with the work to be done, in place of the present and irrelevant "male" and "celibate" criteria; recruitment, training and ordination in closer relationship to the local church to be served; models for diocesan clerical lifestyle more appropriate than the monastic one; and opening the ordained ministries to women and to the married.

These and many other areas of church life and practice are all involved in attempting to deal with the innocent-sounding complaint in the letter to which I referred at the beginning of this column. "It all goes together." Basically, that's gratifying. We would be suspicious if it didn't. But it also means struggling in all these areas at the same time and with heavy opposition from the leadership in many of the churches. So we aim high and we are lucky if the gain is measurable. I, for example, still expect "something better than we got," or something better than we have yet achieved with God's help.

To stay sane and sober, one gets philosophical. Is progress *ever* easy for mortals to see? Our lives are short, and the creaturely resistance to inevitable change so tenacious that the slightest evolution is almost indiscernible. Like Becket's "friends" we "argue by results" . . . we want results. We want the fruit, the flower, the end. And all God ever gives us is a little tiny bit of the means, the aim, today. Jesus warned: "Enough, then, of worrying about tomorrow. Let tomorrow take care of itself. Today has troubles enough of its own" (Mt 6:34). Our today is and has been a wonderful time to be alive: lots of good seeds being planted. The hope that is very like our faith suggests they will survive . . . even in very unpleasant weather. Our generations may not see them in bloom, but they will be hardy perennials. And it has to be enough (just as, understandably, it never is) for mortals to have a small part in such a process.

6

"Translating" the Vernacular Liturgy*

My handy dictionary lists several meanings for the transitive verb
"translate." Among them: ". . . 2. to put into the words of a
different language. 3. to change into another medium or form (to
translate ideas into action). . . ." Against odds which not long ago
appeared formidable, the Western churches in communion with
the Roman church have accomplished for their liturgical celebrations at least the basic part of #2. That work continues, of course,
with the emendation of terms incongruous with a subsequent understanding of the fundamental meaning of the texts and also
with an unending quest for greater nobility and grace of form.

There is another, more important kind of translation, indicated
by meaning #3 above, which has not yet captured our imaginations in any general way: "ideas into action" . . . or the classic
liturgical expressions referring to the marks of God's reign, justice
and peace (liberation and reconciliation), into a concrete, contemporary agenda for the lives of believers and believing communities. Biblical faith must issue in a way of life. Its capacity for
enabling, inspiring and stimulating that way of life depends on
the classical nature of its expression in liturgy (Bible and sacrament). Liturgy's classical character is what enables it to serve all
times, all places. This kind of translation is our discovery of mission, witness, purpose; it is the permanent task of a pilgrim
people, both as persons and as churches, different and new in
every time and place.

We have recognized the need of translation #2. I wish we could
say the same, with any confidence at all, of translation #3, because, more than doctrines, commandments, or sacraments, that is
what Christian life is all about.

*Worship, March 1989

Before I get into that, a recent reminiscence might be helpful. When I looked in my "Vernacular" file for some reminders of that "radical" struggle, I found not only several copies of The Vernacular Society's quarterly *Amen*, dated from '51 to '60, but also the N.C.W.C. News Service's translation of beloved Pope John XXIII's apostolic constitution of 22 February 1962, *Veterum Sapientia.*

Now there was a pope who wore the office in a manner that did not cry out for a court jester. A friend who had been in Rome at the time of John's election told me (with appropriate affection and appreciation) this story of one of the new pope's first audiences. The Bishop of Rome came into the room, sat down and said to the assembled group: "So you came to see the pope. Here is the pope." Taking his nose between a forefinger and thumb, he began, "Il naso!" Holding up an arm, he continued, "Il braccio!" And he went on through an abridged list of parts of the human anatomy. The atmosphere John created in his ministry discouraged idolatry from the start.

In *Veterum Sapientia* the tone was more formal, for example: "After having examined and carefully pondered what has so far been outlined, we, fully conscious of our office and our authority, establish and order the following: . . . 2. That the same authorities (bishops and superiors general of religious orders) see to it with pastoral concern that none of their subjects, moved by an inordinate desire for novelty, writes against the use of Latin either in the teaching of the sacred disciplines or in the sacred rites of the liturgy, nor, prompted by prejudice, lessens the directive force of the will of the Apostolic See in this matter or alters its meaning . . . ."

But the voices of renewal and reform were persistent, and the erosion of the historical domination of those churches by Europe had been long in the works. Even in that document there was a brief nod in the direction of Eastern, other-language traditions. And when the Second Vatican Council, called by the same pope, decided it was past time to insist that all the baptized again possess the liturgy as their own and that they grow up, mature, as believers, with a full ownership of that incomparable source, the church's "Counter-Reformation" resistance to change had to yield, and happily did so.

If such a development is possible in a relatively short time, because of a general sense that it is required by the church's deepest reality, then the conciliar vision of a pilgrim, always-reforming church is clearly not as unrealistic as it may seem today. Far more is happening now in every aspect of the lives of local churches around the world than was the case before the Council. To mention only what may be the most important of many contemporary ecclesial phenomena, the recovery of the Christian Initiation of Adults as normative and as the permanent agenda of every local faith community is critical for moving attention to translation #3 ("ideas into action") from its present limits as the preoccupation of a spiritual elite to the center of consciousness in all the churches. For that recovery cannot but awaken us to the primary importance of that kind of "translating," which must occupy both our individual consciences/action and our corporate search for consensus/common action.

And what a transformation (however slow and gradual) that will be when not merely a live parish here or there but most of our thoroughly domesticated churches will begin to stir, to find their assigned social roles confining, to risk the alienation of those "members" who had become securely confident that the structures of "religion" would always buttress their power and wealth against the powerless and the poor. In this matter, predominantly black churches in our country are way ahead of the rest of us, simply because they know they are oppressed, they taste it every day, and the celebration of liberation and reconciliation in the eucharist both evokes ecclesial spirit and demands social action. By recognizing the more subtle idols that oppress all of us without exception and by identifying as the gospel insists with all who suffer, RCIA can enable that same dynamic to characterize every faith community, as we bring the signs of the times and the light of Christ together.

It is a great gift to have a liturgical tradition (biblical word and sacramental action inseparably joined) which reveals God's design for the world and makes us partners in its realization — one that does this in a classic way which can be applied anew in every succeeding time and in every different place. There are no blueprints or party line or concrete steps revealed, for such imprison the truth in a transitory moment. The concrete steps we have to work out with our imaginations and with the rest of the human race. But the direction, the orientation is clear in the word of God, liberator and reconciler. Everything is to be measured by that orientation. It is that clear direction in our sources, as well as their ambiguity about concrete steps, which invites the different interpretations and applications of different believers. And out of all our different insights, with the reconciling will of the community, we make a bit of progress here or there toward a consensus . . . *sensus ecclesiae.* That's why, at our best, we are so loath to stifle controversy, because it is fruitful. And because we are all, individually, so very limited.

That classic character of revelation illumines a way, an aim, without defining our steps. So it also involves temptations, to which we have corporately succumbed. We have created a disjunction between liturgy and justice/peace. One of those sins is our successful diminishing of the meaning of the message by reducing it to the dimensions of the after-life. "The reign of God," "the holy city," "eternal life," "heaven," and other synonyms have been robbed of their biblical and liturgical meaning and equated only with fulfillment. All or nothing. If we can't have perfect peace and perfect justice here and now, we don't want to be bothered with the aim, with the steps (risky and small) that incarnate. So we lose the meaning of human life in God's covenant. And our habits, customs, social institutions, political/economic structures can continue their idolatrous reign as long as this life lasts. Baptism ceases to mean the beginning of eternal life and God's new creation and becomes a mere family occasion. Eucharist becomes escape. Tragically, this has become the common temper of the churches, along with a fatalism about the world and its ills. Ask most of us Christians what our mission is and the reply will reveal the narrowest notion of evangelization: getting more members for the church. This is hardly the mission assigned by covenant, Law, prophets and the Christ. "Justice and justice alone shall be your aim" (Dt 16:20). "Your strength is not in numbers, nor does your power depend upon the stalwart; but you are the God of the lowly, the helper of the oppressed, the supporter of the weak, the protector of the forsaken, the savior of those without hope" (Jdt 9:11). These texts are not isolated. They are the refrain of the message.

Another of our sins in taking the teeth out of the liturgy is the privatizing and individualizing of God's design for the world. The loss of the full social dimension of revelation and mission has, of course, something to do with our acceptance as institution by the powers-that-be, but it has persisted long after those powers became supremely indifferent to us. Privately I am a member of the church and reap the benefits of its sources and its life. But my participation in social/cultural, political/economic organization and activity as a member of society and a citizen of the world and of a country is quite another thing, free of the influence of revelation. What a parody of the covenant and of faith's vision! If we want to think that the way of the Lord, morality, is merely the way we manage our sex lives, we can — obviously, we have — and so we remain the slaves of the institutional idols of our time: the military, big business, money. It simplifies life when you don't have to contest these powers, but it is also unfaithful.

As the Second Vatican Council taught, a new kind of human being is emerging in the new kind of world which human progress has opened up and brought close to all of us, with a new sense of responsibility toward all the sisters and brothers and toward history. No wonder there is moral confusion. Our consciences are tangling now with the whole immense and complex world. And its problems have developed faster than our capacity to deal with them. But the biblical vision is adequate to the new scene and our mission finally has an appropriate arena. So the simple, family, tribal, relatively isolated ways in which justice and peace took flesh in the various ages reflected in our biblical-liturgical sources must be translated in a new way. Among other things, it means seeing government (and taxes) as the only instruments we have for doing together what we cannot do alone. It means taking governments in hand, with active subsidiary associations, and using our participation and power to see that through them we serve the needs of all, not merely those of the powerful. As theologian Joseph Sittler wrote, justice is love operating at a distance.

Yet we still want to believe that philanthropy, noblesse oblige, our handouts, our benevolent giving out of our abundance to the impoverished are somehow the fulfillment of the Law, our proper mission. On the contrary, our sources are quite clear that what we do not need belongs by right to the impoverished. It is not ours to ''give.'' Our mission is to create a world that enables the liberation and reconciliation of all. Leonardo Boff spoke to both sins:

48

"The reign of God, the eschatological liberation of the world, is already in process, is already being established. It takes shape in concrete modifications of actual life" (*An Advent Sourcebook*, ed. Thomas J. O'Gorman [Chicago: Liturgy Training Publications] 1988, 10).

Recognizing our sinfulness in ignoring our covenant mission is a large and courageous step. For it means accepting a constant tension in our lives between our at-homeness in the world and our faith-vision of what it must become. Like our spiritual ancestors, our moments of faithfulness are fewer than the periods during which the idols of the day enjoy our almost undivided allegiance. We are always falling away . . . and coming back . . . holing up for a while . . . and resuming the journey. Israel's biblical story is the story of believers and believing communities everywhere and always. We want to think translation #2 is enough, but translation #3 is the heart of the matter. We can be patient with ourselves as long as we keep repenting, keep resuming the pilgrimage, keep clear the orientation to the reign of God's liberation and reconciliation, keep opening our habitually closed selves with the help of our imaginations to new possibilities.

When the next attitude poll brings the depressing news that church members share the same prejudices, hostilities, greed and the same lack of responsibility for using political-economic-structural tools for a contemporary mission, as the larger society, our sinfulness is not the issue. But our placid confidence that our piety remains intact should scare the wits out of us.

7

Sorting Out Our Ways
of Common Prayer*

One of the many gifts of the Second Vatican Council in my
church is the attention it drew to the local church — parishes, dioceses, and larger areas or national units of cohesion. It had to do
this for the sake of the other reforms it mandated. It recalled a
forgotten part of our tradition that valued decentralization and the
principle of subsidiarity. Just as Michael Harrington and some
other promoters of economic reform in our society have responded
to the lessons of modern history by proposing a socialization that
has to be built from local constituents and not imposed by political
authority's force, so we in the churches cannot afford to overlook
or minimize the Council's appropriation of that basic human institutional principle (and of the church's own earlier tradition).

That conciliar gift was not bestowed at the expense of our unity
as local church with the other churches. In fact, it was given as
the only healthy basis for the universal communion to which all
Christians are committed. (And which my church, like others, had
been pursuing with some success until recent Roman developments.) In my old age, it seems more and more clear to me that
the Council will be remembered and celebrated for that gift more
than for any other. And hope assures me that it will come into its
own some time in the future: " 'Watchman, how much longer the
night? Watchman, how much longer the night?' The watchman replies, 'Morning has come, and again night. If you will ask, ask;
come back again' " (Is 21:11b-12).

Vernacular languages and other liturgical reforms, coming out of
that concern, are obviously aimed at the local churches' making

*Worship, May 1989

the liturgy their own, possessing it, becoming comfortable in it —
which, it seems to me, means making the liturgy their popular
worship, their popular devotion. The recent interest in what are
called "popular devotions" needs to be examined carefully in relation to the liturgy. We are all well aware of Western theology's
fondness for distinctions (and no one can doubt that many of
them have served us well). But the distinction between liturgy and
"popular devotions" creates at least as many problems as it solves.

If the way we pray is the way we believe, and if we are not immune from the classic temptations of the covenant people since
Abraham and Sarah, then we had better take a second look at that
distinction and its consequences. If "popular devotions" and the
faith life out of which they grow are formed by the liturgy (where
Bible and sacrament come alive in the proclamation and action of
the Sunday assembly), there is no problem, except perhaps one of
time and schedules and the extra-ecclesial obligations and mission
of believers. If they affirm a local people, an ethnic group in ways
which "put down" no other people or group and which create no
"enemies," there is no problem. If they give priority to praise and
thanks, if they are fiercely monotheistic in feeling as in doctrine, if
they are totally devoid of miraculous pretensions, there is no
problem. If they serve the full, active and conscious participation
of all believers in the liturgy, there is no problem. If they are also
truly popular and not merely the interest of "leaders" who are
either inimical to liturgical renewal or unwilling to work at it,
there is no problem.

The recent publication of *Household Blessings and Prayers* by the
National Conference of Catholic Bishops' Committee on the Liturgy (Washington, D.C., United States Catholic Conference, 1988,
$18.95, 433 pp.) offers households, families and other small groups
forms of prayer which meet those criteria and more. If one must
use the phrase, "popular devotions," it is what I would call the
best. How marvelous it would be and how much it would change
things, if bishops, parish staffs and other leaders would actively
promote its use!

Its Foreword reads in part: "Prayer must happen in the 'little
churches' — the households, the families — if the Sunday assembly is to become a community of prayer . . . this book is devoted
to that 'bond of prayer' that joins the prayer of the Sunday as-

sembly to the daily prayers of every Catholic, the bond between Roman Catholics of all descriptions and our bond to other Christians and, in many ways, to Jews from whom we have learned so much of our prayer. . . . Wear this book out with use until you know much of it by heart . . . '' (pp. 2–4).

Virginia Sloyan, of The Liturgical Conference, says of it: ''Put in the hands of adults or children in the setting of their homes, it will say: 'Stand tall. What we do together is important, and lovely!' For their dignity, form, simplicity and occasional unpredictability, the prayers and blessings that appear without attribution are rich supplements to the cited selections: from Judaism, the Christian Scriptures, the saints, hymns, bishops' pastorals. . . . For all the teachable moments, big and little, in our households, the book is a mine of gold'' (*Commonweal*, March 10, 1989, pp. 148–49).

In Chicago's *Liturgy 80*, Gabe Huck discusses its virtues and its limits, concluding in part: ''Perhaps the two most important things about this book are the recognition that the prayer of the church is the responsibility of all the baptized and the assumption that we must deal well with ritual. These are not new ideas in the Catholic tradition. In most times and places the baptized have had their vocabulary of rituals: song and gesture, seasons and occasions, short prayers and verses. . . . This book is a gift that invites all to consider anew their baptismal task. . . .'' (February/March 1989, p. 80).

In contrast to the gospel fidelity and vigor of such prayers, ''popular devotions'' which arose out of liturgical alienation or petrification in whatever quarter tend not only to reflect but also to teach and perpetuate that sad state of affairs. If our lives were liturgically-centered and rich in biblical and gospel terms, we might be able to afford such luxury. But, of course, that kind of life would not feel the need. No ethnic flavor (which, when appropriate, we should be finding in our liturgical celebrations) can rescue common prayers of that sort from their debilitating flaws.

When believing communities in general are not being actively involved in and formed by the proclamation and action of the Sunday assembly, we can hardly blame them for looking elsewhere and for coming up with ''popular'' worship that is both privatized and bizarre. But I am not thinking about blame. I am thinking about the terrible loss of Christian orientation when such forms are used and begin to dominate our consciousness and begin to take the place of "right worship" (orthodoxy).

Liturgy, with its biblical base and motif, is acutely sensitive to the temptations that beset the believing community, the local church. Idolatry remains the principal one and all the others are its aspects: the hunger for a manageable god, for some kind of control, some kind of manipulative power with respect to divine blessing and benevolence, for a god whose ways are our ways and whose thoughts are our thoughts, for a pantheon of creature-gods and its consequent diffusion of our responsibility. Another is making petition and intercession primary, in place of the praise and thanks which have a crucial priority in Jewish and Christian tradition. Another is the shamanizing of the clergy, making them exclusive avenues of grace rather than pastors in a faith community with common avenues. Another comes close to the liturgy but makes its secondary aspects primary, hopelessly confusing and perhaps losing the latter.

When devotion takes flesh in the words and actions of a community alienated from liturgy, it reveals all kinds of more or less subtle yieldings to these temptations. For example, to make what is clearly secondary in the eucharist more important than its primary meaning is to inflict the kind of spiritual and symbolic damage from which conciliar reform is trying to save us. We have all seen and are still seeing the effects of devotions which made an *object* out of what is primarily a sacrament, a symbolic *action*. This happened innocently enough, because the eucharist had ceased to involve and form the faithful. So a dynamic sacrament of proclaiming the word of God in assembly and eating and drinking together in Christ, joining thereby as one in the spiritual sacrifice which is acceptable worship before the one only God — that action is for all practical purposes lost to many, along with the mission it commands. All is reduced to a veneration of its increasingly distant element, as an object.

A "time of the great sorting" is what one commentator called the post-conciliar decades. And, since reform is now the permanent life of the church (in theory), the sorting will continue to be part of its vigilance. It seems to me that we have an unparalleled opportunity to fan the flames of human liberation and unification (justice and peace) already ignited by a happy combination of traditional influences (including the Bible) and modern developments and technology. But we cannot afford the luxury of diversions and amusements which might be acceptable in an ecclesiastical ghetto. We started out after the Council quite serious about this sorting out of things. Vernacular languages in the liturgy (merely one of the requirements for the full, conscious, active participation of all) led us deeper and deeper into the waters of baptism toward a recovery of conversion (of life rather than of loyalty), catechumenate-initiation and a community of faith with serious counter-cultural implications.

Admittedly in this pontificate the sorting seems to have been stopped, or reversed, but one must hope that this will appear in history only as a sad interruption. What some church leaders and the media curiously regard as a contest between "orthodoxy" and a less fervent commitment, looks to me like something else. I think it is rather a contest (no denying there is a contest afoot) between a conciliar and reform commitment, based on the church's sources and the signs of the times, on the one hand, and, on the other, the predictable second-thoughts with respect to the Council of administrators quite naturally made nervous and even frightened by the prospects which that conciliar commitment had opened up.

All through our scriptural and subsequent history, Jewish and Christian faith communities have known this tension, this contest between the prophetic and the institutional. To choose one or the other is to depart from the tradition, like choosing liberation or reconciliation (either-or instead of the orthodox both-and). It is also too easy, inhuman and unreal. To keep them together and indissoluble is what the covenant tradition of the Bible is about. Its responsibility is also to prevent the institutional from its sometimes overt tendency to smother or kill the prophetic, whose dynamism and truth are the institution's reason for existing (and which are found nowhere else). What scares the elected guardians of the household (to the extent that they have subordinated the pastoral basis of their offices) is what scares us all: the biblical refrain of repentance, letting-go, opening up in faithfulness to the Spirit — Jesus' refrain of repentance, growth, change, newness. They need the help that a passive and consumer-type body of faithful cannot provide.

On St Valentine's Day this year, *The New York Times'* "Quotation of the Day" was from Prime Minister Benazir Bhutto of Pakistan. Commenting on some of the "Fundamentalists" (another euphemism) in her country, she said: "The dying order always likes to give a few kicks before it goes to rest." The churches which sadly now seem associated with the "kicks" nevertheless have at their heart and center the bread and wine for which a dawning consciousness in humanity is hungry: faith's vision of the reign of God, the table from which no one is excluded, where all are one and all are free. Our eucharist like the church itself is but a sign pointing to that fulfillment.

But it's pretty cloudy now and it takes a lot of "sorting out." And time is always and by nature limited.

8

Liturgy's *Sine Qua Non:*
A Sense of the Holy*

One of the several advantages of having lived and partly lived through the greater part of this remarkable century is the sobriety which experience lends to recollection, its tempering of nostalgia. Personal experience of "the good old days" is not a guarantee of fidelity to facts, but it certainly helps avoid outrageous romanticizing. Whether the topic of conversation is education, politics, or public worship, our tendency to berate the (unquestionably dismal) current state of affairs by attaching a certain aura to a previous era seems to be a feature of the human psyche.

It is not Pollyannish to suspect that generalized deploring of the present in comparison with an imagination-colored past is merely one of the ways in which we make our lives more comfortable and shun our responsibility for change and growth. But that is another subject.

The readers of this essay are acquainted, I am sure, with the lament that the liturgical movement and the reform of liturgical texts and actions in recent decades have adversely affected our experience of "a sense of the Holy." Overt or implied, that lament is part of the currency of references to liturgical renewal in conversation, literature, and theater. One hears it not only from the many whose only relation to church is nostalgic but also from many active believers. It is more complicated than it sounds and it is not easy to dismiss. In fact, no criticism could be more serious, since it strikes at the very heart of what the faith community is about.

For the weekly worship assembly is the heart of covenant community life. And that public worship's sine qua non is its orienta-

*Worship, July 1990

tion to the only One who is Holy, to God. It is the faith community's self-realization, enabling a true "sense of the Holy" in its participants. It celebrates the revelation of the Unknowable and the symbolization of the Unutterable. It relates the worshipers to one another as one subject, a body, a reconciled humanity because it relates all of us, without exception, to one Holy Source and Lover, thereby liberating all of us from the idols we are forever making, from the absolutizing of any other allegiance, from oppressions recognized and unrecognized. It cannot benefit God. Liturgy exists to give us access to these gifts. To miss a conscious experience of these gifts is to make liturgy meaningless. That is why full, conscious, active participation by all is the aim of any and every renewal effort.

The Holy — revealed in the covenant history of Judaism and Christianity, according to the condition of a humanity slowly evolving, as Love surpassing understanding — is celebrated whenever the faith community gathers for the proclamation of the biblical message and for sacramental worship action. Those are the basic symbols given to enable our "sense of the Holy": the assembly, the Bible and the action. In a sense, all three are one, because the faith community gathers for the worship action, precisely to do that action, and proclaiming/hearing the biblical readings is as critical a part of the action as the baptismal, eucharistic or any other rite. The symbols do not capture God but rather open us to a vision of God's will for us — a developing vision attuned to our developing capacity. With the signs of succeeding "times" they are the earth and the sun and the rain which foster that development.

The depth that faith sees as revelation in Judaism's development and, for Christians in its Christ-fruit, was visible even in the earliest stages of covenant history, when a tribal and nomadic group somehow glimpsed the unity of "the nations" and the freedom of all persons inherent in acknowledgment of one God's sole dominion over all that is — that depth could continue to animate and orientate our seeking only because its symbolic communication is classic, applicable to all times and places. The Holy One is revealed as "known" in the command to do justice . . . and then in the command to be reconciled with those unlike ourselves . . . and then to be Love, which includes both (liberation and solidarity).

Those liturgical symbols effectively preclude our idolatrous wish to make the Holy One our tool or our instrument for whatever purpose . . . or even an agent with whom we can bargain. So great is the mystery of the covenant that believers' "sense of the Holy" sanctions on our part only modesty, humility, openness to receiving, thanksgiving and praise. No proud assertion, no smug assurance, no self-confident rhetoric, no judgment of others, no inflation of ourselves or our official leaders (servants).

Isn't this the only kind of "sense of the Holy" to which believers dare aspire? And if we do not experience it in the Sunday assembly's scriptural proclamation and eucharistic action, if we do not find it in that symbol, is it possible we are looking for something else, something that may comfort us but is either unrelated to the faith we share or its enemy? Or is it possible that we are not looking there at all — to the public face of the church in its liturgy — and are instead seduced by today's mass media interpretations which (even from ecclesiastical leaders) sometimes evidence a less firm grip on the essentials than we might hope for.

Surely we are only beginning again to learn how to employ the symbol fully and fairly and finely, how to celebrate (and create an appropriate environment for) public worship. We must continue to work hard on those practical problems. But "a sense of the holy" must be the basis and the atmosphere of all such efforts. Like our Jewish forebears, we Christians are always going after strange gods. The Bible makes it clear that most of us most of the time and all of us some of the time are on the wrong track. We are sinners. We are creatures with limits. We are pilgrims moving toward something not yet realized . . . and without blueprints. This is not a lament, but simply a fact of life. And, because it is a fact of life, it is a fact of faith. It is not only in 1990 that the churches are not a pretty sight. We are never a pretty sight. But it is the dynamite of meaning in our sources, in the liturgical symbol, that makes the unpalatable institution more than merely palatable: necessary, our spiritual home, the place where our hunger and thirst for the Holy can find nourishment.

Sometimes I wonder whether the apparent insensitivity of some of the clergy to that basic hunger and thirst is not a by-product of sad developments in church history — the clericalism frequently addressed in these pages. Unless they fight the alienation consciously and constantly, clergy can so easily lose their membership and involvement in the day-to-day economic, political and cultural life of the world. The tiny ecclesiastical system can become their world. "Protections" and privileges and, sometimes in urban areas, a steady stream of ritual services can almost totally isolate them from the experience of the rest of the Sunday assembly (in which they preside). In such a "sacred" ghetto, it is bound to be more difficult to sympathize with the need most serious Christians feel for a Sunday assembly that is neither pro forma nor another session in group therapy.

Recently it was my privilege to attend a gathering in honor of Father Gerard S. Sloyan, priest of Trenton diocese, biblical scholar, liturgical renewal promoter and benefactor, Jewish-Christian reconciler, ecumenist, writer, teacher, one of those rare thinkers whose specialization loses sight of nothing. In one of the several rejuvenating papers that day, Dr Carolyn Osiek spoke on the contribution of biblical studies to our common life in terms of *access*. Simply, the word indicates much of what we all owe to the liturgical movement as well as to biblical scholars: the access to sources, which every student knows is indispensable to genuine inquiry, no matter how many authoritative and gifted interpreters are available.

Access to the mediated glimpses of the Holy in liturgy's symbolic action is the aim of liturgical renewal in every age. If such access seems an impediment to "a sense of the Holy," then we can dismiss the feeling, or we are victims of the deprivation of our immediate past. Nor should such feelings surprise us, for human nature tends to prefer the misery it knows to any new and unfamiliar relief.

Access, of course, is always in particular contexts, in concrete faith communities and their celebrations — which asks a lot of the particular Sunday assembly. What may be called the "style" of celebration may be so impersonal and rote and ideological, on the one hand, or so capricious and manipulative and idiosyncratic, on the other, that it conceals rather than reveals the sources.

Many Christians are so accustomed to the former distortion that "a sense of the Holy" is equated with dim lighting, privatized "attendance," the evident proprietorship of a clerical caste, and other marks of liturgical decadence and stagnation. We have to confront the idolatry and superstition which always lurk around the edges of faith. There is almost nothing we like better than to relinquish our responsibility for accepting and living faith and hope and love's justice and peace, by trading this precious access for the private and quiet glow of a shrine, or the bargaining of a novena, or the party-line interpretation of a guru. Growing up is difficult. Straining for the Holy Who remains beyond our reach is somehow less attractive than reducing the Holy to dimensions we can handle.

Baptist Harvey Cox described the two styles of liturgical perversion I mentioned above: "Ritual becomes *ideology* when it is used to throttle creativity, to channel religion or fantasy into safely accepted molds. Organized religions in periods of decline, nations anxious to enforce patriotism and obedience, individuals who feel they are losing a grip on themselves — all become self-conscious and meticulous about ritual proprieties. . . . Ritual becomes *idiosyncratic* when it ceases to be shared by a group or to emerge from historical experience, when it becomes the property of just one, or of just a few people. . . . Ritual does for movement what language does for sound, transforms it from the inchoate into the expressive. Therefore an idiosyncratic ritual is ultimately frustrating and self-defeating" (*The Feast of Fools*, Harvard University Press 1969, pp. 71–73). Jewish and Christian liturgy belong to that ritual genus.

Both finicky ceremonialism and careless disregard of traditional structures are fatal to a liturgical celebration which would provide access to revealed sources. Structure here means the patterns of our rites as they have developed through centuries of faithful use. It does not, of course, mean the building or space for worship. Some of the current contexts which give rise to complaint are a natural result of assemblies still attempting to renew their celebrations in unreformed architectural spaces. If a parish's idea of "renovation" is merely the placing of an altar facing the people in a worship space built as a shrine for sacred objects rather than an arena for communal symbolic actions, no wonder that its efforts to involve all the people sometimes descend to the ridiculous, the idiosyncratic, the imitation of theater or sports events or therapy sessions. A crazy environment encourages crazy actions. Places built for a clerical liturgy and its audience make the liturgical recovery of an initiated assembly (understanding itself as the body of Christ and its specialized ministers as parts of itself as well as leaders) well nigh impossible.

I think these are all considerations related to the complaint about a diminished "sense of the Holy." Assuming, however, that "the Holy" comes to mean for all of us God's oneness and sole dominion, any diminishment of that "sense" is the end of worship, public or private.

9

The Relevance of the Liturgy*

It is natural, too natural, in any movement of reform and renewal
after a long period of stagnation, that repair efforts should make
some mistakes. Some of the paths we follow in our attempt to get
back on the pilgrim trail turn out to be blind alleys. The many
who do nothing, because they are tired or because they do not see
the problems, make the biggest mistake of all.

But we should not ignore mistakes-in-progress in our own
camp, even when their advocates are motivated by the same desire that moves us: to make the Sunday assembly's liturgical
celebration fully participatory, alive and relevant as "the primary
and indispensable source of the true Christian spirit." The *desire*
alone is not enough. Liturgy is a tradition, not a concoction, and
its relevance is on a deeper, more universal, more effective level
than the action-interpretations of any individual or group bound
by inevitable limits of time, place, knowledge and experience. Our
best efforts at incarnating the reign of God's liberating/reconciling
will at this moment must be modest, humble, open to the further
steps (political, economic, cultural) which we do not yet see.

The mistake-in-progress I am concerned with here is hard to
identify in abstract terms but unmistakable when one experiences
it in celebration. When a single "theme" or action-issue dominates
the entire rite and one's attention is drawn to the planners and
leaders rather than to the biblical God, participants are deprived
of the reign-of-God breadth for the sake of an agenda, deprived of
the stimulus to use all of our gifts in the work of interpretation for
the sake of ready-made and only momentarily cogent "answers."

When any oppressed group turns in upon itself, forgets that its
experience should make it the advocate for all, indulges "liturgi-

*Worship, September 1990

cally" in self-promotion and self-pity, the relevance of liturgy is ir-retrievably lost. Single-issue zealots are sad enough in the political and economic spheres. They are a total disaster as liturgy planners. The rightness of their cause is not in question. The nature of liturgy *is*.

As readers of this column know, I never tire of quoting theologian Joseph Sittler's remarks about imposing "themes" on the liturgy, which conclude: "We must not . . . declare a premature calm over the boiling sea of the biblical witness. That body of water is a tumult of oppositions, a disclosure of tensions, a mighty music instinct with the thudding of matters that cannot be made completely harmonious." We have no right to avoid, by forcing the community's liturgy into a mold that seems momentarily apt to the planners, the human responsibility for activating all our faculties (especially imagination) in a continuing work of practical interpretation in every new day and situation. The liturgy stimulates that work but never substitutes for it. The work is ours, with the rest of the human family, and therefore is always tentative and modest and open to correction.

Perhaps it should not be necessary, but I think it is, to preface these remarks with the statement that the writer's conviction about the church's task today, our mission, is to make the little, time-bound steps toward justice/peace which a consensus of our current perceptions of appropriate action suggests. That's part of our service to the rest of humanity: to speak and act on concrete issues. The liturgy, however, cannot be bent to replace our human and fallible activity or to lend it the aura of God's word without surrendering its character and power.

We are a people of biblical tradition. Our faith is a common faith, the faith of the community. Individually and in our sub-groups we are different in countless ways, which differences (when they are valued rather than feared) are part of our glory. They enable us to learn from each other, as persons and as groups, and to transcend the dreadful limits of every person's and every group's current perceptions and interpretations. And we are pilgrims in history needing the big aim, the big picture which stimulates and invites creative imagination, and much more than we need dictation about the next, immediate step, a liturgy reduced to the narrow dimensions of one group's current perceptions.

This may be a hard saying, but it is so fundamental to the meaning and spirit and power of liturgical celebration that it makes one want to scream quite as desperately in some "progressive" liturgical celebrations as in *all* pro forma, rote and clerical ones. It illustrates our cultural difficulty with symbol and with the inefficiency, playfulness and contemplation symbol requires. It exacerbates that basic problem. It encourages the illusion that liturgy's verbal texts are meant to supply the "answers" to the immediate problems of daily life, whereas the entire liturgy (whose nonverbal elements are *at least* as important as the verbal ones) is concerned with our life's orientation to the reign of God. Liturgy is thus catholic, unifying, comprehensive, seminal, productive of growth and development beyond our present condition. It forms us and stimulates our imaginations to deal with today's issues without offering blueprints, or a specific agenda. It trusts us to develop these and to keep on revising them.

It is such a liturgy that has kept faith alive through millennia of Jewish and Christian history: millennia during which both biblical groups have been idolaters in one way or another most of the time, preferring a god in our image who will provide a list of do's and don't's for every occasion, afraid of the mystery and ambiguity of the vision of God's reign (the end which stimulates our continued seeking and which refuses to permit us to be satisfied with today's "cutting edge"). A culture insensitive to symbol and disinclined to accept political and economic responsibility is severely tempted to measures of "crowd control," "party lines," the imposition of one interpretation upon all. Inspiration and stimulus be damned, we say, we want an agenda. But actions imposed prove to be neither liberating nor reconciling, and those two aspects of the biblical God's love are indissoluble (a word we like only when we apply it to our doing). Like so much else in our culture that is throwaway, what Harvey Cox calls "idiosyncratic" treatment will make the liturgy throwaway as well.

Liturgy's classic character on the whole enables it to offer moments such as the homily and the intercessions when the assembly's here-and-now interpretations should be expressed, when such expression is legitimate and appropriate and necessary. We need these moments of relative spontaneity, when the present stage of the assembly's pilgrim journey is the focus. Students of

the berakah, model of our eucharistic prayer, tell us that tradition-
ally it was not only a thanksgiving for God's deeds but one
framed in the precise time in Jewish history when it was offered.
All this, however, without sacrificing the liturgy's classic character.

So in our tradition the biblical readings enjoy a clear primacy
over the homily, and the local assemblies are asked to include certain broad categories in the general intercessions. Isn't that subordination of interpretation in the rites also the reason why homilies
are not the last word of interpretation but rather the first, the
priming of the pump, encouraging all of us to continue that work
with our own consciences, in our thoughts and words and deeds?

All of us except the most supine are aware that the rich and the
powerful in each succeeding age have claimed ownership of the
liturgy, as well as of the church in general. But for the liturgy's
ambiguously classic, "far-off" vision of God's design for utter justice, perfect peace, their claim might at some point have seemed
cogent. Since they are as innocent of the power of God's word in
symbolic communication as the rest of us, they have satisfied
themselves with their influence upon the way we preach and the
intercessions we make. They always impress the crowd, for we
are obviously more awed by wealth and power than by divinity
. . . most of the time. But, whatever the general temper of the
churches, it is our liturgical sources (far more than any other aspect of church life) which raise our eyes above the rich and
powerful and enable singular, prophetic voices. In the long run
the rich and powerful are defeated by the very liturgy they claim
to own.

One of the most obvious examples in American history is the
defeat of slave-owners, who mistakenly thought that exposure to
their church traditions would induce a more passive and docile
mood among the African workers, whose bondage was making the
"owners" rich. Instead of fulfilling the wishes of the "masters,"
however, the biblical stories and songs (the language of the liturgy) to which the slaves were introduced became the language of
a revolution that is still going on. In other words, it is not the liturgy which blesses the status quo . . . now, or at any point in
the evolution of human institutions. It is our satisfaction with the
way things are *for us* that renders us almost incapable of understanding the liturgy we celebrate. Hence we resort to the superfi-

cial and self-defeating measures under discussion (the idiosyncratic domination of public worship by ideologies, by our limited vision, by our self-consciousness, self-pity, self-promotion) to supply what we fail to perceive the traditional rites are already supplying.

Our rites supply not the answers, not the concrete socio-economic steps today toward justice/peace, but rather the sanction, inspiration, orientation, and dynamic to move believers to join with other people and groups who want to make the world a better home for all. Our rites do not excuse us from work, they impel us to work, to create the local, "intermediate" (in Bellah's terminology) institutions without which democracy perishes and economic socialization goes the way of the imposed communism of Eastern Europe. God's word does not supply what we have the brains and the imaginations to create. Liturgy moves us to use our brains and activate our imaginations, if we work at it with love and with dissatisfaction; if we adapt the language of the readings, songs and prayers to be not only inclusive but incisive and compelling; and if we open up the symbolic action until the gestures and the acts have no need of "explanation."

People who know they are oppressed and divided as long as any of their sisters and brothers are oppressed and divided perceive what satisfied and socially dominant types fail to recognize. The rich and powerful may call the shots for many preachers, teachers and ecclesiastical officials (whose occasional or frequent lapses into sycophancy are legend). But the traditional, classic, slowly-evolving-through-countless-generations-of-believers liturgy keeps undermining their foundations, keeps washing away the sand on which their castles are built. Unlike fads and fancies sometimes imposed upon the liturgy by good-willed, superficial, impatient planners, liturgical tradition respects every member in every assembly engaged in doing the rites far too much to indulge in manipulation of brain-washing.

C. S. Lewis wrote in *The Chronicles of Narnia* ("The Horse and the Boy," Book 5): " . . . in Calormen, story-telling (whether the stories are true or made-up) is a thing you's taught, just as English boys and girls are taught essay-writing. The difference is that people want to hear stories, whereas I never heard of anyone who wanted to read the essays."

And W. H. Auden said it another way: "You cannot tell people what to do, you can only tell them parables; that is what art really is, particular stories of particular people and experiences (M. K. Spears, *The Poetry of W. H. Auden*, p. 13). (Thanks to Don Wardlaw for the two references above.)

Stories are the Bible's and Jesus' and the liturgy's way.

10

What Should We Ask of the Liturgy?*

It seems to me that the growing number of worshipers expressing disappointment and frustration with their Sunday assembly's eucharistic celebrations is one of the healthiest signs of these early days of ecclesial renewal. It is evidence that the possession of liturgy's biblical traditional sources through the full, conscious, active participation of all is becoming the desire of some of the faithful. When people become aware of the critical part played in liturgy's symbol-language by what were formerly called "externals" (environment, music, choreography/movement/gesture, distinction of roles, engagement of all, etc.), they realize that a mere pro forma ritualizing is a profound injustice, a denial of their baptismal rights, to say nothing of the fact that the rote or casual performance of presiders and other leaders insults the rest of the assembly.

The resulting disenchantment is healthy when it leads to corrective action. Serious believers are no longer satisfied with the feeling that they have fulfilled a duty or an "obligation." They see more clearly that the object of our worship has no need of it, and that worship is not barter but thanksgiving, praise and orientation. So they understand better their need for common expression, inspiration and experience. Entrenched habits, clerical weariness, and a euphemized institutional inertia conspire to resist the demands of the thoughtful, to turn their disappointment and frustration into anger, and to build the vast army of non-practicing former Christians. . . .

We have a right to ask much more of the Sunday assembly's liturgical celebration. But we have no right at all to ask anything

*Worship, May 1991

that will undermine its symbolic, classic, ambiguous character. For the biblical message, the message of the liturgy, is not a series of specific answers to the specific problems of our time. Rather, it is durable because it is our orientation to God and therefore to each other — our orientation to a common and mysterious Source in relation to whom we find our dignity/liberation and our reconciliation/solidarity. In the former we find our freedom from all other powers and masters, our conscience. In the latter we find our common bonds with all other human beings as sisters and brothers. A pilgrim people's problems are different at every stage of the journey. Liturgy offers the basis for all these stages, refrains from offering the specifics that might mire us in some former stage of the journey, and invites all of our different imaginations and other gifts to grapple with the problems of the day.

Liturgy inspires this human work in offering this basis and in providing for the mere beginnings of interpretation in the light of the signs of our times (homilies, general intercessions, etc.). But its great gift is the raising of human hearts and eyes above (or their penetration deeply below) even the "cutting edge" of today's causes of justice/peace. Thus God believes in us, loves us, far more than our limits believe and love God. It is the lack of dictated packaged answers to specific current problems that trusts and dignifies us by laying upon us all the duty of bringing our gifts to bear on the problems of today — many different interpretations coming together to make another common step on the pilgrim journey.

I remember an address by Gregory Baum delivered to a Dignity convention in 1981, where he encouraged gays and lesbians to be leaders in the broader struggle for human rights in every sphere, not merely in their own. He pointed out that ideological unity in any society always means a heavy pattern of conformity. For example, "Jews can be well only in an untidy society." People who know oppression, if they are believers, should be more concerned with generic oppression, for their own particular case has its roots in what Baum called "the real relation between the political order and the psychic order." In order to keep society moving and to prevent stagnation (and that is part of what our pilgrim community is about), any oppressed group is able to see (better than most) current hypocrisies and injustices and therefore has a vocation to be a social critic, to be a pressure for and seed-planter of social change, to be in the forefront of a common struggle against sexism, racism, classism, homelessness, joblessness, neglect of the poor, and the rest.

What Baum said to that group is what the liturgy says to all believers. To attempt to make the liturgy a tool of any one current cause, therefore, is to undermine its basic, classic role and its real power. Of course, we use in liturgical celebration the tools of the cultures of the assembly involved: language, music, etc. But the thrust is not local pride or the pride of our group, but universal, reaching toward the other, solidarity with all and reconciliation. Justice for ourselves is only a part of justice for all.

This danger of asking the wrong thing of liturgy is related to the modern, Western fact that our questions tend to be articulated in terms of individualism and a private spiritual quest. When the question so misses the point, any "answer" is useless. For the biblical tradition understands faith in one God as a gift through a human community of believers, a covenant community, *not* as either a private gift or a private acquisition. And that biblical community is a pilgrim, in a constant process of corporate growth, development in understanding, worship and mission, the last being its reign-of-God witness for justice/peace, liberation/reconciliation in the world.

Our pilgrim progress or evolution is painfully slow for our brief lives, because, although stimulated by individuals or the few, it must become a corporate growth. Which means we do not see "the results" — our small, tentative, fallible, liberating/reconciling, public and private steps toward the ultimate fulfillment of God's reign of justice and peace are the only "results" any generation sees. Humans must be content to be and remain tiny parts of the unseen God's mysterious vocation-process. Like all social/political/economic developments, the growth is not steady, even, balanced, universal, every-day-in-every way onward and upward. Rather, it is in fits and starts, here and there, sometimes spawned in the most unlikely quarters, not welcomed at first by the community as a whole, in time becoming its consensus.

The biblical tradition has certainly played a seminal role in the development of the very individualism which now makes it so difficult for Western types to appreciate its corporate process (and its corporate worship). In that part of the world, certainly, many other forces have been at work: creating an atmosphere in which not only the dignity and rights of the individual person have gained a hitherto unknown respect and legal sanction, but also, and tragically, the commonweal has suffered disinterest, neglect, and even contempt.

For communities of biblical faith, the latter effect is devastating. For such communities, whether Jewish or Christian, find their "primary and indispensable source," their inspiration and their vocation in corporate worship, in the ritual action of liturgy, in symbol, where the Bible stories live in the proclamation/hearing of the community and in the deeds of rite.

What we dare not forget is that the liturgy assumes that the assembly which celebrates gathers with a profound sense of its corporate unity: in other words, not as a random meeting of individuals, but as a single entity made up of many members, whose bonds are stronger and more real than any bonds of family, tribe, blood, color, nation, or other human social category. The unbalanced nature of our pilgrim's progress, then, can itself be a handicap to further development, unless we recognize its partial and transient character and compensate for it — that is, keep our feet on the terra firma of liturgical tradition and refuse to be swept off them by any momentary "cutting edge." It seems to me that only that kind of profound fidelity can keep us moving and open to further progress.

"What should we ask of the liturgy?" is a healthy question only when members who are articulating expectations have freed themselves, or allowed themselves to be freed, from the rugged individualism of our culture as well as from the inebriation of always-limited temporal successes. This means a humble, bonded relationship with the rest of the community of faith and with the rest of the human race, for all are called and all are potential members.

Such a relationship does not mean that we agree with all the others, that we all interpret our sources in precisely the same way, that we like all the others and find no enemies among them. The different gifts and different interpretations which different members, old and new, bring to the community are essential to its life and to the process being discussed. Were it otherwise, we would still be offering sacrifices of animals and crops instead of the *thusla logike, oblatio rationabilis,* the sacrifice of the Cross, the sacrifice of being and life-orientation, the sacrifice of obedience and praise. Were it otherwise, we would be even more unaware of sexist, racist, classist elements in the very biblical tradition that strains against them and enables us to continue the struggle.

Our bonded oneness is moved by God along its pilgrim way not only by saints and prophets, persuasion and prayer, but also by very earthy argument and discord, non-violent resistance and struggle, by the interaction of different schools and ways of interpretation — all of which are enabled to serve the progress of the whole by a common humility before the mystery of God, before the vision of God's reign, and by our clumsy efforts to love one another in spite of disagreements and enmities.

The ecumenical movement is an important recognition of the earthy unity appropriate to a faith community whose ministry with the rest of the world is biblically defined as reconciliation/liberation. Until recently that movement showed real signs of fruition, although its progress seems to be currently and temporarily thwarted by officials and other members who are too attached to administration and housekeeping, to historical animosities and pride. Its great gift, meanwhile, to the continuing pilgrimage is strength for the realization that the church of God is sufficiently aware of its limits and sufficiently large in faith and hope and love so that many different ways, interpretations, schools, and ecclesial traditions can live together with common respect and contribute to each other and the rest of the world as one body.

I think these are some of the things of which we need to be aware before what we ask of the liturgy can make much sense. The raising of human consciousness to hitherto unobserved issues of justice is the most rewarding aspect of our lives. Communities of biblical faith, by celebrating in liturgy, a fulfillment that is not yet and by occasionally daring to resume the pilgrimage for which they were founded are a seedbed of consciousness-raising in the very long run, in potency, even though (as the Bible testifies) most of us are idolaters most of the time. To ask of liturgy what we should ask requires the cultivation of a faithful patience. . . .

11

" . . . No Use Running . . . on the Wrong Road"*

Country music songs have some great lines. One of them, in the seventies, went: "There's No Use Running If You're on the Wrong Road." Everything I do is opinionated, so it is no great departure if this column is simply a letter of opinions addressed to other clergy and all who hold pastoral offices in the churches. . . . It seems to me that a lot of us good-willed and reform-minded clergy find ourselves running on the wrong road, especially at the core and heart of the church's life — its worship.

We are somewhat better at dealing with mission, with the gospel's concern for the marks of God's reign: liberation/reconciliation. In this area we know we have to be countercultural because the reign of God is the pilgrims' promise given to a status quo that remains (no matter how much progress we make) oppressed and divided. We have a long way to go, of course, in adding the teeth of economic/political organization and action to our concerns, but at least more of us seem to be on the right road. With regard to liturgical celebration, however, there seems to be less awareness of faith's countercultural requirements. We recognize the need to employ different languages and different cultural modes of communication in celebration, without facing our current culture's poverty in the world of symbol and imagination (the stuff of liturgy, the world of our biblical and sacramental sources).

As long as we are stuck in a cultural rut which is so one-track, so preoccupied with the cerebral and the "productive," with regarding human beings only as workers and as thinkers, the contemplative, playful, inefficient, imaginative character of liturgical

*Worship, November 1990

celebration will continue to elude us. That is why it seems to me so much of our running is on the wrong road. We try, but our cultural habits and preconceptions render us helpless for the important renewal work of fully opening up the symbolic action which is Christian public worship . . . in any of the rites. We tend to think that more or different *words* are the answer, or that jazzing worship up with pop materials of one sort or another is the answer. Meanwhile the powerful symbol language of the liturgy remains unspoken and unused. We say, "The old symbols no longer speak to modern folks," forgetting that modern folks celebrate occasions by a special meal with friends, vacation at the seaside and the lake, put fireplaces in urban dwellings, etc. You don't have to be a Jung to know that the "old symbols" speak to and cause deep resonances in human beings (who may think they are merely little scientists and capitalists and pragmatists).

I am afraid it is we who prevent the symbol language of worship from communicating, by allowing it to remain so desiccated by an unkind history, so shrivelled up, so minimized for the sake of pro forma and efficient "handling" that we feel we must "explain" it with more of our confounded and stubbornly literal words. As a consequence, what G. K. Chesterton is reported to have said about Christianity we can apply appropriately to our celebration of public worship: It has not been tried and found wanting; it has been found difficult and not tried.

This should be everyone's concern. I appeal especially to clergy and other pastoral ministers because their roles within the churches include a special responsibility with regard to planning and leadership in celebration. While renewal breezes are clearing minds and hearts of many unnecessary and heavy burdens in our time, they also have a price which touches leadership roles in a particularly painful way. Liturgical, biblical, patristic and missiological studies of comparatively recent times are now commonly shared. Those rediscoveries, along with the signs of our time, not only enabled an ecclesial council of a large part of the Christian world in the sixties, but also enable a general and unprecedented access to our Jewish and Christian sources, to the roots and development of our faith tradition. They contend, however, with a proud human obduracy familiar to all of us, which resists any challenge to our habits. It's hard enough to get rid of *bad* habits.

So when habits have been generally judged, for a long time, to be "good" and "spiritual," our tenacity is fierce. Conversion is a constant necessity in the Christian life.

Profound clergy reforms are certainly in the cards, although one can understand why the first decades and generations of a massive renewal effort concentrated on the more basic liturgical participation, ecclesiology and the peace/justice mission. Clergy reforms, implied in and demanded by all of those concerns, naturally follow. For the clergy are, first of all, part of the church, members, and then ministers, servants in the churches, of the churches, for the churches. Deep-seated changes in the churches' self-understanding, worship and mission clearly require revisions, new approaches, changes equally drastic in everything connected with the churches' preparing, supporting and working with clergy: recruitment, qualifications and talents of candidates, training (in closer relationship to the communities to be served), call and ordination, lifestyle, continuing education, etc. A number of pioneering organizations, movements, meetings have been engaged for decades in consciousness-raising on these issues. They probably have the same relation to the broad canonical reforms yet to come as the Liturgical Weeks of the forties and fifties had to the concrete reforms which came later (and will continue to come).

Clergy (the episcopal and presbyteral pastoral orders particularly), other pastoral ministers and other church leaders — all have responsibilities which cannot be deferred until those broad reforms become realities in all the churches. Our preaching, our other pastoral work, our example are still important influences in the communities of faith. We owe the communities to which we belong a critical re-examination of all that we do in preaching, teaching, liturgical celebration and community building, because we are all stuck to some extent and some of us to a disastrous extent in habits of speaking and acting which contradict and sabotage our recovery of a common liturgy-and-mission ecclesiology. The price exacted by renewal should be a daily price for all of us, and therefore more easily dealt with. When reform comes thundering in so rarely, after so long a rest from our pilgrim journey, the pain can be excruciating and the conflicts generated by any efforts toward consistency debilitating. Pain, discomfort, strained relations with adamant standpatters, and conflicts are in themselves neither good nor godly. In our world and church, with our mixed bag of history, however, any effort to be good or godly may require us to endure them.

Until we begin to *feel* (not merely to say) that church as a whole, all the baptized-and-presently-committed (on the local level, the Sunday assembly) *is the primary minister* of worship-and-mission, we continue to carry and spread the virus-view of church-as-pyramid, or of a clergy-"above"-the-church. A decent ecclesiology (a decent idea of what the church is) must have been a lot more common before the mass media made stars of the prominent clergy and called their every spoken thought "the teaching of the church." At any rate, wherever clergy exist in the service of faith communities, clericalism has reared its ugly head and spawned its host of ills. We need constant self-examination and resolution (to say nothing of a sense of humor) to combat it. And we need to realize also, it seems to me, that there is little support in "real life" for the optimistic trust that bad habits, upon encountering a good principle, will simply dry up and blow away, and will some-how remove themselves without the pain and conflict of excision. The harshness of the latter is softened by its Spirit-sanction and the churches' atmosphere (at least in intent) of love and personal humility, of general listening for that "tiny, whispering sound" of First Kings 19 in each other's words and postures.

Even now — before basic clergy reforms and before the recovery of a communal Christian initiation becomes the primary agenda of every local faith community and the experience of every member, old and new — the clergy's leadership can do a lot. Simply by dealing vigorously and honestly with our own self-understanding and with habits which have many of our words and deeds fight-ing against the liturgical participation and sense of church we are trying to celebrate and preach and teach and live. Clergy qualifica-tions, training, lifestyles, and many other non-essentials will have to change, as they have in the past. Tradition, liturgy and com-mon sense require a clergy role. All of the churches, excepting only those which have abandoned sacramental worship, ordain full-time or part-time specialized ministers (commonly called bishops, priests and deacons) to build the faith community; then invite the different gifts of their different members, gather all in common mission, preach the word and preside in the symbolic community actions we call sacraments.

Clergy are, like the rest of the baptized-and-presently-committed, *members* of the body of Christ, the church, whose general ministry has through ordination made them its instruments for a specialized ministry. They are ministers (servants) of Christ because they are ministers (servants) of the church, the body of Christ, not because they are shamans, gurus, gnostics, magicians, or fortune-tellers. And not because they possess any private avenues of grace or enlightenment, or hang suspended from above.

Any habit, then, which distances these clergy from the other members of the faith community or suggests that, once ordained, clergy may operate independently of the church and communion of churches to which they belong is a habit which undermines reform, renewal and progress. "Floating clergy" are consequently a contradiction in terms. And what about the practice of concelebration? In the intervening years I have discovered no reason to qualify what I wrote in my book on presiding in liturgy: "The liturgical problem is twofold: 1) they (clergy without specific function, different from the rest of the congregation) have no necessary function in the rite and therefore might be considered to be among those superfluities which a firm, strong, clean ritual action abhors; 2) because they have no necessary function they tend to accent, visually and experientially, the separation of clergy from church, a separation which will be discussed in this manual as one of the principal obstacles to an improved style of presiding" (*Strong, Loving and Wise: Presiding in Liturgy.* Washington, D.C.: The Liturgical Conference 1976, p. ix. Now published by The Liturgical Press, St John's Abbey, Collegeville, Minn.).

What does it do to people's understanding of sacraments as symbolic actions of the whole church, the entire assembly (including and employing its specialized ministers) when we tolerate habits which imply that sacraments are the acts of clergy alone? When one wishes to present someone for baptism, or desires to celebrate matrimony, or needs a funeral for a loved one, the instinct (even in 1990) is to "find" a clergy person. There can be exceptions, of course, when a clergy person who is also close friend or relative is invited to preside. But the first thought and instinct should be the faith community, the church, the parish. It is the community which celebrates sacraments, especially at great moments, and the normal presider is the normal pastor of the community.

What of the habit of "Mass stipends" in parts of the Christian world? It is a habit which contradicts basic principles of worship renewal. We all know that economic reforms in the church, which should be the first step, are always the last and most difficult step. And we know that the general intercessions are where those intentions belong. We might even have read what Francis Mannion wrote in the May 1983 issue of *Worship* about the Mass stipend system, calling it "ecclesiologically and liturgically pathological."

Then there are habits of sheer clergy laziness, which continue to cripple liturgical experience in countless communities, which trivialize the very heart of the Sunday sacrament of love and unity: gathering at a common altar, eating from a common plate, drinking from a common cup, nourishing the bond of our oneness in Christ at the table of his body and blood. What about bread that is real bread, broken for all to share? How many clergy and liturgy committees make absolutely certain that all candidates for ministries of leadership in worship (acolytes, musicians, readers, eucharistic ministers, etc.) are persons whose example of full reception in both kinds will help supplant the bad habits of those who ignore Jesus' invitation and will help open up again this precious and primary symbol? In how many Sunday eucharistic celebrations do the clergy care enough about the integrity of the rite and the experience of the community to prepare enough bread and wine on the altar before the Great Thanksgiving for all those present, so that there need be no (i.e., *no*) traffic to or from the place (tabernacle) of reservation during the liturgy? In how many church buildings where a pre-reform font does not permit the immersion of adults and children, are the clergy sensitive enough about the power of symbol language to use a temporary portable basin, tub, or pool for the immersion of a candidate, a bathing from head to toe, and the sacramental experience this enables for the community that prays with, accepts, shares the Spirit, supports, clothes and welcomes the neophyte?

These are only a few of our bad habits, our largely unexamined, partly unconscious counter-renewal habits. They deal with *basic* problems, not with the periphery which seems to attract so much of our running. We've got plenty of it to do on the right road. "There's No Use Running If You're on the Wrong Road."

12

Individualists Are
Incapable of Worship*

South African playwright Athol Fugard spoke (no, *witnessed*) at
New York University recently about his love for his strife-torn
country, some of the moving influences in his life, and his work
as a writer. "All I know of loving I have learned from South
Africa and South Africans." Of his plays, he made this comment:
"People who look for political statements are looking in the wrong
direction. I am a storyteller. . . . Any story, anywhere, is going
to be 'political.' . . ."

It seems to me that profound truth should be part of the regular
meditation of all of us who are committed to church reform and a
living liturgy. We can't afford to waste time blaming liturgy for
our social ills. We can't afford to ignore the patent fact that the
most threatening "liturgical problem" we face is not in the liturgy
but rather in our privatization of everything, in our country's and
our culture's individualism-run-riot.

The awesomely corporate act of public worship assumes, requires, demands a celebrating assembly of believing persons who
have not lost the sense of being part of humanity, the sense of relation to, interdependence with, even identification with every
other human being — as consequences of the love of God. People
who approach that act, who gather on Sunday as self-contained
units, individuals for whom all others are merely competitors or
marks, are simply incapable of it. Any sensitive pastoral minister
has long since observed that the Sunday assembly's liturgical
problems (participation, engagement, understanding, experience)
cannot be solved by liturgical reforms alone.

*Worship, January 1991

Of course the church needs continuing liturgical reform. The bed of a living tradition has to be dredged constantly, as a maxim has it. One of the glories of this confusing and promising century is the resumption of that invaluable service in so many parts of the faith communities of Judaism and Christianity. No question about it. Pressing those issues is a most important contribution to the life of faith.

But it is insufficient in itself. The cancer of Western and American individualism infects that Sunday assembly and produces a church that is barely capable of celebrating the eucharist or any other liturgical rite. We cannot blame the liturgy for the fact that we who celebrate it, the faith community, are so mesmerized by the idol of rugged individualism that it is dreamy to call us a "community" at all. It is quite impossible to see in our corporate life a community of biblical faith committed to witnessing in the whole world the advent of God's reign of justice and peace.

This is being written in November. God knows where our country's arrogant and violent and greedy acts in the Middle East will have us all by the time this issue reaches you. We are in charge. We will make a "better world" our way, regardless of the cost to others or to our own young. Just when the United Nations was showing some maturity, some ability to deal with the international issues it was organized to deal with, our government had to step in and take over. Instead of a United Nations' police operation, then, we have the unleashing again of a military machine traumatized by the threat of peace, with unimaginable weapons and hundreds of thousands of disposable young lives (whom our government and its machine classify as an "option"). And we continue to engage in our Sunday assemblies, committing ourselves to the ministry of reconciliation, without batting an eye! Is it our fault? Have we been misled? Whatever . . . it is so very, very tragic. We simply do not, apparently cannot, identify ourselves even with our own fellow-citizens, much less with other peoples, other cultures.

This is being written in November. We voted again — the increasingly diminished minority of the eligible. Most did not vote, and that "most" may include most believers. Even this minimal democratic right and obligation is not considered worth the effort by those who do not see an immediate and private (very private) stake in the potential results. We who celebrate the eucharist lack a sense of being part of a community! Talk about "liturgical problems" . . . !

Did you listen to the mass media during the campaigns? It is as if any thought of politics and taxes, of the means of doing together what we cannot do alone, constitute an invasion of our privacy, our individual rights, our terrible arrogance. Taxes are the necessary way we share the cost of doing together all those things we must do together or not do at all, as cities, as states, as nations, eventually as world. But our individualism makes taxes an evil and an affront. And this is dominant.

One would hope that the argument of believers regarding taxes would be the ways in which the majority decides to spend the money. That would be congruent with biblical faith, for presently our common resources are devoted to military might and to the defence of the status quo economically, the defence of the power of the wealthy. But one hears little of that argument. Rather, taxes are simply evil, because "they" are taking it away from "me." And "me" is not part of "they." In no way am I a part of anything bigger than myself. That, of course, makes liturgy either a fraud and a lie, or merely a diversion without meaning.

We could go on and on with this list of cultural horrors. A recovery of Christian initiation processes is finally afoot and promises an eventual antidote to this disease, but it is not yet sufficiently advanced, general and intense to be effective for us now. Long term cultural and psychological losses are not quickly regained. Attention to the individual is one of the beauties of human evolution, for which we must all be grateful and in which Judaism and Christianity have played a seminal part. The individualism discussed here, however, has become an absolute, an idol, destroying the human capacity for love, solidarity, and reconciliation, and reducing the human thirst for justice to private dimensions. This is not evolution or progress, but insanity. There is no point in individual dignity and freedom if the necessary community of reconciliation, common support and action is lost.

With Eastern Europe apparently now prepared to surrender the insights as well as the ugliness of its communist experiment, Donald Nicholl suggests where hope may lie (for the church as well as for the rest of the world) in the 13 October 1990 issue of

The Tablet (London): ''. . . the spread of this disease of individualism . . . in the shape of colonialism, slave-trading, missionary arrogance, and so on, until it explodes in epidemic proportions in America, where it destroys land, animals, and native people. From there it now threatens the whole earth as, like some giant combine-harvester, it mows down one traditional culture after another — cultures which enshrine a wisdom about how to live in community which it has taken thousands of years to learn. . . . We, the human family, are these days in virtually the same situation as the people of Israel in biblical times when they were on the verge of extinction . . . when God saved a 'remnant' (*sheerith*) from which the salvation of the world was to spring. So also with us there is still such a remnant, composed of all those broken, battered, despised, marginalised little people whom the combine-harvester of individualism has not completely uprooted . . . '' (pp. 1300–01).

Sometimes we speak of ourselves, euphemistically, as ''formed'' by our biblical/liturgical sources in saving, regular ritual actions of reading and singing and praying. It would be more truthful to say we are in liturgy ''exposed'' to those saving sources, perhaps even desiring formation, but all the while enclosed in a cultural shell so thick and so resistant that only in relatively rare instances are we able to either really *go to* these sources, or really respond to the equivalent of *Ite, missa est*.

It is not only in our attitude toward political life, community life, national and international world life that our rugged individualism has crippled us. It is evident in every aspect, every layer of our life and experience as church, in its liturgical heart and center, where we are supposed to find the inspiration and strength for liberating and reconciling action in and for the rest of the world.

It is in our leadership (sometimes euphemized as ''conservative''), where even pastoral offices/functions (episcopacy, presbyterate, diaconate) become privatized, popularly assumed and frequently exercised as if these community functions had no dependence on the community whatsoever, as if the Holy Spirit were a clerical preserve, the sacraments of initiation meaningless, most of the church merely consumers. As if popes and other bishops were functioning in ways and with sources entirely unknown to our rites of ordination.

It is in us all, occasionally evident even in groups appropriately committed to and agitating for the church's freedom from the status quo, the powers that be, from archeologism and attachment to outdated ways and interpretations. Oppressed groups are usually those who see these problems most clearly — not because of their virtue but because of their oppression. Jewish and Christian liturgy, worship of the one God who liberates/reconciles, doesn't really grab people who feel the need of neither, who think the status quo is just fine. For the biblical message is a way of life, a pilgrimage, a seeking, and not a hunkering down. The satisfied and the comfortable may recognize the "obligation," but are happy to miss the point.

Groups and individuals who are trying to be pilgrims, who are alive, awake, aware, are people who *feel* oppression and division, especially their own, and sometimes that of others. In our society, they include obviously women, Afro-Americans and other "minorities," lesbian and gay persons, etc. Such groups and individuals, therefore, can be and should be natural leaders in our struggle against this cultural problem of individualism and our recovery of a living liturgical tradition. Many of their groups and individuals and many other reform groups in the church are such leaders. Their experience, or their sensitivity to the experience of others, has made them advocates for all and their groups a powerful social and political advocacy for progress.

However, we cannot expect that they will be immune from a disease that infects us all. *Corruptio optimi, pessima.* So sometimes we in reform movements turn in upon ourselves instead of becoming advocates for all. We become self-centered, maybe even self-pitying. We go further. We set up our own little eucharist, therefore inventing our own little church. We escape those awful "others." We forsake the classic sources that liberate and reconcile without specifics, inviting our responsibility and our imaginations, and we substitute our tiny words and deeds. Thus we rid ourselves of responsibility to the living tradition that is never finished, always beckoning on. And we also rid ourselves of our real task: in the political and economic world.

In this connection, I may as well conclude with a letter I wrote a month or two ago to "Call to Action" regarding their advertisement for a November gathering in D.C. during the bishops' meeting (R.C.): "Your brochure on the conference arrived in today's mail, and I want to explain why I am so disappointed. Our Ash Wednesday Call for Reform . . . was so good and so promising that I had hoped we would finally have an organized voice for a broad Catholic Church reform education and advocacy effort. I speak only for myself, of course, but the message I get from the conference brochure is that the planners have become so discouraged with such an effort that they have abandoned this focus and have gone the way of every sectarian movement in history.

"One can understand and respect that way. Many great souls have chosen it. But Catholic tradition with its intimate relation between ecclesial structure and sacramental liturgy remains a compelling value for many of us. For us, church reform is not the substitution of an ecclesial structure to our momentary liking for the basic ecclesial structure of Catholic tradition — a basic structure that was respected in the 'Call for Reform.' . . .

"We need lots of interpretations, movements, ideologies within that basic structure of unity, peace, reconciliation. But it seems to me that to make one interpretation, one movement, one ideology the whole cheese not only stifles the progress that a living tradition involves, not only limits the imagination to today's 'cutting edge,' but even more importantly is only another manifestation of cultural egocentrism. The answer, it seems to me, is to center the church where Catholic tradition does in a eucharist which is an ecclesial feast, bringing together and reconciling all kinds, types, interpretations of the biblical/liturgical message — not a eucharist of people who imagine they have arrived.

"It's hard to say this in a short space. Anyway, God bless you. Thanks for all your past work. And try to understand why I (and, I hope, others) cannot rejoice in what seems your current direction. Peace!"

13

Some Premises of
an Experiential Worship*

. . . That an experiential public worship is our right as initiated
members faithful to the Sunday assembly is not in doubt. Nor is
the complexity of the quest for that right's satisfaction. For the
kind of experience we individualists seek depends upon the formation of each of us: always various, since Christian church tradition
has opted for openness; childish when catechisms (interpretations)
assume the place of our biblical/liturgical sources; chaotic when
our histories jumble shamanism with the gospel and regularly prefer institutional peace and prosperity to an unending pilgrim journey toward the justice and peace of the reign of God. The faith
prospect of always having to upset the way things are in order to
achieve something better is one which sets the teeth of any house-
keeper on edge.

Nor is it only housekeepers who disdain the quest. One cannot
read the human heart, but one suspects that the larger part of any
contemporary church is with its housekeepers rather than with its
prophets and its Christ — as in the Bible's frank admission of the
idolatry of most of the Jews most of the time and our own experience's confirmation of our dependence on lucid moments in
Christian history as well. So one cannot define the experience the
liturgy should offer contemporary people by merely asking
around. Isn't that obvious fact the reason why we need the liturgy
so much, need it as our primary and indispensable source, need it
for growing up in Christ, need its biblical/sacramental orientation
to the one, only, jealous God, through Christ and in the Spirit, so
that what we feel we need begins to correspond just a little bit to
the letting-go and the imaginative quest it demands?

*Worship, September 1991

The power of the status quo's domination of our lives coupled with a non-existent or misguided church initiation makes it far from certain that we will look for (and therefore find) anything in the Sunday assembly but a reassurance that we are all right and a feeling that we have observed the proprieties of "religion."

That critical, basic notion of Judaism and Christianity — that this covenant people has a corporate pilgrimage and journey on its hands, in service to God's design for the world as a whole, and that the gift of faith frees us from the status quo's domination so that we can imagine and effect possible ways of advancing the realm of our liberating/reconciling God — is demonstrably absent from the formation of many. How, then, are people inculpably innocent of the covenant of faith supposed to articulate the needs of the believers' Sunday assembly?

No wonder the best we can do most of the time is to desire "good music," or "good preaching," or "good environment," or "a sense of mystery," or "warmth and hospitality," and so on. Habit has us so firmly in its clutches that it does not even occur to us that we need, farther and deeper and apparently more elusive than all those good things, a new conversion every Sunday, an orientation, courage and inspiration for living day after day in a remarkable way: exercising the freedom God gives us in questioning any of the ways and mores of the period which seem either denials of or obstacles to the liberation and reconciliation of all human beings in God. When God means something else to us, we have already capitulated to one idol or another, we have already lost the pilgrim trail.

The faith community's prophets and saints are our leaders in this fundamental sense, in Christ and after Christ. Theirs is the freedom and the reconciling love which image the hunger and thirst for justice/peace that are the foundation for experiential liturgical celebration. To recognize this, however, is not to fall prey to the current fashion of decrying "the institutional church" and church officials, whose housekeeping chores too frequently get the best of them. Add to this the fact that we all live in a media, starstruck culture. In everything, we tend to be audience, idolizing the "stars." Our political campaigns are not about participating in deciding the issues, but about the star personalities. Instead of nourishing and feeding our understanding of, responsibility for and participation in our political and economic and cultural institutions, the modern technology of communications seems only to make us more impotent.

So we make too much of church officials also. And those of us concerned with reform and renewal must be wary, lest that mentality capture us and we begin to measure everything in terms of the moment's stars. There is no faith community (no good news people, no liturgical tradition) that is not an institution. While the tautology "institutional church" may soothe the wounded feelings of self-conscious prophetic types, it is not terribly helpful in our quest. The ordained officers, ministers, servants, guardians, housekeepers of the churches are as necessary as bread. While one laments the tendency of many of them to exercise a preferential option for the rich, the safe, and the established, one cannot afford to entertain the illusion that they can or should be eliminated. Adlai Stevenson once pointed out that our much maligned politicians serve us better than we know or deserve: they prove to be our servants in more ways than one and illustrate for all of us the lives we lead and the atmosphere we create. The same can be said of church officialdom in general.

Perhaps, when we have made a little more progress in our recovery of a baptismal ecclesiology and a catechumenate/initiation involving the whole faith community, we will be forced to make much-needed ministerial reforms. We will make the revolutionary step of employing appropriate qualifications for the selection of candidates (rather than "male" and "mainstream" and "celibate") and will find ways of training them in close relationship with their sponsoring churches. We will be able to communicate to those we choose for leadership (servant) functions a less easily shaken grasp of the good news and a trained sensitivity to the terrible temptations of institutional office. The paradox of institution-as-easily-corruptible and institution-as-sine-qua-non is one that believers have to live with, always uncomfortably. Where else but in the faith community can one find such thumbnail appeals to human imagination and progress as Hillel's "What you yourself do not like, do not do to any other — this is the whole Torah" or Gerard Sloyan's "Things are not as they seem"?

When occupants of ecclesiastical office talk more about the church and its officials than about Jesus Christ and the reign of

God, when they propose to bind us to an authoritarian party line of interpretation instead of to the classic faith tradition's sources and challenge to creative imagination (with its possible variety of interpretations), then we know we are in the kind of trouble that is almost sinking the old ark today. "Almost" is the key. We need it too much to let that happen. And we do have, in our sources, an even more authoritative promise.

Harvey Cox, in a recent address to a large *Corpus* convention in New York City, remembered how Pope Paul VI, while archbishop of Milan, answered Cox's question about the church's "new" minority status with another question: "How can we be a minority without being a sect?" Montini's successor is apparently untroubled by such questions, but they will keep cropping up, thanks to the Spirit in the churches and their radicals and agitators. Have we learned enough from our history so that these latter will not leave us? So that their blood and sweat and tears turn out to be the leadership which officialdom so often denies us?

What John Oesterreicher writes of Jewish suffering in his preface to Flannery's *The Anguish of the Jews* is a humbling and saving prescription for all of us who are graced by discontent in the churches as well: "No doubt, to cry out against an injustice we ourselves endure is fully legitimate. By itself, however, it remains an instinctive reaction and is not yet a moral stance. A moral attitude comes to life only when *all* lose thought and speech, *all* ready-made opinions, *all* judgments shrunk to the size of nutshells, *all* forms of bigotry are shunned and fought. Nothing, after all, seems more consistent with bitter reality than to meet it with bitterness, nothing more realistic to the sufferer than to let sorrow become his tomb. Absurd though it may sound, history's bitterness and sorrow call rather for wisdom, for goodness, for a lasting openness of heart. There is, I think, no truer answer to the anguish Jews have suffered through the centuries than such grace, no better way to honor the victims of what Maurice Samuel has called 'the great hatred.'"

We need the old ark because, as Martin Luther King Jr said, "The church is all we have." The faith community is the only corporate reality and institution in the world which constitutes and realizes itself in worship, in the public worship of a mysterious Other, a universally liberating/reconciling Other. It is the only institution which grounds and bases itself on the creatureliness and dependence of every mortal being and every institution, including itself. Its liturgies' good news and classic message is the compelling sanction of our freedom in spite of all oppressors and oppressions and of our reconciliation in spite of all barriers. Whenever it seems to make an idol of itself, its worship brings it back to earth, restores modesty and sanity.

And, as we dare to try to let these gifts form us, we can also dare to hope that they will be contagious.

WORSHIP IN THE SUNDAY ASSEMBLY

14

"So Knit Thou Our Friendship Up"*

The liturgical schedule of most Roman Catholic parishes is at odds with the vision of church and Christian life which parishes awakened by the Second Vatican Council are seeking to promote. One problem at a time (the daily liturgical schedule is quite another — and is serious, too): the Sunday Mass schedule is a counterproductive concession to bad habits. I suspect that one of the greatest services most urban parishes could offer their members would be to reduce the number of Sunday Masses until a correspondence is reached between the worship space (assuming it is of human size) and the assembly of the people. That service might not be appreciated immediately, but it would teach and create the conditions for deeper understanding of what we are about more effectively than our homilies.

We cannot seem to make up our minds whether our schedule of Sunday liturgies is going to be determined by the practices of the merchandise mart or by the vision of the covenant community's worship assembly which we find in scriptural and liturgical tradition, in sacramental theology, in initiation and ecclesiology.

As a consequence, one urban church after another maintains even now a Sunday Mass schedule inherited from a period when faith, worship, mission were privatized, clericalized, and when the convenience of individual members viewed as consumers was the guiding principle. Now, if we are fortunate, we find ourselves rediscovering the local assembly of believers as church, as a covenant community of mutual aid, strength, support in prayer and faith and mission. And our schedules remain a major obstacle. In-

*Worship, September 1984

stead of gathering the believers together, they disperse them. Instead of one or two celebrations into which we pour our time, energy, money, talents, artists and care, with a memorable and inspiring effect, we prefer a half-dozen perfunctory, dutiful and depressing rites. Since a *good* habit (the canon law of Sunday eucharistic celebration) still keeps many coming and makes this almost their sole experience of faith and church, the foreseeable result of what we are now doing is a prospect about as happy as that of the nuclear arms race.

Thus it is terribly important that we look at the problem, discuss it thoroughly, and do something about it. Among the many habits which today's (temporary) ecclesiastical tide of reaction tends to affirm — and which therefore continue to impede, subvert or stifle the renewal of the church at its primary source — is this needless multiplication of eucharistic celebrations on the one day on which that celebration is most appropriate.

This habit subverts renewal at its primary source because the primary source of Christian renewal and spirit is the Sunday assembly where we celebrate those twin symbols of faith: the biblical word and the sacramental deed. The celebrant of that inspiring, healing, restoring rite is the assembly of baptized persons — not as individuals, but precisely as assembly, community, covenant group. (This is why "presider" or "presiding minister" is the preferable term for the bishop or priest who appropriately leads, and helps identify by a collegial ministry, this church with the other churches in one communion.)

This assembly, this corporate celebrant of Sunday Mass is the creation of the good news that all of our variety, our differences, our distinctions (sex, age, class, color, nationality, physical or mental condition, economic or political status, trade or profession, lifestyle, etc.) are reconciled in Christ and in God. At this moment we are nakedly daughters and sons of God, and only that. Our rock-bottom human and baptismal unity is what makes church. Our coming together to realize church before the one All-holy, our being in one place at one time for one common prayer-action — this is what Sunday Mass is all about.

While liturgical texts have always reflected the priority of the assembly, our practice demonstrates a deafness to their too familiar refrains. And much of our eucharistic hymnody (medieval and modern) echoes not that basic Christian tradition but rather our contrary practice: a great deal about the sacramental elements and objects, little about the unification and reconciliation of God's daughters and God's sons in a gathering-made-church.

Percy Dearmer's hymn is an exception, and gets to the heart of the matter:

"Draw us in the Spirit's tether,
For when humbly in thy name,
Two or three are met together,
Thou art in the midst of them;
Alleluia! alleluia! Touch we now thy garment's hem.

As the brethren used to gather
[better, 'as believers used to . . . ']
In the name of Christ to sup,
Then with thanks to God the Father
Break the bread and bless the cup,
Alleluia! alleluia! So knit thou our friendship up.

All our meals and all our living
Make as sacraments of thee,
That by caring, helping, giving,
We may true disciples be.
Alleluia! Alleluia! We will serve thee faithfully."[1]

"So knit thou our friendship up!" Until this kind of phrase, this idea springs to mind whenever we think of Sunday Mass, we are only playing with renewal. Its bits and pieces have not yet jelled to reveal the truth, goodness and beauty of their integrity, their wholeness, the way they fit together. Instead of appropriating the Council's reweaving of the fabric of covenant community, we have too often simply tacked on "the changes," hanging them haphazardly on a tattered garment of contradictory practices.

In "Chronicle," from the May 1984 issue of *Worship*, Aelred Tegels discusses Saturday evening Masses in particular and the needless multiplication of Sunday Masses in general, saying that celebrations not required by the exigencies of the space available impair "the reality of assembly, so vital to the full symbolism of

---

[1] *Worship II* (Chicago: GIA 1975), no. 67.

eucharistic worship . . . . Indeed early Christians generally seem to have perceived 'togetherness' as an essential attribute of worship. And rightly so. Dispersing the assembly violates the integrity of worship."[2]

Quite apart from the question of when the Sunday liturgy is most properly celebrated (whether Saturday evening or Sunday morning or Sunday afternoon or Sunday evening), my concern here is to encourage the reduction of the number of such celebrations, whenever and wherever possible, in favor of a critical emphasis on getting the sisters and brothers *together*.

The *norm* is clearly that all those persons who have been initiated into the community of faith and who constitute a particular concrete church should gather in one assembly to celebrate the Sunday eucharist. This is clear in Christian tradition, as Tegels shows. This is clear in a sound ecclesiology: baptism is into a specific community of persons, who, as members of Christ, have no private ecclesial function but need each other. This is clear in the nature of the eucharistic sacrament: corporate action expressing common faith, "sacrament of love, of peace, of unity, of reconciliation." This is clear in its climactic holy communion, when it is our eating and drinking together with and in the Lord that is the decisive moment of our public worship.

As a result of the Second Vatican Council, we have come to recognize more generally not only the gifts of our ecclesial history but also some of its distortions and blind alleys. Forces at work in the life of the church and the surrounding culture diminished the place of the assembly and its constitution through initiation and liturgical participation — forces of ignorance, privatization, clericalization, false priorities. Outside the bounds of our discussion here, they nevertheless all go together. Even the architecture of the worship space showed the change from a traditional preoccupation with the assembly of believers to a distorted preoccupation with objects.

The Council in the sixties put us on the road toward regaining some of what we lost in those processes. One of the most important gifts of that Council was its emphasis on the concrete local church, the existential community of believers. Not to deny the

---

[2] *Worship* 58 (May 1984) 258–59.

importance of universal solidarity and communion but to strengthen, balance and complement it. But our Sunday Mass schedules had been firmly fixed by that time. And we had long since forgotten how great the loss had been when we went from one assembly on Sunday to multiple assemblies in one place.

We had long since adjusted ourselves and our view of what it means to be a Christian to the practical realities of urban church life. From branches on a living vine and members of a living body, we had become private and individual clients of an international spiritual corporation. From communities of friendship, prayer and mission, our "churches" had become buildings spread about to serve us spiritual consumers. So it no longer mattered where I went on Sunday or with whom I gathered — one outlet was as good as another, like Montgomery Ward or Esso. I had adjusted myself to being a "layperson," a patient, a client of a clerical class which had the proprietorship of the buildings called "churches." I was adrift, without a local church of friends, an existentially isolated "part" of an ecclesial entity thought of only in the singular and only as universal.

Humans are almost infinitely adjustable. We can get used to practically anything — even to liturgical schedules which do not serve the faith community but instead effectively prevent it from a true development, growth and maturity. There was a time, though, when it must have been different.

We can imagine how painful it must have been at first, when the baptized who were used to assembling as one family on Sunday found themselves too numerous to meet together in the space they had at their disposal. Certainly their first inclination would have been to start another community, another church, so that the integrity of both the old and the new celebration could be preserved. That may seem difficult, but it is surely the most sensible solution. It is one I would propose for all those crowded suburban church buildings (with ten Masses all jammed to the rafters), whose "proprietors" have been thinking that this column is not for them.

Their situation basically is not much different from that of the urban church buildings half-empty for multiple Masses on Sunday. Chances of a genuine assembly — of being missed if you aren't there — are dim in either case. As Tegels suggests in the article mentioned above, dioceses should assume the responsibility of seeing to it not only that urban churches do not have more celebrations than are needed but also that crowded suburban parishes are divided into human units, where friendship and "togetherness" are at least possible.

We seem to have acquired the habit of creating parishes without regard for the human size and condition of the Sunday assembly when we made the parish school the center of church life and the source of our Catholic identity. Parishes were defined in numbers that by any truly ecclesial standard are monstrous, so that the educational institution could be adequately supported. While that might have seemed practical in the short period, it has not served us well in the long run. We no longer need to supply an educational system in toto, and now we discover that our enthusiasm for schools vastly diminished our character and vitality as a church of worshiping, believing and world-changing adults.

So the Sunday assembly, always the keystone of the church, has to be brought out of the closet. We had consigned it there in favor of concentrating all our time and money and energy on the kids. Now millions of those kids have left us because they found no adult church to relate to when they grew up. I think it is still hard to find an adult church. And one of the reasons is the problem under discussion.

An adult church requires an adult Sunday assembly, one that brings its members not to a clerical caste that has private sources of divine information and guidance, but face-to-face with each other and face-to-face with the primary sources of faith for all of us, clerics or not: the twin symbols of word and sacrament. Those symbols and fonts ask of us that we grow up, that we stop asking for the perhaps too specific "answers" which secondary sources like parish schools, catechisms, clerical edicts were reputed to indulge in, that we listen to the scriptural word and act out the symbolic deed and find in them and in the signs of the times the formation (certainly with the help of all of our secondary sources, homilists, teachers and each other) that enables us to make good and holy decisions and choices.

Such a Sunday assembly is not to be had in quantity. That is why it is so rare an experience. And why the visage of the church is so uninteresting, except to those of us who have benefited from the gifts of great experiences or great teachers that pushed us deep into the heart of the church and the gospel, beneath all the camouflage and all the overgrowth. For it is those twin symbols we celebrate in the Sunday assembly that do for Christians what the Constitution does for citizens of the United States. They save us from ourselves; they save us from victimization by fads and fancies; they save us from the vagaries of succeeding administrations (on parish, diocesan, national or world church levels), some of which do not take kindly to their vision and their promises. Especially in this media and television age, when a pope or another bishop, or any leader in the church, is too much swayed by personal limits, by cultural prejudices, by the inevitable constructions of a particular time and place, it is the Sunday assembly and its symbolic sources that rescue the faithful and set us all on firmer ground.

A number of parishes have begun this necessary work: reducing the number of Sunday Masses (and of Masses in general) so that they can increase significantly the meaning and the power of the Sunday assembly. The scriptural word and the sacramental deed are always there, but they can be rendered dead or alive, vital or perfunctory, personal or remote, sweet or sour by the attention and participation of the entire assembly and by the preparation, the talents, the time, the energy, the resources, the arts of those who care for the space and of the planners and ministers of the celebration.

A kind of devotion to breathless, nonstop ritualizing simply has to be succeeded by a new kind of devotion to bringing the sisters and brothers together, first of all, and then spending ourselves, utterly spending ourselves, on what we do once we are together. From quantity to quality, a giant step, for God's sake.

"What life have you if you have not life together?
There is no life that is not in community,
And no community not lived in praise of GOD.
. . .
And now you live dispersed on ribbon roads,
And no man knows or cares who is his neighbour . . . ."[3]

"So knit thou our friendship up." One assembly filling one church building, a building full of church, rather than four or five

[3] T. S. Eliot, "Choruses from 'The Rock,'" *Collected Poems 1909–1962* (New York: Harcourt, Brace & World 1963) 154.

Masses with a scattering of private individuals in a barren and unfriendly space. And no more breathlessness, no more excuses. No excuses left for allowing that time to be anything less than a moving experience. No excuses left for not spending hours on a homily that takes the faith community, its primary sources and the world we live in with equal seriousness. No excuses left for not searching (and paying) for musical talent, both instrumental and vocal. No excuses left for not attending to the environment of worship and the beauty that bespeaks God's transcendence/immanence. No excuses left for not making sure that everything we use in celebration is appropriate and well-made: from the bread (to be broken and shared as the missal says) to the hymnals that are placed in the hands of the assembly. No excuses left for not carefully screening and training all ministers, insisting that the public readers and proclaimers of a scriptural word must be excellent speakers and communicators.

And, best of all, no excuses left for forgetting for one moment that the Sunday assembly is for the purpose of making a church out of all of us rugged and ragged individualists. The Sunday Mass schedule is to be tailored to bring me together with the others of my faith community. It is *not* to be tailored to my convenience, my habits, my work schedule, my date book, my recreation, or the way I have privatized the sacrament of love and unity, of reconciliation and peace.

15

Real and Worshipful General Intercessions*

The Lord told us that beginnings would be hard and that it is more important to worry about today, where beginnings are supposed to happen, than about some future date, result, or end, because the latter depends upon, follows from, the former. So an essential part of the biblical message is that we must always be beginning, becoming new, starting afresh, repenting, open to the possibilities toward which the Spirit moves us. Our experience confirms the warning — current ecclesial experience especially. The perennial task of church reform and renewal, finally resumed on a more general scale in recent decades, has now met a reaction so clear, direct and ferocious that it frightens us into a standstill.

However, one does not overcome a paralysis by refusing to exercise the rediscovered muscles. Rehabilitation requires the overcoming of one's fears and the prudent and regular employment, development, strengthening of the atrophied faculties. Such exercise inevitably involves a certain disarray, a certain groaning and struggling appropriate to creation's contingency, and appropriate also to the faith community whose mission is to help the rest of the world experience the same groaning and struggling (we call it pilgrimage) and thereby conform to its purpose — making ready the way of the Lord, the reign of God's justice and peace. History assures us that these processes are messy and time-consuming. But in the biblical message this is the object of time and must never be misinterpreted as waste.

This deadly fear, reaction, lack of faith in the Spirit affects liturgy as well as all else. The messiness of a living church, a living tradition, a pilgrim entity is as evident in its liturgical foundations

*Worship, November 1986

as in the rest of the structure. Renewal at this heart and center of the church's life, in its primary theology, is perhaps hardest of all, not only because we rightly see the liturgy's joining of biblical and sacramental sources as our ecclesial identity, but also because the resumption of liturgy's long-interrupted development has graced us with a lot of gifts we do not yet know how to use very well. We fumble around with these gifts for a long time before we reluctantly acquire facility in their employment. That characteristic of human nature, while it is exasperating in the extreme, is at the same time responsible for a gradual refinement in our apprehension and appreciation of each gift. The refinement seems to occur in the process of our fumbling.

One of these important gifts in our central eucharistic rite is the recovery of the ancient practice of the assembly's offering a series of "general intercessions" as a distinct part of the Mass. The conciliar constitution put it this way: "Especially on Sundays and holydays of obligation there is to be restored, after the gospel and homily, 'the universal prayer' or 'the prayer of the faithful.' By this prayer, in which the people are to take part, intercession shall be made for holy church, for the civil authorities, for those oppressed by various needs, for all people, and for the salvation of the entire world" (Constitution on the Liturgy, no. 53).

After the Council, implementing documents taught us more about the history, characteristics and forms of the general intercessions (as they are now commonly entitled). Most of us in ministry studied those documents twenty years ago, put them into practice with varying degrees of conviction, and then left them on our shelves with other specifics of reform. What we did not pick up at that time we thought we would learn in regular celebration of the rites. But what we really learned in regular celebration was the truth about the difficulty of beginnings. We learned that our *ex opere operato* fixation and formalism are easier and therefore more powerful than our desire to repent, start afresh, and work at making the Sunday assembly the source of inspiration and the dynamic of Christian lives. Sparks tended to be smothered by inexorable routine.

Even in the rare places where pastoral adaptation and the work involved were taken seriously, there was at times an absence of liturgical sense and feeling. A sentimentalism foreign to the spirit of the Roman Rite or a kind of juvenile rally syndrome which ignored liturgical mien, rhythms and structures were mistaken for progress. Mistakes are inevitable in a living organism; and these are understandable, because we were so unaccustomed to this responsibility. So twenty years later the fumbling is still more evident than the refinement.

The general intercessions became part of the Mass, almost universally. But the dutiful passivity of the assembly's "audience mentality" was in many places hardly shaken by the introduction of these intentions — nor by the other "changes" so subtly slipped into its Sunday fare that nobody was required to notice. People still "bought a Mass" to express their real concerns, and the stipended intentions (a corruption which should have disappeared with the recovery of the intercessions) were still listed in the parish bulletin, as if nothing at all had happened. The inertia of habit, so different from the organic development of a living tradition, had conquered again.

However, twenty years are as an hour in the mammoth project of getting us back on the pilgrim trail. Nor can one speak of any of reform's particulars helpfully without reminding ourselves constantly that "it all goes together." Any item belongs in the context assumed by the Rite of Christian Initiation of Adults — a community committed in faith, worship, and a daily life and mission that serves the world by prodding it along toward its goal. "Your kingdom come on earth as in heaven." Perseverance in both the whole agenda and the individual items is the key. It is perseverance in the appreciation and use of reform's gifts that will bring us back to life again, corporately, as church. Perseverance in beginning — always beginning. Perseverance in involving the Sunday assembly *today* in an experience that will touch our hearts. The past is past and the future will take care of itself, if today is what today should be.

Our need is always to look freshly at what we are doing, in worship as in other activities, but in worship especially, because, for believers, worship is the primary and indispensable source. There we "play kingdom" (act out our and the world's goal) and give the Bible and sacrament a chance to form us to read the signs of our times as grownups, with consciences.

As part of that fresh look, a reminder of a few relevant historical facts seems appropriate and necessary. The first explicit reference we have in available literature seems to be in Justin's *Apologia*, about A.D. 150. He indicates that on Sundays, after the readings and homily, "we all stand together and offer prayers" (these prayers are distinguished from the "eucharist and prayer" later uttered by the presider with the assembly's "amen").[1] And the oldest surviving example in the Roman Rite is the series of solemn prayers at the conclusion of the word part of the Good Friday liturgy, probably dating from the third century.[2]

In the development of the general intercessions in regular Sunday use, the general structure had three main parts: 1) an invitation addressed to the entire assembly (which may be omitted); 2) a series of general and particular intercessions, in litany form, between the deacon or other reader and the rest of the assembly; 3) a conclusion by the presider, usually in the form of a prayer (and limited to a petition that God will hear us).

The invitation, when used, is addressed to the rest of the assembly and is *not* a prayer and should never be in the form of a prayer. It should be worshipful and brief, and it should invite the community's intercessions.

The essential part is the series of intercessions, with the people's response to the prepared intercessions being crucial. Options and freedom are encouraged, both in the formation of the series of intercessions and in the assembly's response to each. They may be sung or said and the responses may be vocal or a period of silent prayer. Some use the simple "For . . . ," while some use the "That . . . " form. Some combine them in a longer form: "For . . . that . . . ." These are prayers and must be recognized, felt and used as prayers. Tradition suggests four classes of intercessions which should always be represented, except in special votive situations, e.g., marriages, funerals: 1) the needs of the church; 2) national or world affairs; 3) those beset by poverty or tribulation; 4) the congregation and members of the local community.[3] "The principal element in this prayer is the participation of the people."[4]

---

[1] *Documents on the Liturgy, 1963–1979: Conciliar, Papal, and Curial Texts* (Collegeville: The Liturgical Press, 1982) 599, no. 1914.

[2] Ibid., 600, no. 1917.

[3] Ibid., 596–97, no. 1899.

[4] Ibid., 239, no. 1903.

The presider's conclusion, usually in prayer form and limited (as indicated above), does not attempt to recapitulate the intercessions but rather modestly, worshipfully and briefly affirms them as the church's prayer, Christ's prayer, and acknowledges our total dependence upon God.

The basic assumption behind the general intercessions is the same as that underlying the liturgy as a whole. It is a keen sense of the relation of this assembly not only to the other churches but also to the world God loves. Even though localized in the place and time of its members, this assembly is a microcosm of Christ's body, a community of baptismal commitment and solidarity, trying to make faith's vision of God's reign serve the rest of the community, the nation and the world. So this assembly has a special relation of representation and advocacy with all those sisters and brothers in the human race whose freedom, dignity and opportunity are curtailed and oppressed by the powers that be, with all who suffer tragedy or misfortune, with all whom the mainstream scorns, demeans, excludes. Our ministry is one of reconciliation.

In Jewish and Christian tradition, liturgy is primarily praise and thanksgiving. "Eucharist," as we must not tire of repeating, means thanksgiving. This is the thrust of the whole rite, particularly of its eucharistic prayer. But the general intercessions (as well as other, less organized intercessions echoing in the psalms, hymns, readings and other prayers) also have a place in worship, a modest place in this service whose priorities are thanks and praise.

Because it is a modest place, and they are subordinate, it is important to respect their character so that they fulfill their function. One of the problems one notes in taking a fresh view of current practice is a lack of sufficient care that they be both prayerful and intercessory. "Thanksgivings" for this or that are thrown in willy-nilly and weaken the litany's strength. The words "For a special intention" are heard, privatizing what is meant to be an intensely communal experience. Little speeches on various subjects, whether prepared or spontaneous, are masked as "intercessions," effectively destroying the God-focus of prayer and reducing the exercise to a kind of self-assertion and contention.

We want *intercessions* here, and we want them to be *prayer*. We also want them to be real, engaging, recognizable as representing this concrete faith assembly's witness and advocacy. They stand for the daily life of the corporate church assembled and its individual members. The sins and failures implied by any of the intercessions are *ours* — our own, our communities', our world's — not another's.

Ancient forms of these litanies have much to teach us, just as our new world has much to teach them. Many of them were remarkable for their prayerfulness, the brevity of their petitions (lending themselves to litany), their poetic quality, their sobriety. We want to regain these qualities without copying them in other ways, for they reflected a world in which the justice and peace of the biblical message were indeed a given vision but without the keen sense of human co-responsibility which modern developments have enabled. Our world and our consciousness of responsibility in it and for it have changed, as the great Second Vatican Council reminded us. Now our human race is marked by a quite general awareness that we are not merely the victims of fated institutions but the creators and supporters of the institutions in which we live. So we can change them. And this new consciousness and responsibility must be expressed and nourished in our intercessory prayer. Thanks to the word of God, we are catching up to the word of God. The Bible is freshly relevant in our kind of world.

Even though we see more clearly now how we are called to prepare the way through structural changes, the reign of God remains grace, gift. So we are striving for a series of prayers — *prayers* — expressing a lively sense of our dependence upon God, a sense as common and communal as it is lively. For the faith community this means a solidarity of such catholic breadth that it can accept and welcome the varying approaches of different consciences and the limits of all our interpretations and formulations. We are different members of one body bringing our gifts in search of consensus, not promoters of division, self-assertion and the putting-down of each other. If our attitude is one of prayer, this should be easy, for in prayer God is the focus and we are nakedly nothing but sisters and brothers, daughters and sons. Our distinctions are simply different gifts (and no one present lacks a gift) and our common need of grace and Spirit overshadows everything else. But it does take attention, striving and work, because the human family has not yet progressed beyond its slavery to violence and tribal (national) sovereignties.

In her positive review of Jeffery Rowthorn's two-volume collection, *Prayers for the Church* and *Prayers for the World*, Liturgical Conference staff editor Virginia Sloyan commented on a defect apparent in many of the contemporary examples. I suspect it is prevalent in current formulations of the intercessions and should be kept in mind by those responsible: "Many . . . are also mundane. There is nothing of true poetry about them — no good images that invite us to go beyond the actual prayer words. They don't allow our hearts to soar, to take flight. Good prayers should do that. True, there will be an instructive dimension to all litanies: they will help us know ourselves and others better and they should deepen our perception of God in Jesus Christ through the Spirit. But they are primarily vehicles of worship — God's praise expressed in the most beautiful and the most authentic words and gestures available to us. In a sense, prayers are nonrational. They should evoke love and feelings and commitment more than thinking, analyzing and judging."[5]

In faith we believe the end is reconciliation — the unity and solidarity of creatures whose only god is God and who are therefore free. We believe the means to that end are reconciling means. But this is far different from having blueprints or some specific advantage over unbelievers in working out with all of the world's people the concrete ways and means for inching our human enterprise along. So modesty and humility become us in our prayer as elsewhere. The general intercessions are not there to impress the world with our knowledge of what is best for everybody. They are there to help worshipers rely more heavily on God's word and God's Spirit than on our own devices — or on the mass media.

Other qualifications being equal, it is helpful when the cantor or reader of the intercessions in the Sunday assembly is a leader in the community's ministry with all who are on the "outside" of the social-economic-political-cultural "mainstream." Originally the deacon was such a minister, so the gospel and the intercessions were entrusted to the deacon.

It will take more time than the churches have yet spent on this project to work out formulas which can be proposed as models. But we can at least share our primitive efforts. Out of a long pas-

[5] *The Living Light* 22 (June 1986) 372–73.

toral experience, my own preference at the present time is for a combination of prepared and spontaneous intercessions, with the prepared ones including all classes of petitions and in the simplest, briefest formula, the unvarnished "For . . . ." After they are sung or said, with responses, the reader invites the rest of the assembly: "Your other intentions," or "You may add other intentions." Sufficient time is allowed for this, and then the presider concludes with a prayer. The invitation to spontaneity is an important element in ritual structure.

Some appropriate intercessions might be: "For churches, for synagogues and for all other faith communities, let us pray." "For justice and peace in the world, let us pray." "For persons in public office and those who hold economic, cultural, or military power, let us pray." "For victims of oppression, persecution, violence, or prejudice, let us pray." "For the unemployed, the hungry, the homeless, the lonely and all who endure inhuman conditions, let us pray." "For prisoners, refugees, exiles and those uprooted by war and tyranny, let us pray." "For children and their opportunities, for old people and their dignity, let us pray." "For those with AIDS, serious illness, and disabling handicaps, let us pray." "For those addicted to alcohol or other drugs, let us pray." "For those who have died, for _____, let us pray." "For this community, our worship, our ministry of reconciliation, our service to the coming of God's reign, let us pray."

16

Some Steps Toward
Appropriate Sunday Liturgy*

A recent invitation to speak about "steps the average parish could take to improve its Sunday liturgy" forced me to think about problems of renewal in a way which I usually avoid. Speaking of "steps" in this matter has always seemed to me a bit unrealistic. The change of heart and of ecclesial consciousness involved is hard to outline. I am not averse to practical and concrete suggestions, but they all go together. The vitality, immediacy, experiential quality of the Sunday liturgy depend so very heavily on the health, the common mind and heart of faith, the common sense of mission of the church that does it. The notion of "steps" seems to imply that there is a ladder somewhere, with numbered rungs, the employment of which will bring us to the heights. And, while we can talk about parishes, the samenesses and differences among the churches of any area defy averaging.

On the other hand, that request invited an effort to assemble an organized list of actions and consciousness-raisings which seem basic to an old and presumably sage type like me. As long as the reader is conscious of my limits, aware that none of us (young or old, ordained or not) has the whole picture, such an effort, I began to think, might be mildly useful. I came up with some twenty-two steps under five major headings (economy, assembly, mission, ministries, rite).

ECONOMY

1. *Set up authority for stewardship of community property and other resources.* Economics, as Gerard Sloyan has pointed out, is a pri-

*Worship, January 1987

mary theological datum. A Christian community has a corporate moral responsibility in this matter which is at least as imperative as that of the believing individual. We must make sure that our buildings, land, savings, investments, purchases are fully utilized for inching the world toward the justice and solidarity of God's reign, the biblical message. The way we spend and use our wealth, corporate or individual, shows where our hearts are. (Even though my focus here is the local parish, these "steps" call for an evolving collegial action with other parishes and units of the church in area, diocese, nation and world.)

2. *Abolish Mass stipends and other "donations" related to sacramental ministry and prayer.* With notable exceptions, Catholic preaching and teaching on the eucharist have improved dramatically since the Second Vatican Council. But it is extremely difficult for anyone to believe we mean what we say when the "ecclesiologically and liturgically pathological" (Francis Mannion, *Worship*, May 1983) custom of "Mass stipends" is tolerated and even encouraged. Such "intentions" belong in the general intercessions of the liturgy. This obviously means serious attention to salary schedules and other economic matters, so the abolition would force needed reforms which might not otherwise be undertaken.

3. *Relate money offerings in the Sunday liturgy to the church's mission.* This must be done very concretely, with *one* collection at the appropriate time, presented with the gifts of bread and wine (then carried to the credence table), of which an agreed upon and known (by the entire assembly) percentage goes to a cause or causes clearly identified with "the poor" (Roman Missal: "for the poor and the church"). As long as believers regard those offerings as merely taking care of their own parish expenses, giving will be as stingy and celebration as devoid of this spark as both are. An assembly with a sense of mission *has* to express it in the money offerings of its Sunday celebration.

4. *Budget realistically for the priority of the Sunday assembly.* Providing a suitably hospitable and beautiful environment for the Sunday assembly, with professional musical leadership as well as competence in other roles of ministry, with furnishings, books, vessels, vesture and other materials which reveal the eye and hand of artists — these are among the economic bases which must be in place before a living community can maximize its experience

in Sunday celebration. Resist the temptation, therefore, to use human misery as an excuse to disparage this other human need. Oppressed people understand better our need of festivity's excess and engage in it with more delight than the comfortable.

ASSEMBLY

5. *Make initiation processes the continuing and no. 1 item on the church's interior agenda.* RCIA is not a "program" — it is the way the church is, the way the church lives. The kind of local church that it assumes and requires — one engaged in the constant process described by Ron Lewinski as a lifelong and ever deepening spiral of gospel-conversion-baptism-eucharist-mission — is the key to everything that community is and does, including its liturgical celebration of its primary theology and sources. These processes, a pattern of corporate renewal, are the basis of the church's year and are as much for old timers as for prospective members.

6. *Express in all possible ways the variety-in-unity and the different gifts of the members of the assembly.* Express it especially in roles of specialized ministry and leadership in the Sunday assembly, but also in every other aspect of the church's life and mission. Make visible appropriate competencies (for each role), which exist among women, minority groups and the culturally disenfranchised just as frequently as among men and dominant groups. It is this mix and the different insights into the gospel coming out of it which make our pilgrim journey (growth) and faith development possible.

7. *Reduce the number of Sunday Masses to the minimum which the size of the local church and the space and optimum conditions for worship indicate.* This, too, is critical, so that believers are *brought together* and not dispersed. We must begin to look at the Sunday assembly as an extended family looks at the gathering of all its members for a festal dinner. For in our Sunday tradition, joined hands, mutual support, attention to each other are essentials, and are as basic in the rite as its sharing of holy word and holy supper.

8. *Substitute other services of common prayer for the weekday eucharist.* Catholic liturgical tradition is not limited to the Mass as a common and public expression of faith and devotion. Mass is above all the act of the gathered community, the Sunday assembly. And the collegial bishop or priest presides as the *climax* of a pastoral role of faith-community-building, enabling, eliciting of gifts. The litur-

giologist who concluded that Protestants had struck a blow at the Sunday assembly when the eucharist ceased to be a regular, every Sunday celebration and that Catholics had struck the same kind of blow when the eucharist became a daily rite was, it seems to me, profoundly correct. No ministerial leader and no community can or will put the time, money, energy, imagination into the Sunday assembly which it deserves if eucharist is also a weekday, everyday responsibility, and, with funerals, weddings, etc., sometimes a several-times-a-day event. It also means that pastoral work does not get done. Adaptations (with fewer words and more action) of morning prayer and evening prayer are quite capable of serving the spiritual needs of the small proportion of believers who can gather daily.

9. *Make sure that the environment and artifacts of the Sunday assembly are appropriately simple and beautiful.* The competence of the artist/ designer cannot be assumed in either clergy or liturgy committees. Both must seek the guidance of artists for the making or selection of everything used in the Sunday assembly's space and celebration, as well as for the creation or renovation of the space itself. This requires more than the budget mentioned above. We must be aware of our need and desirous of that help, and careful in selecting the still rare person with appropriate talents and training. If the seating and arrangement of the assembly as a whole do not have priority in any building or renovation project, then we are on the wrong track.

MISSION

10. *Resist every temptation to isolate, ghettoize, separate the local church from the rest of the world.* Just as initiation is our interior agenda, so mission, our call to be a sign in the world of God's reign and a servant to the rest of the world in prodding our baby steps toward that peace and justice, is our exterior agenda. The biblical faith of Jews and Christians sees the world as a developing epiphany of God, its creator, source, heart. The local church's purpose therefore is not to consume the lives of its members or to fill up their schedules, but rather to inspire the community for living elsewhere. Even the retreat, or the cloistered community of prayer, is for service to the rest of the world. Being part of the world, at home in

it, happy to bear the tension between its present reality and faith's vision of God's reign — these are essentials of our mission.

11. *Raise the local church's consciousness of the tension between the status quo and the peace and justice to which we are called.* When conversion/baptism declined in our consciousness and we began to speak of "Christian countries," it was easy to forget that the faith community is a countercultural force and to privatize its moral imperatives of seeking human liberation and human solidarity with means that are reconciling. Our obsession with sexuality (a private matter) and our neglect of other moral areas (economic, political, military) are sufficient evidence. You can't get blood out of a turnip and you can't get living liturgy out of communities which lack this sense of social mission.

12. *Interpret mission in contemporary terms,* that is, in terms of creating the structures and institutions that will advance the peace and justice of the world, of achieving a global rather than a family or tribal or national view of human problems and solutions. Private and individual palliatives and remedies for persons and groups whose lives have been deprived or ruined by our systems must continue (almsgiving), but a new human consciousness makes new demands: preventive rather than remedial action on the structures, institutions, systems which determine so much of our lives.

13. *Risk taking corporate steps out of community consensus on issues of prudential judgment.* Only a community that has made RCIA its life will begin to understand why not only individual believers but also corporate bodies of believers, as church, are called by the covenant and by their sign function in God's world to risk even possible missteps in the effort to interpret and prepare the Lord's way, to incarnate the reign of God in the still primitive stuff of human economic and political structures and institutions. Covenant history, Jewish and Christian, proves this development and evolution, slow as it is. We are not party-liners, and orthodoxy is a deeper unity than our interpretations and applications (despite what these unhappy 80s and the mass media keep telling us), but we do believe that the liturgy in which Bible and sacrament live and which nourishes us with primary sources calls for action in concrete steps toward the freedom and the solidarity of all God's children.

14. *Consistently evoke and employ the gifts and responsibility of all members of the church.* The community of the baptized and presently committed is the church (parish, diocesan, national and world) and the ministry of the whole is basic and primary. The entire church, the body of Christ, is the minister both in its liturgy and in its sign and servant relation to the rest of the world. A major part of the pastoral task is the encouraging, enabling, supportive, reconciling building of this kind of corporate sense out of all our different gifts.

15. *Make visible in every Sunday assembly a variety of specialized ministers.* Already mentioned under assembly, this distinction of roles needs constant attention and nurture. Seeing is believing. For example, to see women regularly in roles of liturgical leadership will do more to overcome our patriarchal prejudices than anything else, even though we need other sorts of efforts too. Competence for the particular ministry is, of course, the primary requirement beyond that, making sure that we find such competence among women members, among minority group (including gay and lesbian) members, among economically disadvantaged members, etc., as well as among the dominant cultural groups. This is not only our reconciling business as church; it is also gospel preaching and assembly involving.

16. *Situate all specialized ministries in the church rather than above it.* All of them, ordained, commissioned or delegated, are parts of the body, the assembly, for the doing of things that require special talents and training as well as individual hands, voices, energies, time. Thus what these ministers do, the whole body does through them, and therefore Christ does. If ministers appear alien or foreign to us, then all is lost. Such an understanding of ministries (and it is also that of the new ordination rite) follows our recovered ecclesiology and will be followed by ministerial reforms in recruitment, training and more.

RITE

17. *Open up the symbol language of liturgy, especially all nonverbal elements of our ritual tradition.* In this we have to free ourselves both from our immediate liturgical past (which kept the symbols but in a desiccated and petrified fashion) and from our capitalistic, ra-

tionalistic, literalistic culture. We have to learn how to contemplate, enjoy poetry, see God in creation, let things speak to us in their own language of being. Then the imaginative, playful, symbolic language which is liturgy will heal our "worker-thinker" diminishment of humanity and show its real power. Symbolic communication is classical, seminal, comprehensive and sufficiently ambiguous to touch us all, every type and heart and mind. It is a communication more adequate to mystery than is our prose. Now we are called to open up this great symbolic tradition again and let the Christ-meal of plate and cup, the baptismal bath, the oil massage, the laying on of hands, lights and incense, color and form — in other words, the whole dance of liturgy — communicate in its own incomparable way.

18. *Employ professional music leadership, with competence in liturgy.* To save space, I refer here to my column in the September 1986 issue of *Worship.*

19. *Insist that presiding ministers give preparation for the Sunday assembly top priority in their time and energy.* This will mean relieving them, not of the pastoral tasks of community building, reconciliation, and enabling of different gifts, but rather of some of the managerial and financial work which others can handle more efficiently. Bishops and priests are supposed to be *pastors.* The Sunday assembly is the climax of the pastoral role, the gathering of the clan, and demands priority not only for preaching preparation but also for careful planning and adapting the entire rite for the maximum experience of all.

20. *Place in the hands of all in the assembly appropriate materials for their full participation.* Not throwaway missalettes which reflect a throwaway attitude toward the liturgy, but a good hymnal which feels in the hand and looks to the eye like something important. And a small sheet inserted, with hymn and psalm numbers for the day and any additional music or responses needed. Materials which do *not* contain the readings and prayers. Folks who are deaf or hard of hearing can easily bring along their Sunday missals, but the assembly as a whole should be bent on common participation in a community action, with heads up and attention to the assembly's common ministry and the different specialized ministries in their particular functions.

21. *Begin renewal efforts with the essentials of the rite rather than with its subordinate elements.* I remember a pamphlet on baptism which contained innumerable suggestions for the celebration of that rite but did not once mention the actual bathing in water. To miss the point of a thing — that totally takes some doing. Immersion in baptism, conviction and reaching out to the hearers in the proclamation of the word, eating from the common plate and drinking from the common cup — these are essentials. Start with them! Don't leave the shriveled and neglected essential elements untouched while concentrating on the periphery!

22. *Cultivate both hospitality and the things that make for a sense of awe/beauty/transcendence as equal necessities and happy tension.* The Sunday assembly needs a strong sense of collectivity and solidarity in order to engage in liturgy. It also needs the reverence, humility and Other-centeredness of worship. So we must maintain and treasure the tension between hospitality — making people welcome, at home, comfortable, seated close together and fully participating — and the equally important experience of transcendence, awe, wonder, mystery, without which worship is meaningless. The quality and beauty of the space and everything used in celebration are part of the latter. And specialized ministers must themselves give the example of being part of the worshiping assembly — worshipers first throughout the rite and only after that having a specialized function at certain moments. A swaggering, self-conscious, proprietary presider or other minister is a disaster.

17

Cautionary Tales About
Liturgy's Verbal Parts*

There was a time not so long ago when we tended to identify liturgy with the words of the texts in the ritual books. If we had the book in hand, we felt we had the liturgy in hand. Perhaps our experience in recent decades, even more than conciliar teaching, is responsible for the fruitful and growing recognition that liturgy is much more than that. Liturgy is a complex of acts. And these acts — all necessities of the one symbolic action we call liturgy — include not only rendering the texts of the rite but also a number of other equally significant and essential deeds: music's elevation of both word and action; other arts' supplying of implements, furnishings, decoration; architecture's provision of basic environment and space; a body language of posture, movement, gesture; a social organization of different ministries and roles; and, fundamental to all of these, Christian initiation's formation of an assembly that believes and therefore has a mission in the world and a capacity for celebrating liturgy.

None of these elements and acts can be neglected in a serious effort to get the local church, the flesh-and-blood Sunday assembly, out of the cul-de-sac in which we had become so very comfortable and on the pilgrim path again. And only the local assembly, including of course its pastoral servant-leaders, can do it. Especially in a time of ecclesiastical retrenchment like the present, we need to work hard on the development of that sense of local responsibility.

So we need to return, again and again, to the most trustworthy authority we have for this task: the emphatic imperatives of the

*Worship, May 1987

Second Vatican Council's Constitution on the Liturgy: for example, " . . . that all the faithful be led to that full, conscious and active participation in liturgical celebrations called for by the very nature of the liturgy. . . . Such participation . . . is their right and duty by reason of their baptism. . . . In the reform and promotion of the liturgy, this full and active participation by all the people is the aim to be considered before all else. For it is the primary and indispensable source from which the faithful are to derive the true Christian spirit . . . " (no. 14). "Pastors must therefore realize that when the liturgy is celebrated something more is required than the mere observance of the laws governing valid and lawful celebration; it is also their duty to ensure that the faithful take part fully aware of what they are doing, actively engaged in the rite and enriched by its effects" (no. 11).

The familiarity of these phrases is like an anesthetic for the many churches which, a quarter of a century later, have yet to respond in any significant way to their imperatives. And, one must add, for an administrative leadership which, despite its pastoral title, is positively ingenious in exposing other priorities.

In other words, the ritual books of a particular tradition and period and the church customs and laws governing their use are only part of the picture. In a living liturgical tradition, the other part (the *more* that is *required*) is, precisely, what is happening in the public worship of the local churches' Sunday assemblies toward "this full and active participation by all the people" ("the aim to be considered before all else"). For it is we, in our concrete existence as church, as the living subject of a living action, who bring that tradition to life in our own words, music and other arts, in our own body language, roles of leadership, initiation practices — all growing organically out of our past yet bearing the unmistakable imprint that comes from this meeting of the signs of our times with our ritual expressions up to now.

These developments are probably not even discernible as they happen; hence the special difficulty of this responsibility. A local mutation becomes truly, fully ecclesial only as it appears authentically relevant and helpful over a period of time and wins wider use in other churches by persuasive appeal. Nothing careless, crude, or immodest is helpful in these processes of life, so the local church needs strong initiation and self-discipline in its uncompromising thrust toward the prescribed full awareness, conscious engagement, active participation of all. But there will be no thrust at all in an atmosphere of legalism where the specifics of rite have become idols, where we continue to insist that people exist for the sake of the sabbath. Or where the job of ecclesiastical authorities has been corrupted from a service to all the churches — a service of coordinating and sharing for the sake of testing and sifting — to a domination imposing all the specifics of a full-blown rite.

Like any homilist's reflections on how the readings of a particular Sunday illuminate the signs of the times, this columnist's reflections on current verbal problems in liturgy are hazarded on the supposition that the author is not unique. In preaching I have found that when an insight into the relation between the text and the signs of the times seems to me helpful, it will also seem helpful to other people (much of the rest of the assembly). So common are we all! In the same spirit, I offer the following expressions of gratitude to churches exhibiting exceptional care for the verbal elements of rite:

1. Thanks to the churches who make evident in celebration the importance of the three biblical readings in the Sunday assembly and who search for, find and commission readers able to *proclaim* the texts in an attention-getting and convincing way that reaches out to the rest of the assembly. And who train their readers to take care of at least the more obvious examples of exclusive language in our English translations.

2. Thanks to the churches who undertake the work of adapting liturgical texts for inclusive language now, even as we hope for and await the refinement and elevated language of common texts from the International Commission on English in the Liturgy and other agencies. The latter will eventually improve on our provisional pastoral efforts. Meanwhile these efforts need to be as careful, sensitive, and respectful of the meaning of each text as our local resources can manage.

The biblical message of liberation (freedom, justice) and unification (solidarity, peace) — those two, inseparable sides of salvation, of the vision of God's reign — is in our time spawning offspring all over the place in movements for human rights, liberation and sharing (with the help, as always, of God's word). No matter how much the status quo (including much of the ecclesiastical status quo) resists that vision, the liturgy keeps generating it afresh.

Anyone who has read church history or lived very long knows how ambivalent the church as a whole (locally, nationally and worldwide) is in the face of such consciousness-raisings. The gospel spawns them, but we rush to disown our children. We aren't "ready." And we accept them finally only when they refuse to be excluded. I remember that it was so with the black movement for civil and human rights earlier. Prophetic oases in the churches provided its dynamism, but the feet of the churches in general were clamped on the brakes. So it is with the women's movement, as with every movement for peace and justice, for the liberation of groups, minorities, victims of society's put-down and prejudice.

While the dynamic message of God's reign ("on earth as in heaven") is in the liturgy and its scriptural basis, it is immensely helpful to us all when the verbal texts express it as clearly as the action, for verbal texts are always more limited by the time and place of their formulation than the other more comprehensive and universal symbol-language of rite. So that we no longer need a microscope, or encyclopedia, or course in biblical interpretation to sense and feel and be energized by it. We do not need to tell lies about our past or to pretend that the covenant transforms society instantaneously. We *do* need to tell the truth about our pilgrim journey — that we are incomplete, unfinished, and on the move. Then we can understand our history (and God's patience) of slavery and patriarchy and the violence of domination by one group over another. Because then we begin to see that in terms of faith's vision we are still primitive. We see the end, the goal, even though we know no more about the means than that they must have the character of love.

Since the Sunday assembly is the celebration of that vision, the banquet of the reign of God, it needs to express it as clearly as possible in the vernacular of the day. So as soon as it becomes apparent that our verbal formulations are impeding or confusing the development of conscience, we need to express the step we have made in our celebration of the vision. Thanks to those who have not shirked this delicate, sparing, poetic, faithful-to-meaning work.

3. Thanks to the churches who are adapting the texts of some New Testament readings in which the generic "the Jews" is used to refer to only a small group of the faithful of the time. This is a

simple service to accuracy, and it is also the apology of a raised consciousness for identifying the failings or sins of individuals with all the other members of their tribe, sex, religion, class, or color. "I was mugged by an old lady; therefore, all old ladies are probable muggers." The general lack of awareness of our roots in and dependence on Judaism and the disturbing frequency of anti-Jewish epithets and offhand remarks among Christian believers evidence a deep sickness that demands attention. The language of liturgy is one element in a comprehensive work of building up Christian appreciation of, respect and hunger for relations with Judaism and our Jewish forebears and faith companions.

While the texts of liturgy must never be regarded as mere catechetical devices, neither must they be permitted to make us comfortable with our prejudices and hates, to militate against liturgy's vision of the reign of God, of love and reconciliation.

4. Thanks to presiders and other specialized ministers serving the ministering assembly who refuse to say more than is absolutely necessary. The human ear is under almost constant assault in our culture. The fact that less is more — more penetrating, more striking, more memorable — is particularly evident in an assembly gathered for the worship of God. The kind of running commentary in which some clergy indulge (and occasionally other ministers as well) tends to numb the aural sense, weaken the impact of liturgy's significant verbal elements, and drown the total experience of the symbolic act in its flood of trivia.

In addition, the rhythm, flow, relation of spoken or sung texts in the rite is severely damaged by the interjection of sergeant-like directives of any sort. "Please stand," when a lifting of the hands would do. "Please sit," when a lowering of the hands would do. "Please sing hymn number 275," when a hymn board or a printed program would do. "Please come to communion by way of the center aisle," when the silent action of ushers or a printed program would do. Points of definition, like the beginning and end of a rite and its moments of transition, appropriately resist arbitrary change, as do the brief formulas which call for a response from the rest of the assembly. No "Good morning, sisters and brothers" is as worshipful an orientation after the opening song of the Sunday assembly as the sign of the cross and the scriptural greeting. The former spotlights the speaker; the latter, the purpose of the gathering. And thanks to the presider who greets " . . . be with you all" rather than " . . . be with each and every one of you," as if we were not already sufficiently fragmented, as if our need and hunger at this moment were not to feel and be as one. Custody of the tongue and the humility of worshipers on the part of presiders, cantors, readers and all other specialized ministers, are priceless blessings for an assembly whose culture has fed it up to its choking neck with stars.

5. Thanks to the churches who employ hymns as the poems and faith confessions and proclamations they are, and not as Muzak interval-fillers. Almost all hymns are poems of faith, thanksgiving, etc., whose integrity and common sense demand that they be sung in their entirety. If for some reason that cannot be done, then they should not be sung at all. There are a few hymns, written with optional verses for special occasions, which can be dealt with accordingly, but they are rare. Hymns are liturgical texts which require the "full, conscious, active participation of all" no less than any other part of the rite. To halt a hymn before we have completed its verses is to ravage that text.

The return of Bob and Ray to radio (remember how they used to say songs?) reminds me to include a thanks to churches who resist that strange practice, who do not say songs. While the ritual books are lenient in this matter, elements of the Sunday liturgy like the Gloria, the responsory psalms, the acclamations (all of them) really demand music.

18

"Priestless Sundays" Reconsidered*

Convenient habits are powerful forces in human corporate as well
as private life, so it is not surprising that they effectively undermine reform and renewal efforts in the churches all the time. They
cast doubt on any attempt to correct distortion and peel away
camouflage and overgrowth. They dull perception and displace the
growth and progress of a living tradition with suspicion, fear and
caution. Consequently, they sometimes prevent and always discourage us from examining proposed solutions to liturgical problems carefully and from all the angles which have made the
Sunday assembly central and crucial in the life of the church.

Unlike the times we older types remember, when The Liturgical
Conference, with its annual "Liturgical Week," was (apart from
Worship, then called *Orate Fratres*) almost the only national promoter of liturgical renewal, now our country is dotted with diocesan liturgy agencies, academic courses, pastoral conferences,
ministerial training programs and publications in the field. That
comparison should offer some relief to our current depression. It
is only natural that, in a time of basic change, the quality of all
these efforts varies considerably, depending on their personnel,
vision, resources and aims.

The Office for Divine Worship of the Archdiocese of Chicago
and its Liturgy Training Publications division not only have a
longer and more illustrious history than more recent comers in the
renewal enterprise, but also, in my opinion, invite the trust and
confidence that many other agencies have yet to win. Because of
this and because serious work in any liturgical tradition tends to
benefit all liturgical traditions, the Chicago publications have

Worship, March 1988

earned a wide audience, not only beyond the boundaries of that diocese but also ecumenically, beyond the churches in communion with the Roman Church.

Their list of periodicals, books, leaflets and visual aids avoids fads and fancies, is solidly based, insightful in a common sense and non-idiosyncratic way, and practical in the best (which is rarely the easiest) manner. Gabe Huck's editorial comment, "Priestless Sundays: Are We Looking or Leaping?"[1] in a recent issue is a case in point. It merits considerably more reflection than this brief column can undertake, but at least I can make a start.

Huck looks at a phenomenon which most of us have simply accepted and taken for granted, and makes some fresh and revelatory observations. At the present time and under the present discipline of most of the churches of the Roman Rite, it is clear that many parishes cannot count on the regular Sunday presence and presidency of a bishop or presbyter. Until steps are taken to reform the discipline, the eucharist cannot be celebrated on such occasions. Surely the eucharist as the central sacrament and celebration of the Sunday assembly is of sufficient importance and carries enough traditional weight to indicate a change in discipline so that qualified women and married persons may serve in those roles. That step alone would solve the problem under discussion, as well as a few others.

Given our present situation, however, many churches which lack an ordained bishop or presbyter as pastor but wish to maintain the Sunday assembly have settled for what is called "a communion service," employing one of its members (usually a deacon, a sister, a catechist, or another parish leader) to preside. Scripture readings, hymns, prayers and the sharing of holy communion (in one form only, reserved in a tabernacle from a eucharistic celebration) generally constitute that service. Sometimes it includes a thanksgiving prayer of some length, similar to the eucharistic prayer but without bread and wine and an expressed intent to memorialize the paschal mystery and obey the messianic last will and testament.

[1] *Liturgy 80*, October 1987 (Liturgy Training Publications, 1800 North Hermitage Avenue, Chicago, Ill. 60622-1101) 4–5.

Reflecting on this new practice, Huck comments on the sometimes enthusiastic acceptance of such a radical substitution in the Sunday assembly and on what seems a general lack of appreciation of the difference between the two services (between "a communion service" and the Mass or eucharist). He suggests that such an easy surrender of the eucharist is possible only because of the persistent domination of preconciliar habits. On the practical level of what people observe and experience, perhaps these "communion services" seem little different from their celebrations *with* a priest: "Do you see what is happening? People are applying what they have learned. They are acting the way they have been formed by the practice of their ritual. I mean this. Sunday after Sunday, they see that only the priest or the priest and a few others take the bread consecrated at this Mass, whereas most of them receive from the tabernacle's supply. Is it clear what we have taught? Even under the reformed liturgy, even with a dozen bright rubrics saying to give bread and wine at a given Mass to the people celebrating that Mass, we have continued to act as if it didn't matter about the bread and wine: any consecrated bread and no wine at all will do. . . ."[2]

Those observations are as relevant for believers who have not yet been threatened by priestless Sundays as for those who presently "make do" with "communion services." For many of the former regularly celebrate with presiding clergy who are disinclined to plan and arrange the provision of sufficient bread and wine in each eucharistic celebration for the communion of all those participating in that celebration, or who do not understand the basic need for doing so. Those are the presiding clergy for whom the liturgy has become an object and has ceased to be an action, for whom it is therefore of no consequence whether or not the assembly does and experiences an integrated eucharistic rite: gathering as church or body of Christ to worship; listening and responding to the proclamation of the readings; interceding for the church and for the whole world; presenting the money ("for the poor and the church," as the Roman Missal says) and bread and wine gifts of our hands and, thereby, ourselves; offering the

[2] Huck, 4–5.

thanksgiving prayer *with those same gifts*, remembering God's saving deeds in history; making the prayer that Jesus taught and the ministry of reconciliation our own; exchanging the peace with the fresh vision of the assembly and each other gained herein; breaking and pouring *those same gifts*, with their full meaning, that all of us bits and pieces might be bound into one, into their pristine unity; eating and drinking together from the common holy plate and cup, *those same gifts*, confirming and building up our oneness in Christ by grace; being dismissed to witness to the freedom and the oneness here perceived and given.

All those actions are one action, one liturgy, one Mass, one eucharist, and they belong together in the Sunday assembly, the gathering of the baptized and committed covenant community. From that action of Christ's mystical body, the church, reserved elements may and should be brought to believers who, through no fault of their own, cannot be part of the assembly: people isolated by old age, or sickness, or imprisonment, or necessary work or other duties. Where a believer in forced solitude (or any situation requiring absence from the Sunday assembly) has a right to ask of sisters and brothers a sharing in the holy communion of the assembly — *that* is where "communion services" make good sense (nourishment, support, belonging).

We have begun to recognize this in some ways. Unordained eucharistic ministers (of plate and cup) are now common, not only to facilitate the communion procession and to encourage full and appropriate sharing in both plate and cup but also to make sure that ministers in the liturgy, like the rest of the assembly, are present and are part of the action from the beginning to the end. No more do priests who have not been part of this particular assembly emerge from the sacristy "to help with communion" and then rapidly disappear. One hopes that the popularity of that specific renewal effort does not depend on the fact that it subtracts from rather than adds to the work of the clergy. Basic issues of renewal like real bread that can be *broken* and *shared among all*, or like the place of the tabernacle of eucharistic reservation have not fared so well. Until the tabernacle is in its appropriate room, separate from the main worship space — and, where there is a daily or small chapel, separate from that, too — it is clear that we will not take seriously the integrity of the liturgy. As long as we do not, that is, as long as there is any traffic to or from the tabernacle during the celebration of Mass, it is hardly surprising that people do not see the difference between the eucharist and a "communion service."

Taking the time and doing the figuring necessary for making provision for sufficient bread and wine for all those expected at a given eucharistic celebration should be an important item on any agenda of liturgical renewal and full participation. That is part of the job of clergy and other specialized ministers, because the rest of the Sunday assembly is, together with them, the body of Christ, members of Christ, sharers in the priesthood of Christ, doers and celebrators of the liturgy. The bread and wine which that particular assembly presents, with which it gives a blessing in praise and thanks, is reconciled, and shares in holy communion, is central to the entire symbolic action, from beginning to end. To interrupt that continuity and integrity by inadequate provision, importing elements left over from a previous celebration, reveals a symbolic illiteracy of staggering proportions. Yet that is where most of us are.

The Sunday assembly with its eucharistic action wonderfully unites in its symbol language many parts or strands of belief which western theology has dissected or separated (for closer scrutiny . . . and then left lying about). While the eucharistic liturgy clearly does not infallibly elicit the "full participation" of all in the assembly, it does, when properly celebrated, assume, require and provide for it. Its texts, arts and actions bring together in a symbolically lucid fashion what we believe about the importance of the gathering, the priestly character of the assembly, God's saving deeds in history, the entire church as minister not only of worship but also of service and witness to each other and to the rest of the world, and ordained ministry as positively representing, confirming and serving the ministerial responsibility and priestly dignity of all.

One cannot help but think that the lack of a strong sense of mission and purpose in life, characteristic of so many churchgoers in our time, is related to the common assumption that only ordained members really *do* anything in the liturgy, really offer what our tradition says all the baptized offer. It was a long biblical evolution from the sacrifices of animals and crops to the sacrifice of life-orientation urged by the prophets and manifest in Jesus Christ. In Greek the latter was called *thusia logike*, in Latin *oblatio rationabilis*, in English "the sacrifice of the logos, of the spirit, of obedience, of life itself."

It is not just any assembly. It is the church. Unlike the sabbath or paschal meals, to which it is related as deeply as all Christians are to our Jewish forebears and faith companions, it is an ecclesial rather than a domestic celebration. It is not the celebration of the ethnic or family group, but the final bursting of whatever remained of those bonds by faith alone, by initiation alone. The local assembly relates to all the other churches through baptism, to the basics of the rite, to the faith the rite professes and to its collegial presiding minister.

There is truth in what has already been pointed out: that our recovery of a eucharistic practice free of past tangents, distortions and diminishments has been slow and far from consistent or complete. Sunday Mass in many parishes in 1988 does look in large part like "a communion service." But it would be a tragedy if our failure to implement liturgical renewal more thoroughly than we have until now were our excuse for letting the eucharist yield its regular weekly place on Sunday to "a communion service." For the latter increases our problems of passivity and privatization, on the one hand, and, on the other, constitutes a continuing obstacle to appropriate disciplinary reforms.

I think we would be better advised to put time, money and effort into cleaning up and animating our eucharistic celebrations, so that the kind of substitution now being accepted would be felt to be inappropriate. It seems to me that while "a communion service" is appropriate in situations where it extends the community's eucharistic celebration to the isolated individual in circumstances where the church cannot gather, a widespread practice of that sort in Sunday assemblies would be irreparable.

Some will say, "You can have the understanding you are talking about without so much work, because it is implicit in our liturgical tradition and in our consequent theology." But "implicit" is not enough. The gift of sacramental action is that it makes visible, tangible and experiential (*significando causant* — "by signifying, sacraments effect") truth that needs to be explicit and out of the closet.

Huck's article does not ignore the desirability of a Sunday

gathering even when it cannot celebrate the eucharist: "A better temporary answer (to the 'priestless Sunday') would be to keep Sunday and keep the assembly, but to assemble for Morning Prayer or Evening Prayer and to include a reading of the lectionary's scriptures for the day. It seems to me less important to have some ritual element that is supposed to resemble the eucharistic prayer than it is to have assemblies who take responsibility for rites that belong to our tradition. . . . Eucharist *should* be missed."[3]

[3] Huck, 5.

The Body Is One and Many*

19

Perhaps it is like whistling in the dark, but I keep saying (to myself as well as to others) that this pontificate or period or moment is an exception that proves the rule; and that the reform and renewal which the blessed Second Vatican Council accepted from the hands of the few and made the business of the many cannot be subverted by a mere decade or two of mortal fright and retreat.

For example, the clericalism which assumed long ago the place vacated by the disuse of initiatory processes and the consequent decline of a sound ecclesiology seems to be again rampant. But, like so many other features of the moment, is this not merely one of those neuroses which tend to follow a trauma, the trauma being the end of an ecclesial paralysis with which we had become too comfortable? If so, the answer is neither to fret nor to despair but to treat the moment as one would any illness and to keep alive the useful distinction between sickness and health.

We are not without encouragement and help — always, of course, from our sources, but even from the current practice of the local churches. In addition to the basic recovery in many local churches of initatory processes, potentially transforming, integrating both our self-consciousness and our activities as church, we see now in most parishes a variety of ministries operating in the Sunday liturgical assembly (and many of them serving the entire life of the community).

After centuries when popular notions of ministry had shrunk to the ordained three (and practically to the one in regular view),

Worship, November 1988

this development is not only appropriate and sound but also a constant reminder that a baptismal ecclesiology is here to stay and a clerical one cannot prevail.

It is natural that a recovery of fuller dimensions of church should result in a recovery of fuller dimensions of the church's principal ministries: episcopate, presbyterate, diaconate. A distortion of ministry into status or class elevation, separated from the rest of the faithful not only by function but also and especially by a certain sense of being the "in" group, with private avenues of power and revelation, did even more damage than its evident shamanizing of the clergy. It undermined Christian initiation, baptismal commitment, vocation and mission. In fact, as we older types remember, "vocation" came to mean only one thing — the call to priesthood, extended to include the life of the vows.

When clericalism was attacked by a return to a more traditional ecclesiology, many bishops and priests seemed to feel lost and meaningless. Actually, it was that reform and return which restored the evangelical and pastoral necessity and meaning of those collegial offices and revised the office of deacon. We clergy *found* our meaning again when we began to see that we are made by the community to serve the community's needs for full- or part-time help, for functions requiring certain talents, training and community mission or ordination.

The reappearance of many part-time, community-commissioned musicians, readers, ushers, acolytes and eucharistic ministers, has been one of the most immediately successful of the liturgical developments accompanying this conciliar reform and recovery. Nor is the variety of ministries restricted to liturgical celebration. As a general principle, specialized ministries in the church have found not their raison d'etre but their climax in liturgical function. Bishops and presbyters preside in the eucharist as the climax of their pastoral task, not as its fulfillment. They are pastors, faith-community builders, and their Sunday presidency caps that work off. We see the relation between work and rite reflected in forms for commissioning other ministers as well. As limited as the post-conciliar rites were, they did indicate that persons charged with the office of lector ordinarily exercise that ministry also as a teacher or catechist outside the liturgy. And those commissioned as acolytes represent the community in visits with those who cannot be present in the Sunday assembly and bring them the bread and cup of life from the altar.

Depending on the size and resources of the local church, the variety of ministries now extends beyond those which have a liturgical aspect to include business administrators, social action coordinators, ecumenism agents and educators for both children and adults. For this column, however, my reflections are on those observed in Sunday eucharistic celebrations, the principal gatherings of the faith community. First, some comments about the great gift these revived or new ministries have been to the church, even in the early stages of trial and error. And then some suggestions for making their service even more valuable. All, of course, from the limits of my point of view.

Leadership in human social functions (like liturgy) is an adult role. Children are welcome and important parts of the social function, through baptism sharing in the basic ministry of the entire assembly. Children learn and grow through such participation. But they do not ordinarily assume roles of leadership. Children should be allowed to be children, growing toward such roles. A gift of this visible variety of roles of adult leadership is that it makes it much easier for all of us to identify with these representatives and to understand our own active ministry as assembly. The experience of these other leaders along with the bishop or priest presiding does much to bridge the chasm which clericalism has created and which a lone bishop or priest confronting the rest of the assembly tends to support.

It is a gift, too, to see the broad variety of the faith community in these roles. While the majority of churches in the Christian world do not yet ordain women, the experience of seeing them regularly functioning as readers and acolytes, sometimes superbly, certainly will do more than many words to break down walls of prejudice and custom and to throw our sexual stereotypes into doubt. In communities which include handicapped people or ethnic, color, class or sexual orientation minorities, persons of those groups (possessing appropriate talents) exercising roles of leadership will help us all become the ministers of reconciliation we are supposed to be.

Because every known liturgy developed with an assumption that there would be a distinction of roles and a variety of specialized ministers functioning, this new development brings the churches back into "sync" with their authentic tradition and rescues the liturgy of all the baptized from its clerical captors. The fact that the clergy had no such ill intention does not alter another fact: that on the level of the perception and feelings of vast numbers of Christians the liturgy became a clerical preserve. And it remained so for too long.

Another gift of this development is the commitment with which many of these new ministers approach their task and the new life they bring with their enthusiasm, their practiced skill and their sincerity. What a marvelous encouragement and example for us clergy, whose temptations to a tired formalism sometimes meet little resistance! They have already awakened many of us, and, as the contagion spreads, so may the critical realization of pastors that the Sunday assembly is not a rote obligation but a celebrational event.

I could go on with a thanksgiving for more of the benefits from our early success in this area, but it seems to me there are also a few problems we need to consider. The latter are inevitable in any reform effort. They may disappoint the pioneers who did not sufficiently anticipate them, but they are fundamentally signs of a stirring, a revived life, which is never neat and tidy.

Each of the ministries requires special native dispositions and talents as well as training. Now that we have established a distinction of roles as a liturgical norm, it is important that the faith community work out a method of recruitment and selection which will assure that only those with appropriate talents will be trained for such roles. Volunteering is not a good method, because none of us is the best judge of her or his own talents. Ministries must not be viewed as gold stars to be awarded to those most frequently "in church" or those who seek them most enthusiastically. The difference is vital and critical for the sake of the community, the common good. Fortunately, there are enough ministries with enough variety of talents required to make it possible for those in charge to steer enthusiasm into appropriate channels. But it does not happen without careful planning and difficult decisions. In time this caution should have beneficial effects on our clergy recruitment also.

Training for the ministries is time-consuming work, but the Sunday assembly is an event of surpassing importance in the life of a faith community. Therefore it is worth time and money and energy. More attention to training is an evident need, not only so that each ministry does its own task well but also so that all ministers attend to and are full participants in the entire rite.

Sound systems are necessary in many liturgical spaces, but assemblies which require them must have them in place and operating before the liturgy begins. All ministers must be trained to keep their hands off microphones. Just as one must refrain from moving furniture during the course of a rite, so must one refrain from testing, adjusting and moving sound systems. Like the verbal announcement of changes in posture, or of hymn numbers, or the interjection of irrelevant remarks, this kind of noisy fiddling with equipment destroys both the atmosphere and the continuity of rite.

Let me also plead for anonymity (at least during the course of the rite) for all who are exercising a specialized ministry. Public worship is a poor and inappropriate occasion for the introduction of those in roles of leadership. Performance in these roles is a form of prayer and each minister merits both our attention and our respect as co-prayer. However well-meaning such introductions, they sap the essential strength of the assembly, which is its God-focus and God-consciousness.

Beauty, simplicity, commonness and silence are among the characteristics of a good worship experience. Hurried or frantic movements, private conversations and belated preparations of its parts are among the enemies of such an experience. A common liturgical vesture for all ministers who are in places of focus and high visibility throughout the rite is part of their service. Just as the presider's chair is important for the sake of welding and keeping an assembly together and acting as one, so the vesture of those leading (presider, musicians, readers, acolytes) is important for the visual definition of the rite and for the beauty that hints at transcendence.

Vesture is not for the sake of the clergy, not for the sake of setting ministers apart. Vesture is for the sake of the liturgy, for the sake of identifying with the rest of the assembly as its voice and hands and body for specific acts. Our screaming individuality and competitiveness are sufficiently devastating in our economy. We do not need them in the liturgy.

Whether you agree with me or not about the problems involved, I hope you share my delight at the broad acceptance in our country of the many ministries appropriate to liturgical celebration and the healthy ecclesiology they communicate.

"Beggars in the House of Plenty"* 20

It would be easy to take off from that title (of a current play) in almost any direction, for it seems to be the lot of most humans in our still-primitive social "order." It is a classic, all-purpose phrase, mirroring the gap between the world's material achievements and our underdeveloped social consciences and institutions. It sums up an attitude and a condition defended by the super-rich, the reigning powers of every institution, and accepted by the weary, the overwhelmed, the non-voters and the dropouts — rapidly swelling categories . . . and omens.

Biblical faith communities and their worship of a jealous God who reduces all those reigning powers to creature size, for the love of beggars, have been and are a source of sparks which threaten establishments of injustice and discrimination. We, too, in those communities, of course, are sinners. We quench those sparks as fast as we can, protecting ourselves and our ways and our security, but they prove in the long run to be, like God, unmanageable. The liturgy saves the alert from the typical diversions of our faith communities: idolatry, superstition, folk-way tangents, culs-de-sac, romanticism.

When we have our wits about us, the liturgy is our inspiration and the source of meaning for the lives we lead. Our living liturgical tradition, biblical roots in the context of symbolic action, continues to develop for the sake of communicating in successive ages the advent of God's reign. The house of plenty is the worship of a God who is liberating and reconciling love. The classical biblical messages of our Jewish forebears and Christian symbolic action, witnesses communicated not merely in word but in symbolic ac-

*Worship, January 1992

tion, an act of such justice and peace as the world does not yet know. It is our orientation for life, for the faith covenant pilgrimage to God, to the marks of God's gift and will and reign: justice and peace. And when liturgy's sparks are experienced they burn and purify our imaginations, our interpretations. They unveil possibilities, alternatives, of liberating and reconciling developments (always according to where-we-are and by our small steps) in human relationships and institutions.

My point here is that those sparks must be experienced by the members of the Sunday assembly. Sacraments are here to *signify*. "The sabbath was made for humankind, and not humankind for the sabbath" (Mk 2:27). And we are taught by the liturgy constitution of the Second Vatican Council that there is a special and heavy pastoral responsibility for facilitating that experience: "But in order that the liturgy may possess its full effectiveness, it is necessary that the faithful come to it with proper dispositions, that their minds be attuned to their voices, and that they cooperate with divine grace, lest they receive it in vain. Pastors must therefore *realize* that when the liturgy is celebrated *something more is required* than the mere observance of the laws governing valid and lawful celebration; it is also their *duty* to ensure that the faithful take part fully aware of what they are doing, actively engaged in the rite, and enriched by its effects" (no. 11).

Pastors and other pastoral ministers are asked to do many things for which they are not trained. This is one of them. Unless there is a trained liturgy director on the staff, this job tends to be a back-burner item. There are reasons for this, but none of them is good enough. For nothing is more important in any pastoral agenda than concentration on enabling and facilitating the very best experience possible for the believers who make up the Sunday assembly. That is the one time we have the Church together. Leadership in that Eucharistic action does not exhaust the pastoral role, which is to be the chief agent in the community's solidarity in faith and in a sense of mission. But that leadership is certainly the climax of the pastoral role. If we pastors fail in that, we fail period.

Committed Christians, like committed Jews, rather expect to play the role of beggars in the world's house of plenty. To believe in and proclaim a liberating/reconciling God is to accept a liberating/reconciling mission as the meaning of our lives. It is to be pledged to that kind of love — never fully achieved in time, always beckoning on. But we should not be beggars in the liturgical assembly, the churches' house of plenty. What we see in the martyrs, saints and mystics, present and past; what we hear in Martin Luther King Jr's "The Church is the only thing we have"; what we learn from a Latin American experience of oppression which has rescued Christian theology from a long and exclusive academic confinement — all these come from the sources we share in the Sunday Eucharist. These classic sources orientate and inspire, activating our interpretations and our imaginations to find the specific steps of our pilgrim path for today.

Even an inattentive ear cannot avoid the chorus of complaint about the human experience of that assembly; they arise, not from peripheral Christians but from many of the most caring. Why is it so hard to experience the sparks we know are there? Why is it that only the few who have confidence to dig and dig and dig, or who have an extensive liturgical education, find in the Sunday assembly the nourishment we all need? Why is it that pastoral ministers and other parish leaders, many of whom work so hard at other aspects of the Church's life and mission, seem unable to find the time, energy, talent, money (and, most of all, vision) to facilitate a stirring experience for all in that precious moment?

While we continue to work on long-range ecclesial problems like initiation, the local church in relation to the other churches, ecumenism, mission, liturgical studies, and ministerial reforms (recruitment, qualifications, [more] election, training, lifestyle), we dare not neglect today what we can do today to make the Sunday assembly the first item on the pastoral agenda. It is the soul of the Church.

My point is not that pastors or other liturgical leaders can "provide" or "guarantee" good experience for the other members of the assembly. No one can do that. But clergy and other leaders are the assembly's delegated agents in preparing for and serving in the Sunday celebration. The environment and conduct of the rite are their special charge. And their work is never neutral. They either facilitate the worship experience or they militate against it.

Many of us are so accustomed to an *ex opere operato* view of rite that we simply do not realize the power (even when we are not conscious of them) of influences such as the manner of leadership, music and environment and the other arts, talents suited to the particular roles and functions, and even the various materials used in sacramental worship. We may think we are, or trying very hard to be, good servants of the gathered Church, but we fail in this critical part of our job.

To blame the rites for our ineptitude is a convenient diversion. The nature of ritual action is such that it does not need to be — indeed, it cannot be — reinvented every Sunday. We will be the problem until we rearrange our pastoral and ministerial priorities. In other words, until we see that our liturgical functions depend on the fundamental desire to enable a profound worship experience in the assembly we serve. That is what quickens the words and actions of any rite. When we want to share that experience more than anything else, we will be on the right track and we will find ways to do it.

Those ways may differ in different cultural and linguistic contexts. Just as no two persons are the same, no two Sunday assemblies are the same. Nevertheless, it seems to me that there are basic human and faith needs in people, whatever their cultural identification, which leadership will try to meet. While the pastoral specifics will be worked out in the local situation, there is space here to recall a few of the more important elements of such an effort.

One of these involves reflection on the extent to which leadership in any common action slants one's experience of the act. Clergy (and any others for whom these roles are professional duties) are particularly vulnerable to an unreal assessment of a rite's impact on the rest of the assembly. It helps get our feet on the ground if we can at times be a part of the Sunday assembly without our usual specialized function. It helps, too, if we can witness via videotape our own functioning and that of the other ministers in the rite.

Another fundamental one is the need of the whole assembly to experience itself as one in worship, undivided, orientated solely to God through Christ. This means that the presider and other leaders must be (and appear to be, and *feel* like being) worshipers, first and foremost, before any advertence to one's special function. We are members of the assembly who have been delegated for specific roles, guided by the same liturgical tradition as all the rest. I can think of nothing that is more damaging to the experience of the assembly than any hint of self-centeredness, self-promotion, self-aggrandizement in the presiding minister's manner or speech, or in those of any musician, or reader, or other minister. Or any suggestion that the presider is the proprietor of the establishment.

The sense of community solidarity and the equality of its members before the mystery of God, without which there can be no common worship, is another element. Besides pastors and other leaders who understand that they are agents of the whole assembly, which is the body of Christ, the Church, that sense can also be enabled and supported by architecture, by the environment or space of the Eucharistic action. It must be evident that the space is designed for the people who gather; that every person has easy sight and hearing with regard to altar, ambo, presider, cantor, choir; that the liturgy is an action rather than an object; and that the liturgical space is an arena rather than an auditorium or a shrine. All of this requires expert consultation and competence, and an artist's eye.

A spare beauty must add awe and wonder to a human scale's hospitality. People need to be made to feel at home (unlike strangers, or clients, or outsiders), without surrendering the worship character of the assembly. It is not merely another gathering, and the space must speak of transcendence as well as welcome. Even when we say the right things about the Church, as the People of God, if we feel otherwise, if we feel Church is a pyramid, substantially the pope and the other bishops, or the clergy and religious, then that is the message we communicate both by the space and by our manner.

Another element is budgeting for music. No liturgy and certainly no Sunday liturgy should be without music. Unlike the ministries of reader, usher, acolyte, etc., the ministry of music requires professional training, time, practice, planning, group work, and therefore just wages according to whether it is full time or part time. The other ministries require training and practice but not to that professional extent. And all candidates for the non-clerical ministries should be commissioned by the community on the sole basis of their talents and training for the specific function in question.

Finally, although it may be unrealistic to expect it, we who are clergy or other liturgical leaders simply have to wake up to the limits of our literal and book-centered minds and begin to understand that the symbol-language of biblical liturgy is a far more powerful communicator than our tongues. We can help each other achieve a careful custody of all our tongues, appropriate silences in the rites, printed directions when directions are needed, and the doing of every ritual gesture and action as a reaching-out to the rest of the assembly, as if the gesture or action touches people in its own way (when we don't water it down or smother it with verbal "explanation"). As indeed it does, when it is allowed to escape from the prison of the shrivelled, desiccated forms our decadence had allowed those gestures and actions to assume. It happens when they are allowed to become free and full and open and playful and real: initiation with a water bath; refreshment with a common eating and drinking from the common plate and cup of Christ; absolution and solidarity with the laying-on of hands; care with the oil massage; light with substantial candles that exhaust themselves; aroma with incense everybody smells and smoke everybody sees; and so on and so on and so on.

We cannot afford to wait for a general contemplative revival to begin using our liturgical tradition in a way calculated to maximize the experience of the assembly. Many of us now know that tradition is a house of plenty. There is growing unhappiness, therefore, in the great number of Sunday assemblies where the many are still made to feel like beggars.

LITURGICAL
PRESIDING/MINISTRY

21

Sunday No Better? —
After All This Betterment?*

Jesus Christ is the same yesterday, today and forever. Since the Council, however, we have been recovering, slowly, the basic gospel truth about the church: that we are constantly reforming, changing, adapting, becoming new. In liturgical celebration, this recovery has placed a burden on presiding ministers for which most are unprepared. The demands and challenges of that role have been multiplied, while its qualifications, training and other obligations have shown no inclination, so far, to correspond. So we have every reason to sympathize with presiders whose efforts to meet the demands of the role so often seem unfocused, ineffectual and even counterproductive.

I think that these problems are a small part but a real part of any answer to what seems a common refrain: "Why does parish Sunday worship remain so spiritless, so careless of the experience of the assembly, so much more a burden than an inspiration?" It does seem odd, doesn't it? While the shape of the liturgical books, insight into the modes and meanings of the Bible, and the churches' theoretical recovery of an evangelical sacramental tradition have seen a progress, a betterment, surprising in its speed and depth, nevertheless the parish Sunday assembly is slow to profit.

Of course that is an outrageous generalization, and I know many exceptions. But I also believe that the complaint merits attention and is supported by a broad experience of Sunday celebrations. People otherwise well disposed towards the currents of reform and renewal find their liturgical activities a source of discouragement and doubt. It is easy for those of us who are profes-

*Worship, November 1983

sionally in the full-time service of the churches to point out that the deep recoveries and discoveries we are working on will take time and patience. I think we are all ready to accept the fact that one of the most significant of these (RCIA, the catechumenate, the process of Christian initiation) will require the persevering commitment of many generations to enable the transformation of urban parishes from spiritual service stations into faith communities of mutual support and corporate strength.

For most of our sisters and brothers, however, the Sunday assembly is the critical moment of ecclesial consciousness. So, again, why after all this betterment of our tools are we no better at using them? Why, when our understanding of sacramental worship, including its scriptural and other traditional texts, has been expanded and illuminated to an extremely gratifying degree, do we see so many dull and inept Sunday assemblies?

In addition to the patience indicated — for repairing some roads that were long neglected — another consideration that affects the question is a certain romantic illusion which colors so many memories of the preconciliar church and its liturgical celebrations. The greatness of our time for Christians is, I think, indisputable. And from our vantage ground there is neither honesty nor realism in an optimistic or nostalgic assessment of our counter-reformation past. Even the present clumsy and inept liturgical practice to which I have referred is — just in its recovery of a popular contact between the community of faith and its scriptural-liturgical sources in the Sunday assembly — incomparably better and more salutary than anything we knew in preconciliar times. The opening up of the biblical books with their uncovering of our Jewish roots through the proclamation of three readings in three cycles and in the mother tongue, as well as a vastly superior visual and auditory exposure of the kingdom banquet, the Lord's Supper, as corporate rather than private enterprise and grace — these advances alone are enough to make comparisons odious.

Conceding all that, what of the clergy who preside at the Sunday assembly's eucharistic celebration? Presiders cannot speed up processes of growth and development which are, by nature, organic, profound, and distressingly gradual. Presiders cannot really compensate in that role for basic defects in the formation of the faith community (including themselves), in its sense of mission, in the environment of worship and its implements. But the presiding role of leadership, as the climax of pastoral work in the community, is potentially decisive in engaging the rest of the assembly, setting its tone, creating an atmosphere and an action that is awesome in its beauty and simplicity, honest and relevant in its prayer and preaching, engaging in its variety of ministries and musical participation, and evangelical in its basic and clear proclamation of the good news.

One of the problems which many presiders apparently have not been able to resolve has to do with the character and style of their role. That role was quite clear in former times, when liturgical celebration had been frozen and petrified to such an extent that every word and gesture was in the book and the leader was simply the voice and hands of the book. The less of oneself that appeared, because one could facilitate nothing, the better. Nothing was demanded of the presider, the other ministers, or the rest of the participants (i.e., practically), because the essentials were all in the book, in the prescribed words, gestures, actions. To concern oneself with the manner or mode of their execution was somehow less worthy, demeaning, trivializing. The act was Christ's *alone*, and the effects were guaranteed, no matter what.

Now the presider is asked to summon every talent and gift one possesses for a service of leadership in a symbolic action that is Christ's because it is the assembly's. Instead of being the voice and hands of a book, the presider is the voice and hands of the assembly, and therefore of Christ, its head, and the Spirit, its animator. The liturgical book offers only the ritual skeleton and structure, gifting the faith community with the biblical and ecclesial tradition. And that structure becomes liturgy when the community does it in solemn rite, in the light of its own place in a tradition that is still being formed, of the signs of the times, and of its own needs and circumstances. Just as the whole church becomes the agent, the doer of the rite, bringing its life, arts, successes and failures in mission, affirmations of faith, so all ministers in the rite, especially the presider, have to summon themselves and their gifts to make their particular services of leadership luminous in communicating and signifying power.

The question is not about what is always present — God's loving kindness and the saving passover of the Messiah. The question is how what is always present communicates with and impinges on believers — by *signifying* . . . symbolically. Because liturgy is for people. It adds nothing to God. It is we who need to be God-centered, both as individual members and as corporate body, church. So our experience in the Sunday assembly is not trivial, not demeaning, not less worthy. Liturgical celebration exists to help us lift hearts that are encased in bodies, senses, imaginations, memories, intellects and all the rest of the human complexity. The communication is a symbol language of words and acts, and the mode and manner of the visible leaders impresses the assembly's spirit.

In their efforts to escape the rigidity and anonymity of the presiding role in the centuries of book liturgy, some clergy have concluded that the alternative is the genial, blustery, social engineering manner of the rally demagogue, or the Sunday breakfast emcee, or the talk show host. And perhaps a few mistakes like this, to break the ice of centuries, are not fatal. But liturgical celebration is an activity at a depth in the worship region of the psyche where any apparent self-consciousness, self-assertion, or self-aggrandizement on the part of the leaders is a source of pain and alienation for all participants.

The only satisfactory alternative to the old ways is paradoxical. When Aidan Kavanagh discusses "An Approach to Liturgical Style" in his recent *Elements of Rite* (Pueblo 1982), the first point he makes is the key: "1. Place yourself in the background." We have to think about that for a while before it sinks in without contradicting the demands already mentioned. Because the presiding role is one of directing or conducting the symbolic action (the ritual "choreography") from beginning to end and all its parts and participants. To do this, I think the presider must be expert in the ritual structure, sharing eye contact with the rest of the assembly at all times, carefully prepared, and leading the community not only when the word or deed is part of the presider's charge but also in attention to every other element and to the group or person responsible for it.

And yet we are well advised: "Place yourself in the background." How can you be in the foreground and the background at the same time? You can. The genius of public worship is the pervasive (in every single thing we say or do in rite) and clear (in every movement, gesture, word) acknowledgment that we are dealing with a mysterious presence in and beyond us all. We are "before God" with a corporate intentionality that makes this moment special. When the presider realizes that one's person is in the foreground, in positions of leadership, so that one may communicate this God-consciousness above all, then the paradox becomes a blessing for the assembly. No matter what role we play in the symbolic action, we are first and last commonly assembly, pilgrims, seekers, humble, sharing this consciousness of mystery. This is the attitude that places the presider's self "in the background." As obvious, simple and basic as it sounds, it demands a level of consciousness and intent that is not always easy to maintain.

Anxiety is one of the enemies of that spirit and attitude, and the confidence that issues from the presider's thorough and time-consuming preparation is the answer to anxiety. Anxiety deprives us of the calm and composure which keep our feet on creature-ground and our manners appropriately reverent and respectful. This is why extensive preparation is now required for presiding in the Sunday assembly. It seems to me there is no way an ordinary human being can undertake such preparation unless a day a week is substantially reserved for that purpose.

The scope of the presider's task in preparation also needs attention. The structures of our rites were organically grown long before there were any "natural food" stores. This growth in the community of the Spirit and the buffeting they have received from year in, year out use have produced a refinement which could not be artificially or intentionally duplicated. In general, therefore, the presider and all other planners accept with gratitude the structure of the rite and spend the time available not in rearranging elements but in more appropriate pursuits:

1. Assuring the beauty and simplicity of environment, furnishings, implements of worship;
2. Providing for the employment of the full variety of ministries in the Sunday liturgy, reflecting as much as possible the sexual, age and ethnic diversity of the faith community;
3. Organizing these ministries, as well as the musical and other planning, so that the rite is a coherent whole, with smooth transitions;

4. Making sure that symbolic action and sense experience is maximized (e.g., the bread and wine and their vessels, gestures, postures, body movements, books and other implements, etc.), and, on the other hand, carefully avoiding interpolations, explanations, and so on, which would add to the already heavily verbal character of the celebration;

5. Finding what in the readings addresses either a basic faith question or a faith response to a current issue or need in the community, and carefully developing a homily along these lines. This should require more time than anything else. If the direction you choose is helpful to you, to your faith, to your life in the church, then you can bet it will be helpful to others;

6. Adapting prayer texts carefully, modestly and only when necessary for meaning and relevance;

7. Aiding the formulation of prepared General Intercessions, so they are inclusive and represent felt needs of the seriously faithful;

8. Overseeing the preparation of any participation materials (in addition to hymnals) needed by the members of the assembly.

Perhaps number four above is the most difficult challenge (although we miss out on five almost as regularly) for American presiders. Unless we have the advantage of some black (or, at least, other than anglo-type) cultural experience, we have been well trained to be so afraid of our bodies and our senses that we tend to regard care (time, money, energy) for the nonverbal-symbol-body language of liturgy as a weakness or a peculiarity. The seminary has conspired with western cerebral and pragmatic culture to render us impotent for our liturgical task.

So we have a lot of work to do if we would open up the marvelous symbolic action of our liturgical tradition and enable it to communicate with humans on all the levels our words have such a tough time reaching. Talk about this problem doesn't seem to help much. Experience does. Good experiences of fully sensate ritual action, or even of the beauty of nature and of the human arts (visual, theatre, the works) have to rescue us from the pitiful limits of words, ideas and effects. Learning how to contemplate, how to stand back from persons and things, so that we can really see them and begin to receive their communication, emanations, vibrations . . . until eating a sacramental bread that is broken and shared, and drinking from a common cup, and baptismal bathing (with touch and oil and perfume and new clothes), and a felt laying on of hands, and fire and light and earth and incense and all the other sensations which help move the human soul begin to get to us . . . until we begin to share the archetypal sense of pleasure in belonging to a cosmos which is God's, and whose hymn of praise we sing in liturgy.

Any presider who regards these problems as superficial, or as "merely externals," should be permanently retired. Such a one is a menace at the helm of public worship, no matter what other gifts or graces may adorn that person.

22

Liturgy's Many Roles:
Ministers? . . . Or Intruders?*

One of the themes of this column has been the relative success of
at least one aspect of liturgical renewal efforts in this country: the
appearance and functioning of a variety of specialized ministries in
most Sunday celebrations. This development is evident not only in
parishes and dioceses where one would expect it, but also in the
many churches which have not yet learned that the Sunday assembly is our core and critical problem. I refer, of course, to the
increasing visibility and operation (although limited) of men and
women as readers, musicians, acolytes, ushers, eucharistic
ministers, etc.

"Specialized ministers" is a clumsy phrase, but some modifier
for roles of *leadership* seems necessary for the time being — until
we regain a general consciousness of the fact that fundamental
liturgical ministry belongs to the assembly as a whole. It is the assembly which is the primary minister. Until that is our common
understanding, our common sense concerning initiation and what
it means to be church, any roles of leadership in public worship
will continue to appear as intruders, sent to us from outside, foreign agents.

The flourishing of different and many roles of leadership is a
great accomplishment — part of the monumental task of making
our Sunday celebration again the people's *own*. Its promise is that
it will gradually infiltrate our heads, hearts and reflexes with the
realization that such roles (including those of bishop, presbyter
and deacon) are members of that assembly and instruments of
that assembly — voices, hands, arms, feet for such tasks of the

Worship, March 1990

community in worship and in the rest of its life as require individual training, talent and delegation.

Since one of those tasks is to maintain unity and solidarity with the other churches, our tradition insists that the pastoral ministries of bishop and presbyter are collegial functions: that no one exercises these functions as merely an ordained individual, but rather as a member of a college of bishops or a college of priests. So the pastors of the churches are linked not only to the church of which they are members, but also to all the other churches through their respective colleges, thus being personal signs of the solidarity of believing communities. Unfortunately, we have allowed the latter aspect of their office to obscure (and sometimes eclipse) the former, both in our consciousness and in our practice.

Churches exhibiting signs of life are beginning therefore to realize the impropriety of alienating — by qualifications, training and lifestyle — the clergy from the communities they are ordained to serve. Hence the widespread interest, now that we are rediscovering the local church, in again electing our bishops, and in the faith community's involvement in selecting (on the basis of the different talents the different functions of specialized ministry require) and presenting candidates for ordination and for commissioning, as well as having a part in their training.

To regain that sense of the Sunday assembly as organic ecclesial unity, totally ministerial, with its multiple leadership functions (pastor-presider, deacon, readers, musicians, acolytes, ushers, eucharistic ministers, environmental planners, etc.) understood as its instruments, enabling its function as body of Christ — that is what all reform and renewal efforts are about . . . now and at all times. Without that awareness and its implementation in the recruitment, training, talents and lifestyle of the clergy, the clericalism discussed in my last column will continue to infect us. The point here is that it infects as well attitudes regarding and performance of the non-ordained specialized ministries now being happily reinstated.

Because the distinction of roles and variety of specialized ministries is such a welcome recovery, it is important that we avoid mistakes and try hard to keep it free from the vestiges of what has ailed us. We are all prey to the habituated mindset which sees leadership as ownership and the assembly as its clients, patients, consumers — as the *object* of leadership's doing. That mindset is both false and fatal to worship. The assembly as a whole (including as the word "assembly" always does, its specialized ministers) is a church, microcosm of the body of Christ, and therefore the doer in both liturgy and mission.

Until we feel deeply the utter incompatibility of those two understandings of the Sunday assembly, we will be inept, even in what we consider our best renewal efforts. And it shouldn't surprise us that the weight of bad habits and the infection of bad thinking are so persevering. And one must add to this the power of our current culture. While acculturation is a normal and inevitable development in any living social creature or community, the biblical (Jewish or Christian) faith community is charged with the task of resisting certain aspects of any and every human culture — that is, idolatry in its myriad forms.

No doubt our catechumenate and initiation processes eventually will produce communities better able to distinguish between helpful and vicious kinds of acculturation, between those capable of serving the message of human liberation/reconciliation in God and those which undermine that message. Meanwhile constant attention is required. Checking the influence of bad habits in the style and exercise of leadership roles in worship is part of that attention. Our culture's fascination with competition and "stars," its penchant for instant gratification and its garrulousness — these, it seems to me, are enemies of the gospel and the liturgy.

Any practice which communicates the notion that leaders in public worship are "stars" is basically and desperately counterproductive, whether the leaders in question are clergy or musicians or any other ministers. Desirable gifts in the leader are no excuse. If her or his style in the particular role fails to communicate a sense of prayerful performance, of *being (first of all) a worshiper and a member of the worshiping assembly,* then he or she is not a leader but an intruder. And the gifts of such a one or such a group damage rather than enhance worship.

I know that good presiders/preachers are more rare than they should be and that we now realize more generally than in our recent history the importance of music in the liturgy. But the power of worship is that it be worship — common worship. And that means a God-consciousness so awesome, so strong, so powerful that all participants are focussed not on ourselves and our many splendid gifts but on our common and mysterious Source, on the only One who is Holy.

The life of the human community does not lack appropriate moments for recognizing and celebrating individual gifts and arts and skills. The liturgical moment, however, is the time to bring us all together, unselfconsciously, in the sacrifice of praise. For the same reason that makes the ritual embrace of peace different from, more stunningly elemental than, the greeting of another on the street, at home, or at work, the entire worship rite must command a focus and depth-wholeness and solidarity of all its participants. Perhaps it is rarely achieved, but it is the struggle for such that makes liturgy so important for human beings. The difficulty of that kind of centeredness must not tempt us to settle for something less, like the familiar handshake, or a back-slapping bonhomie, or the warm feeling we get when the rest of the assembly applauds us.

We do not need rules about this. Rules are irrelevant. We do need to cultivate this spirit. It is not the applause that is wrong, but rather the "star" focus. A burst of applause may be simply another form of the congregation's "Amen," an assent and affirmation of a truth expressed in word or gesture, the power of which suddenly impinges upon the consciousness of the group gathered for worship of the Holy One (e.g., the clapping and verbal exclamations which punctuate and make dialogue of a tradition of African-American preaching).

Our recruitment, training, delegating and use of specialized ministries must stress that such leadership is primarily by example. The leader's role as worshiper and member of the assembly is basic. Only when that is clear in the mind and manner of the leaders can their gifts enhance the worship event — and when each is fully participating in the entire rite, fully attentive to every part of the rite . . . not merely to those parts in which one is exercising one's leadership role. The satisfaction an artist finds in such service is properly quite different from that found in the lecture or concert hall, the theatre or the cabaret.

Against our penchant for instant gratification, against the "highs" we love so much, the liturgy's repetitive, Sunday-after-Sunday formation of a faith community is a persistent, as-long-as-life-lasts work. Each celebration should be an experience for all, yes, but the aim is a total orientation of our lives, individual and corporate, finding our place and our relationship of creaturehood. Part of the genius of rite is that our different gifts and functions are overshadowed by our sameness and our commonness before the One. They are reduced to creaturesize in that moment of vision.

In public worship it is critical that the roles of leadership (required by any social act, any assembly) are performed by people who clearly demonstrate that they are *not* the masters of the rite, but its servants . . . that they are all other participants. This does not mean an unimaginative, rote performance. Pastoral adaptation is a necessity in a living tradition. It does mean, however, that an assembly cannot celebrate when the structure of the rite is unfamiliar, when it feels directed by the whim of the presider . . . or any other minister. Pastoral adaptation is not merely adaptation by pastors. It is rather a serious effort concerned with the entire community, its cultural situation and experience of the signs of the times, its many different faith-insights, all needed to make that familiar structure live here and now.

Ritual tradition assigns different texts, gestures and actions to different participants — to the congregation, to the presider, to various other roles, and to the assembly as a whole. A good presider will resist the temptation to do everything, as will other leaders. And all leaders will see their roles as enabling the assembly to celebrate. The one who leads a prayer does not lead the "Amen." The one who reads a lesson does not lead "Thanks be to God." A cantor or choir does not always sing the psalm, when a congregation can learn to sing the verses antiphonally or in some other way. And so on. . . .

It seems to me that the vesture of not merely the presider but also all ministers who are functioning throughout the rite is part of leadership's service to the beauty and formality of public worship. Appropriate vestments discourage too much self-consciousness and the "star" syndrome. Liturgical vesture is not decoration for the wearer but part of the environment of a solemn and awesome act and recognition of the roles being performed on behalf of all of us. It proclaims the fact that these people are, in this liturgy, our commonly delegated servants, instruments, voices, hands and feet. In assemblies where only the presider is vested (or only the presider and any other clergy present), we see the old clericalism run amok.

Then there is the problem of our garrulousness. In my opinion, this is a widespread disease, affecting not only those Sunday assemblies in which renewal has not yet taken hold but also many assemblies otherwise devoted to a living and experiential celebration. I think it debilitates all the efforts of the latter. There is not only the habit — disturbing and interrupting — of issuing directions: "Please stand . . . Please sit . . . etc." when a simple gesture will suffice for even a stranger. But there is the apparent assumption that the texts, gestures, movements, music, all the elements of this totally symbolic action, are incapable of communicating as the rite insists they do. So anyone who has a microphone — presider or other leader — must come to their aid with off-the cuff commentary.

What does it say about the readings, when the presider or reader tells us what a reading is going to say before we hear it? Do presiders and other ministers really think that our casual words are more helpful than classic texts, or that rich symbol is "explained" by our verbal interventions? Are we still unaware, we ministers, that our leadership function is to open up and make experiential the scriptural words and actions which have communicated through the centuries? Our responsibility is to drown them in a sea of idle chatter . . . or even careful commentary. We need more silence in the liturgy; we do not need more words.

LITURGY, JUSTICE, AND PEACE

23

Scripture Has It,
Not on Bread Alone
Shall Human Creatures Live*

There is a devil abroad whose ascendancy is especially tempting, and whose masquerade obstructs and diminishes certain essential aspects of church reform and renewal in many of the quarters where serious efforts are happily occurring. It is a devil that pretends to be the friend of the poor and the oppressed, but identifies the faith community's need of festivity's "excess," of beauty and artistry in the environments and other elements of celebration, as the enemy of social justice.

In churches only beginning to be more fully conscious of our covenant call to deal *as churches* with social issues, to grow into a morality bigger than the private and sexual one into which an "official" and then a ghetto church had retreated — in such local churches, the appeal of the kind of mask described, combined with a cultural predisposition to categorize art and beauty as "luxuries," is devastating.

All of us who are appreciative of this conciliar era (and the recoveries, rediscoveries, and prospects of growth which it enables) are grateful for these beginnings of an awakening to issues of justice and peace and to our mission to be advocates of all those excluded or put down by the society at large. To pursue the reign of God, to make ready the way of the Lord, is precisely to understand our individual and corporate identification with poor, oppressed, fringe elements of the larger society as a critical part of the church's mission, witness, and service to the world. The church

*Worship, May 1983

must make real and felt the tension between the world-as-it-is (with all of its unfreedom and division) and the vision of God's reign (with its freedom and oneness for all God's children). Faith proposes the latter as the object of our living tradition, growth, and development.

The private and sex-centered morality for which the churches have been famous is therefore beginning to yield to a morality in harmony with the good news of Jesus Christ . . . and which therefore has a broad public as well as private scope and is less concerned with isolated "acts" than with the integration and orientation of our individual and corporate (as church) lives. This is great progress, and deeply related to all the other signs of life and hope in current ecclesial reform.

Visionaries like Teilhard de Chardin have pointed out that world developments involve the emergence of a new type of humanity — one for whom economic and political institutions are no longer part of "fate" or "destiny," but are generally recognized as mutable, as created and supported by us, and therefore as malleable in our hands. Anthropologists like Margaret Mead speak of the same phenomenon. And the Second Vatican Council related it to mission, implying that the world is now "ready" for the biblical message of the new Jerusalem in ways that were previously unimagined except by the few.

So we are, all of us, obliged to build upon these developments, and to keep raising and extending our consciousness of discipleship as a call to peacefully and justly overthrow the existing order. In other words, to bring the reign of God to bear upon current social organization and institutions. This is part of faith, not merely its byproduct, and we can rejoice that, even though we don't yet know *how* to do it, we recognize more and more widely in the churches that it must be done.

But there is this devil abroad. It doesn't always assume the highly dramatic form of a person vowing to fast to the death in protest against a parish's undertaking a long overdue building renovation (because, in the faster's view, the money the parish would spend on renovation should be spent on food, clothing and housing subsidies for those whom our society relegates to its increasingly large human ash-heap). Sometimes it is manifested simply by the opposition of justice or peace "activists" to any festal expense or any disbursement for the sake of art or beauty in the liturgical celebrations of the churches. Sometimes it takes the more subtle and sickly form of feelings of guilt whenever budgets recognize such needs.

We need to face the issue squarely, because it is a real one, and because dishonesty and masquerading never serve the cause of God. If "wasting" money on festivity and beauty and the spaces and things that shape our lives by shaping one of our most significant corporate acts — that of worship — is sinful in a world where many, many people are hungry, then we should stop doing it. If it is as necessary as bread, then we should stop speaking and acting as if such spending were the enemy.

In a society like ours, one that makes such a "virtue" out of care for "No. 1" and profitseeking and securing economic advantage over other people, it is to be expected that serious Christians are burdened with great guilt. Because we know that we support this kind of society, we make its rules and laws, we elect its promoters and its guardians. If we have attained some "success," we also enjoy its benefits. We have, in general, swallowed hook, line, and sinker, and antithesis that our democracy (under the influence of its economic and military masters) insists upon: an opposition between our liberty and our solidarity, between our freedom and our desire for a more equitable sharing of resources and of goods.

One would think that, from the viewpoint of a person of biblical faith, Jew or Christian, the joining of these two social ideals and goals, clearly identified in the progress of the biblical vision as marks of the reign of God (and each as illusory without the other) would be the major project of political thought and dialogue. However, we have been so absorbed and acculturated that most churches do not even discuss the issues. We simply posit the antithesis and opposition as being in the nature of things, much as we once believed the sun to revolve around the earth.

People who believe in God's reign and therefore in our freedom and oneness as a human family, and who see these goals as fundamental imperatives of our covenant call, and yet who have been sold this kind of "free enterprise" economic bill of goods, are quite naturally somewhat neurotic about their social justice posture. As the gospel's insistence on overthrowing the old order and building the new becomes more clear in our minds, we become not more rational but more frantic about the social sickness of our culture.

And here is where that devil has its day. Instead of seeing the problem as a political and economic project — difficult, no doubt, but not insurmountable — we believers generally still choose to waste our energy by attacking one another or some aspect of our culture more vulnerable than the false antithesis at its economic base. Since considerations of art, environment and beauty are already low priorities in the culture that has consumed us, they are easy targets for our wrath and scapegoats for our guilt.

So it is that an anti-human, very melancholy picture begins to emerge — at first, in faith communities aroused to consciousness of oppression, and then spreading like a dark cloud wherever that consciousness-raising converts people to the aim while leaving them frustrated as to the means. I refer to the cries that are raised in parishes the length and breadth of the land whenever the community contemplates spending any money on the environment of worship and its implements. "How can we do such a thing when our sisters and brothers go to bed hungry?"

It is a rhetorical question, and no answer is expected. But a Christian or a Christian community cannot let it go at that. It owes a clear answer to itself and the world it serves, and it ought to straighten out the kinks in the taunter's head so that her or his goodwill can be channeled into effective social action. We must answer, even though any answer has to be as complicated as human nature and as intricate as our world-grown-small. To allow such a question to go unanswered and unchallenged is to yield the floor to the superficial (at best) and inhuman (at worst) mentality that raises it. The questioner may be a committed believer, but the question is built on the sand of either an irrational oversimplification of our social problems or a materialistic and crass view of human need.

The melancholy picture of this intramural fight among believers has, I think, absolutely no necessary relation to the consciousness raising discussed above — the happy rediscovery of church as kingdom-witness, countercultural and antistructural critic, advocate of prisoners, poor folk, handicapped persons, society's untouchables, and all other non-mainstream elements. All of these must be supported by the church in their just demands for a rightful place in the world and an equitable sharing in its wealth. But that devil made us "do it," made us fall for a phony relation between our gospel reawakening and our (culturally induced) suspicion of play, festivity, senses and the body. Taking these liturgical concerns seriously makes an easy target for the wild flailing about that neurotic guilt entails.

Get the picture? — the picture of the arts and the human search for beauty of environment and implement as "luxuries," as belonging to the class of goods that has no necessary relation to our well-being and that delights the rich whose "real needs" have been met? That picture is false not only because it is a classic red herring in any serious pursuit of social justice, but also because it distorts and diminishes all of humanity. And it is disastrous in the church, which, because of its God-orientation, should be the one institution to insist (in season and out) upon a more integral and wholistic attention to the spectrum of human needs.

Devils like this do not bother with the weak or the anemic. They go for the jugular and the richest, reddest blood. So it is frequently our "best people," our apparently most committed members, who fall for this mask and follow this false scent. So we lose the steam that should be generating both the immediate local aid that a faith community should be supplying to its members and neighbors in special need, and the ecclesial inspiration for and participation in the kind of social-political-economic movements that address the basic problems of our society.

Our modified capitalistic system, with a great deal of government subsidy and support for the military-industrial complex and minimal government responsibility for those in direst need, is one that not only tolerates social evils but seems to require them for its survival. The recent statement by the Episcopal Commission for Social Affairs of the Canadian Conference of Catholic Bishops, "Ethical Reflections on the Economic Crisis," is lucid on this point. Believers must either hide from such assessments or we must move to change the system. Squabbling about the expenditure of comparative pennies for the needs of sacramental celebration must gladden the hearts of those who wish to perpetuate our unjust status quo. It cannot please those seriously concerned with the mission of the church, nor can it earn anything but ridicule from students of social change.

One looks in vain for significant Christian participation in the social movements that are trying to unite the twin biblical values of liberation and solidarity. So far, on the corporate level of parish, diocese, or world church, we can talk up a storm but our power (money, property, votes) remains a solid bulwark of the status quo. Talk is a start, of course, but it is only a first step. And in the painful road ahead, we cannot permit a red herring like the one under discussion to divert us from our continuing search and pilgrimage.

If that devil still beckons, let us enumerate some of the Christian principles and experiences that require us to resist its blandishments:

1. "Scripture has it, 'Not on bread alone shall we live.'" The story of Jesus' temptations treats humanity with all the reverence and respect that the complexity of our nature and our needs demands. Not bread alone. Not even bread alone first, and then when everybody shares bread alone with equity we move on to a subsequent, lesser need. The teaching is that we will never treat the person as we should unless we see and deal with that person *from the first* as all that she or he really is.

Facts reported recently by an American journalist in Russia are highly relevant. The writer described rites and ritual furnishings and forms which an officially atheist government has been obliged to provide for a number of important social events, or "passages," in the lives of its citizens: birth, entrance into the working population, marriage, divorce, etc. The ersatz character of the furnishings and forms, which seem to us modeled on Christian liturgical tradition minus its foundation and its spirit, is sad. But the testimony to a fundamental human need cannot be overlooked.

Dedicating a renovated chapel, Sister Marian McAvoy, President of the Sisters of Loretto, quoted a Latin American theologian: "It is wrong to emphasize the lack of material things in the life of the poor, lack of food, shelter, health care, and not realize that it is the loss of the human as sacred that is the greatest loss of poverty, the loss of dignity and sense of worth" (Kevin Seasoltz, *Worship* [March 1983] 113). The temptation story says, "With bread, the word of God!" The slogan of a contemporary labor union is, "Bread and roses!" Not bread without the word, not bread without roses, not the word without bread, not roses without bread.

Humanity's hunger for the spirit and for beauty is as real, as immediate, and as worthy of attention as its hunger for bread. It is inhuman to separate them, and even more inhuman to oppose them to each other.

2. The local parish or other church community, as a corporate body, is obliged to make offerings and share its goods "for the poor and the church." That should be the clear meaning of the money offerings at Sunday liturgy. And a definite part of them should be earmarked for "the poor," for the relief of human needs either through its own agency or through whatever agency the faith community agrees on. This kind of relief, a social band-aid, is no answer to the problems of injustice and oppression in society, but it is a necessary response to immediate need.

No conflict should be either imagined or invented between that almsgiving and the obligation to provide for the needs of the church's life and worship: professional musical talent and environments and artifacts as beautifully crafted and as ennobling in materials and form as possible. This means paying just wages for the professional talents we require, and using absolutely nothing in public worship — whether in visual environment, in furnishings, in vessels, in vesture, in any of the implements of common prayer — that does not come from an artist's hand and that does not involve the help of artists in its selection.

The search for transcendental beauty in celebration is not a luxury, but a necessity of faith. Nor does it mean necessarily spending more money. Our churches and their ecclesiastical suppliers trade in millions every year to depress our spirits with shoddy, poorly made, ill-designed, pretentious junk.

3. It is no service to human progress to imply that there is any shortcut to social justice in a world in which liberty is claimed by a ruthless economic system that dominates politics and solidarity is claimed by a ruthless political system that controls economic life. Nor to imply that the diversion of common funds to the creation of beautiful environments and artifacts is a significant part — even a significantly small part — of our failure to solve the problem of joining a rational politics with a rational economics, dedicated to both the feeling and the unifying of all God's children.

National sovereignties — the very structure of our countries — are a major impediment to the world planning and world scale of any contemporary solution. And, on the national level, the powers-that-be in each society (especially the military powers) are not about to humble themselves sufficiently to seek real answers. Christians who are serious about biblical imperatives of the reign of God have to join with other people of good will to patiently construct the political organizations and movements that will offer this kind of alternative — in places where there are relatively free elections. In places where there are not, Christians need to learn some hard lessons from Ghandi and from Martin Luther King Jr. A crusade against church renovation, church building, or provision for liturgical celebrations whose beauty and integrity enable experiences of the transcendent is an escape from the real work to which we are called.

4. Oppressed and dispossessed people seem to understand the human need for festivity's "conscious excess" better than affluent or comfortable ones. A party, a festivity, a celebration, a liturgy has, for people who live daily with the aching pain of want, a psychological and social function whose healing power those who do not so live can scarcely imagine. Glimpses of this truth are everywhere, if we open our eyes. When, for example, a committee was planning an ethnic day for black people (many of them poor and all of them oppressed) before the Philadelphia Eucharistic Congress several years ago, a black representative to the committee laughed uproariously at their middle-class concern that the vesture of the participating bishops should not be, in any way, excessive. The black priest, who had lived with American racist oppression every day of his life, thought their concern very, very funny, and said, "If any one of those bishops were felt by the people to be *our own*, really with us and belonging to us, the more excessive the festivity and the more impressive the vesture, the better! Without that feeling, even their presence is an affront!"

5. Finally, let us be honest about what put that devil in our heads. We are all part of a culture that has demeaned the human person, as Harvey Cox points out in *The Feast of Fools*, by a narrow worker-thinker definition: "Human celebrative and imaginative faculties have atrophied." It is not commitment to the gospel that has made us contemptuous of beauty, art, and that reverence for things, materials, forms, that opens us to the language of being. It is rather the diminishment of a culture which has domesti-

cated our gospel and robbed us of our power to serve it. Our mission is to counter that culture, not only with respect to its lack of care for ''losers,'' but also with respect to its failure to value the human needs for festivity and fantasy that liturgical celebrations, among other human events, serve.

The church's service to humanity is principally an orientation to the one true God and the consequent relativization of all persons, groups, powers and institutions that pretend a right to our worship, a right to dominate us. That orientation is accomplished on a human level involving the body as well as the mind, senses, imagination, memory, all human faculties — and therefore involving all kinds of material things and expenditures. It is an orientation that we, whose lives are dominated daily by the ''powers and principalities,'' ersatz gods, must renew again and again through recollection, repentance, prayer and the service of the least of our neighbors. The Sunday liturgy of Christians is a critical part of that necessary renewal process, and the more striking its beauty and integrity and careful celebration the more effectively it helps us gain the orientation that we seek. All of us need it, no matter what our circumstances. Those in circumstances of want need it in a very special way.

To tell a person who hasn't enough to eat, or lacks a decent place to live, or is without a job, or has rags for clothing, or suffers any other elemental want, that all he or she needs immediately is the physical necessity is to be condescending in a very ugly way. It is to imply that Godwardness itself is a luxury, and that only the comfortable and the rich are adequate to it. The gospel reminds us that the opposite is the case.

So let us get on with the job of being church, free of phony oppositions and the narrowness of a production-obsessed and profit-seeking culture. In Eliot's words, ''You must not deny the body'' (*Complete Poems and Plays*, Harcourt Brace 1971, 111) — the eye, the touch, the ear, the scent, the taste . . . as well as the stomach.

24

Where Have You Been? "Peace Liturgies" Are the Only Kind We Have!*

Ever since the American Catholic bishops published, by a virtual consensus, their pastoral letter on war and peace, I have heard (not frequently, but now and then) a question which I found first puzzling and then appalling. "When are we going to get some 'peace liturgies'?" "How about developing some liturgical celebrations which correspond to the import of the bishops' document?" "Isn't it time that our public worship began to reflect our growing justice-and-peace awareness?"

The appalling part was my growing feeling, generated by the seriousness of the questioners and the context of the questions, that they were not merely complaints about the homilies people hear or the apparent lack of pastoral adaptation in the preparation of Sunday Mass. They were really talking about the basic stuff, rhythms, content of the eucharist! After pinching myself to make sure I wasn't dreaming, I tried to understand. Maybe such questions rise helplessly out of habits located somehow in the genes, acquired during those centuries when the gestures, actions, texts of Sunday Mass were remote, foreign, a package to be delivered to God but whose contents hardly required close examination. Maybe, if we still have that "obligation" mentality, it *is* possible to participate for decades in a eucharist that calls for our involvement and nevertheless remain unconscious on the rational level of the patent meaning of what we do symbolically — which, next to thanksgiving itself, is reconciliation, making peace.

Worship, September 1983

It has been a sobering experience — this revelation of how little even our otherwise enthusiastic members connect intellectually with what they do in the Sunday assembly. So that Sunday Mass, which is regularly and always, from beginning to end, a rite of peace and justice in the reign of God, can elude (at least on the conscious level) many who are seriously concerned with the good news and the way of Jesus.

It tells us something about our preaching. Most observers seem to agree that preaching is generally still far from a felt interpretation of the signs of the times in the light of our liturgical-biblical sources. It tells us something about clerical unwillingness to spend the time and money and do the work necessary pastorally to adapt, for example, some of the language of prayers to seek current rather than merely historical relevance, the general intercessions to be the cries of a believing people, the music to seek both excellence and popularity, the environment and implements to be an experience of surpassing beauty, etc. It tells us a lot about our cultural disinterest in symbol and the symbol-language which liturgy is.

On a deeper level, it is a salutary reminder to us all that the common prayer or rite of the Sunday assembly engages and forms us, when we are fully present in it, in ways so basic, so profound, that they steal in upon us, escaping immediate detection. Liturgy is not a teaching aid, or another means of catechesis. Catechesis serves liturgy, not vice versa. And symbolic ritual action forms us deeply precisely because we do not set out to form ourselves — we place ourselves before the Most High, and, in the eucharist, at the table of the Messiah. The symbolic action is interested, not in putting across points one, two and three, but rather in enabling our experience of the reign of God, the new Jerusalem, the heavenly banquet, eternal life (not after death, but here and now, beginning with conversion, faith and baptism). In public worship we are experiencing God's invitation and God's alternative to our status quo. So that we know what it's like — not just in our little rationalistic way, but in the entire being we present in worship, in our guts and senses, in our taste and touch and smell and sight and hearing, in our imagination and our memory.

The involvement, participation and corporate experience we are regaining because of our twentieth-century reforms are not matters of instruction, not a pastoral letter in action. And our tendency to view everything Christian as a matter of instruction is one of the chief reasons why liturgical renewal is so difficult for us. Liturgy is an art, but it had become in the popular consciousness a thing. Despite all that has been done since the Council and before, the questions with which I began this column indicate that liturgy is still considered as a static object "out there," a package or tool to be grasped and used, rather than as the symbolic act we do as faith community and in which we "play kingdom," envision and experience an alternative to the status quo. Rather than as the symbolic art (as well as act) of creating an environment, an atmosphere in which human commonness overcomes all distinctions, statuses (because God is the object and dominion is the Lord's); in which human dignity is felt (not argued); in which human gifts are reasons for thanksgiving (not for competitive comparison); in which Love is the name of God, erasing our neat line between means and end.

Before I go on, I want to make it clear that I am writing about the questions at the beginning of this column . . . and the problems they seem to me to reveal. My concern here is liturgical celebration and what can appropriately be asked of that symbolic action. While liturgy is source and summit, it does not exhaust the Christian life nor Christian values. Instruction is important. The intellectual life and rational pursuits are gifts and blessings. We need good pastoral letters, for example. Like the questioners, I thank God for the pastoral letter referred to: "The Challenge of Peace: God's Promise and Our Response." I have been a pacifist for forty-five years, so I do not agree with all its parts, but its overall appeal to Christians and its tenor — respectful of the past but recognizing clearly the call of the gospel and the reign of God to face both new circumstances and progress in our ecclesial understanding of that call — breathe the Spirit. I urge every Christian to obtain, read and study the full text and make it the focus of adult education in all faith communities during the coming year, for these reasons:

1. The process of its preparation and publication is as significant as its content. In contrast to the medieval and modern tendency to isolate the teaching authority from the rest of the church, its process returns to an organic notion of church and teaching authority

— its consultation, its listening to the actual situations of believers and to different opinions, its attention to the conclusions of experts, its public and open character. This will mean much for all future exercise of the bishops' pastoral teaching function.

2. It is a clear affirmation of the public and political character of Christian morality, and a disavowal of a long period of privatization of moral scope and responsibility.

3. It is a modest proposal of guidance for the formation of consciences in these matters, inviting our attention to Christian sources more basic than the letter itself and rejecting the temptation to make our moral decisions for us or to provide a neat little list of DOs and DON'Ts.

4. It accepts the obvious pluralism in Christian moral response, while welcoming prophetic gifts and positions which go beyond the consensus obtainable at any given moment in the faith community as a whole.

5. It opposes boldly the present stance of the U.S. government in these matters, and thereby recovers the health-giving paradox of a faith-message that is both in a culture, a status quo, conditioned by culture, on the one hand, and, on the other, strongly countercultural in its commitment to the reign-of-God alternative, prospect, hope.

6. It appeals (at last!) for the recognition, study and implementation of nonviolent means of resistance to institutional evil and implies that fostering such developments is part of the church's essential peacemaking ministry.

7. It accepts the special responsibility of the United States for the nuclear arms race and its moral dilemmas, since we were the first — and so far the only — nation to employ nuclear weapons against another nation.

8. It relates the peacemaking mission of the church to the world's still primitive economic-political systems: "An important element missing from world order today is a properly constituted political authority with the capacity to shape our material interdependence in the direction of moral interdependence."

It seems to me that, given the present situation and climate of the churches, this is a remarkable and excellent pastoral letter, and the American bishops should be congratulated for an extremely responsible (and arduous) exercise of their ministry. The purpose of this column is to ask for the same appreciation for the peculiar and inimitable character of our liturgical rites and structures (primary symbols, deeply formative, of the reign of God, the vision of the covenant, the prophets, the Christ, and therefore ambiguous and non-specific with respect to where we are at any given moment). I want the same appreciation for liturgy (on a deeper level) as I have just expressed for the peculiar character of the bishops' letter (important, but secondary and derivative instruction, moral guidance, evangelical proclamation, issuing, as all such ministerial efforts must, from where we are at this given moment).

Before the relatively recent conciliar beginnings of general reform, most Catholics were estranged from our primary liturgical-biblical sources and were therefore dependent almost exclusively on secondary ones — papal encyclicals, bishops' letters, homilies, approximate catechisms, congealed laws and rules, classroom teaching. Even the encyclicals and letters reached relatively few. As a result, we suffered not only from that estrangement from our basic sources but also from ignorance of biblical, liturgical and patristic studies and their revelation of our tradition. And we acquired a wildly exaggerated confidence, quite without historical or theological foundation, in episcopal (especially papal) and even presbyteral inspiration. . . .

Now that we are slowly getting back to our basic sources, the Sunday assembly is again our major Christian contact point — sharing its proclaimed readings, its prayer and action, its holy meal of love and reconciliation, its kingdom-tension with our status quo. Because that assembly is where our faith is chiefly formed and where we discover deeply what it means to be a Catholic Christian and what all those approximate and secondary habits and answers *meant* to convey but frequently did not and do not. The idea is: if you really get hold of a classic text, a classic source, and become comfortable with it, you are capable of dispensing with the old commentary, placing it in perspective, writing a new one. In fact, you have to keep writing new commentaries all the time to incarnate the source in the language, culture, ways of a world that is always in the process of change, some of which is real growth and development.

The American bishops' pastoral letter is one such commentary. We need it. But we must not desire or seek to turn the liturgy into a commentary. And that, it seems to me, is what some of the questions I am hearing ask us to do. We avid consumers of instant causalities apparently do not like the nondirective subtlety of liturgy's transforming power. So, unwittingly, we run the risk of asking liturgical celebration to become what it must never be: a rally, an instruction, a blueprint for action.

God knows (and we must learn quickly) that we need rallies, instructions and blueprints for action. But they become monsters unless they are kept humanly modest and relative to (subject to) God and the vision of God's reign which we experience in liturgy. There is no question in my mind but that our world needs desperately a mass economic-political movement which merits the enthusiastic support of believers. We need its rallies and its blueprints, its definitions of the enemy and its plotting of concrete strategies. These are critically important human activities if we are to catch up culturally and morally with our scientific and technological achievements. They are also quite different from liturgical activity, which offers basic orientation but no blueprints, which claims friend and foe alike, in an experience of the holy city without which demagogues emerge, enemies are hated, and strategies become demonic.

So the questioners I began with do not need "new liturgies" (a semantic barbarism) or different rites to bring their public worship into harmony with their social conscience. What has happened is that their social conscience has finally caught up (in ways appropriate to our particular moment in space and time) with the vision celebrated symbolically in the liturgy for thousands of years. And any student of Jewish or Christian worship, or anyone who has more than a distant and passing acquaintance with biblical ritual tradition, knows that much more than coincidence is involved in the reform-prompted currency of two deeply related transformations: 1) the transformation from reliance on secondary sources and commentaries to a living relation with our basic and primary sources, especially in the biblical liturgy of the Sunday assembly; and 2) the transformation from a privatized and narrow moral posture to a moral outlook sufficiently all-embracing to take on institutional oppression, the military-political-economic powers-that-be, and to challenge them in the light of the biblical-liturgical vision of God's reign.

Like the phrase "institutional church," the phrase "peace liturgy" is a tautology. There ain't no other kind of church . . . and there ain't no other kind of liturgy.

25

Which World Do You Live — and Worship — In?*

All of us together inhabit this planet at a time when its vast spaces and distances are fast shrinking and its cultural variety is being rapidly homogenized. For more and more of its people, the consciousness of place and of belonging has begun to extend to the whole planet. Yet, despite this development, we do create our own "worlds," our own life environments. We reduce the real world's complexity and dimensions, establish comfortable perimeters, recognize a cast of characters with which we can cope, set a feasible agenda, and so on. Some of this is as inevitable as sin, simply a function of the limits of all creatures.

As long as we can see this tendency to create our own "world" as such, as a function of human limits, and therefore struggle against it and refuse to let it blind us to the real world, God's world, where God's children belong, we can accept its necessity and relate it to (make it serve) the rest of that reality. The trouble is, the little world I thus create is a jealous world. It wants to capture me . . . totally. And often all the rest is lost. I become a prisoner of my own construct, paralyzed by its givens, instead of a pilgrim being who grows by challenging the givens and straining against the limits.

It seems to me this problem is related to some of our liturgical puzzles and difficulties and to the extremely slow pace of renewal. So much depends on where we have chosen to live, on our particular "world." And it is an appropriate reflection in the light of the seasons we have been celebrating, Advent and Christmas, both of which focus on the reign of God. "Your kingdom come."

*Worship, January 1984

"Your kingdom come, your will be done *on earth,*" as a matter of fact. On this very planet. Despite the reign-of-God vision of the biblical message and the revolutionary ferment Christopher Dawson linked to it, the human race in general had to wait for other developments to gain a real awareness of responsibility for the world. That awareness has been late blooming, aided immensely no doubt by progress in transportation and communication. Most previous generations in human history were resigned to much smaller, much more constricted "worlds." The great cultural powers (military, economic, political) that defined all roles and imposed the stereotypes that people made their own were quite beyond their grasp. Those powers were in the realm of "fate" and "destiny," and human responsibility did not extend that far. The Second Vatican Council recognized the magnitude of the change in consciousness which the modern world has occasioned. In the Constitution on the Church in the Modern World 55, its accents are bold: "We are witnesses of the birth of a new humanism, one in which the human person is defined first of all by a real responsibility toward all brothers and sisters and toward history."

People in general (not just prophets, proclaimers of God's word, visionaries) are beginning to understand that we create these powers, these institutions and structures that determine our lives to such a great extent, our support keeps them in existence, and we can change them. This is a new reality, described so vividly by Teilhard de Chardin in "The Rise of the Other" (*Activation of Energy,* Harcourt Brace 1971, pp. 73–74): "Up to now, human beings have lived apart from each other, scattered around the world and closed in upon themselves. They have been like passengers who accidentally meet in the hold of a ship, not even suspecting the ship's motion. Clustered together on the earth, they found nothing better to do than to fight or amuse themselves. Now, by chance, or better as a natural result of organization, our eyes are beginning to open. The most daring among us have climbed to the bridge. They have seen the ship that carries us all. They have glimpsed the ship's prow cutting the waves. They have noticed that a boiler keeps the ship going and a rudder keeps it on course. And, most important of all, they have seen clouds floating above and caught the scent of distant islands on the horizon. It is no longer agitation down in the hold, just drifting along; the time

has come to pilot the ship. It is inevitable that a different humanity must emerge from this vision."

What the bishops call a responsibility to the world that newly
defines what it means to be human and what the visionary calls a
"different humanity" — both emphasize the Christian's presence
in and focus on the real world, a conscious choice of the real
world as our "world," our life context. It seems to me this enables modern believers to perceive more (and more deeply) in the
biblical proclamations of God's reign. In this sense, the human
race has finally grown into a capacity for participating more fully
in the revealed divine purposes.

While still a mystery, those purposes and their advent are now
immediate in a much sharper sense. The advent of God's reign
has to do (as I think Scripture and our faith tradition at its best
have always dimly seen) with life today, at the present moment,
and with the world as a whole. So we see the church as existing
in and for the world (of which we are fully parts). We see the
church in service to the world, as salt and light and leaven. We
do not try to make a life "in the church." The church is not our
life but its search for inspiration. Our life is in the world, the only
world we have, God's world. And we are church, not to create
another "world," another culture, but to celebrate together, in the
word of God and the sacraments, the meaning and the vision and
the power we need for life in the world and for orientating it in
accordance with the divine will.

The practical significance of all this for liturgical celebration is
fairly obvious. If church is thus related to the world as a whole —
as servant, minister, dynamic — then the church has to utilize to
the full the limited time, attention, energy which the baptized
community in general can give to its corporate formation and
celebration. Our business is inspiration and vision for a life outside the ecclesiastical sphere. The Sunday assembly, therefore, becomes again very, very important, as our common contact with
the basic sources of faith. And the experience gained in that assembly, in the breaking of the bread of word and sacrament, is
crucial. We not only want but need an experience of transcendent
beauty, awesome worship, palpable sincerity, gripping relevance
— altogether a memorable occasion. And the Sunday liturgy can
be all this, without a doubt, if the pastoral work of building faith

community is going on, and if we put our time and careful preparation, our attention in execution, our energy and money, our artistic and communications talent into that gathering.

But there are other interpretations of the reign of God and its advent — interpretations which are at the root of many of our problems. The cataclysmic figures Scripture uses to describe the fulfillment of God's purposes have come to signify for many only death and the afterlife. The world, in this view, is impenetrable and lost, irrelevant to God's purposes, if not satanic. So we make the church our world, our self-sufficient fortress, our culture. Not the salt, the lamp, the leaven in and for the whole — not at all! — but rather a permanent retreat from life, an island protecting us from mainland influences. The world then is something to be suffered, not changed. And the parish sets about to consume and exhaust the time, the energies, the talents, the interests and the resources of its members.

Is this not the church of Evelyn Waugh and *Brideshead Revisited?* And of much of the Catholic nostalgia of our time? There *is* a certain attraction in that tight little island, that ecclesiastical world. It was terribly beguiling in that exquisite TV production so many of us watched last year. Its "Catholic culture" was an intricate and astounding European and Western achievement, weaving a whole fabric of life out of an ecclesiastical system that had forgotten (momentarily) its Lord's difficulties with such systems.

So the Sunday assembly — in such a church "world" — fades into a daily routine of relatively constant ritual action, distinguished for its dogged persistence but not for the beauty, awesomeness or art which the symbolic action merits. Although frequented by few, this quantitative rather than qualitative public worship supports the illusion that "pastoral work" is going on constantly. It offers prayer-sanction for the faith community's alienation from the rest of the world. Mission becomes building the church rather than the advent of the reign of God. The clergy are protected from tough questions, such as "what is real pastoral work in a time like ours?"

Concern for "the least of my sisters and brothers" does not take the shape of changing economic and military and political institutions and their deeds, so that government serves all of God's people with equity and on a world basis, but remains on the level of handouts. "We" are always doing good to "them," keeping our solipsistic identity inviolate. The church world duplicates (rather than supports) trade, professional, cultural organizations of the world, providing Catholic counterparts for everything from recreational opportunities to health facilities, from general education to professional associations. Many parish schedules reflect this overweening ambition. The list of liturgical services sometimes appears to be a cafeteria of rites designed for individual consumers, instead of a corporate effort of doers to express and confirm a community's faith and praise and thanks. And the rest, in addition to serving essential parish needs, may look like an anxious concern to keep the faithful busy, rather than to refresh us for being busy elsewhere.

To criticize such an alternative "world" is not to denigrate the roles of those who serve the church pastorally, as specialized ministers, or those who serve the entire body by specialized prayer or work through community life in vows. Such persons may or may not be affected by the sickness I have been trying to describe. All of us are limited creatures, with different vocations, and no one life can embody or express the whole of faith's vision or empowerment. Neither of these broad groups of particular vocations alters in any way the world-focus appropriate to believers, nor the church's commitment as servant and sign in and for the world. These thoughts may seem like a denigration of those vocations, but only if we have made the subtle and pernicious mistake of letting conversion and the life that begins with the sacraments of initiation be replaced in our consciousness by those specialized services.

It is evident that we have made this mistake quite commonly and widely. So, instead of being two limited contributions to the total reality of Christian life in the world, the clerical and "religious" (the word itself is a clue to our problem) ministries have come to be regarded as models for all. All Christians have to try to model faith and hope and love for each other, but to make clerical roles or a monastic lifestyle a model for other Christians is to eviscerate the meaning of the church as a whole.

The only challenge in such a self-contained unit as the Catholic "world" I have described is its own maintenance. And its maintenance is a no-sweat proposition. Just keep the bridges drawn, the windows closed, the humdrum and routinized "dispensing" of sacraments endless, the believers occupied. The Sunday assembly, in this "world," is simply another one of those almost constant ritual moments. Why make a fuss about that? Curious, indeed! We've got a whole world created for the baptized! If it happens to embrace at the moment only some clerics, some religious, some of the unemployed, retired and elderly, it is nonetheless the Catholic world. Tough for those who aren't making it! Baptized aliens are welcome, but they can't expect the regulars to get all excited because they turn up only on Sunday (and, increasingly, naturally and unhappily, much less frequently than that).

This description of a closed ecclesiastical world is, of course, a caricature. Useful, as any caricature may be, to describe very real shapes and substances which habit and routine have made obscure. Nobody is perfect, so perhaps no one exhibits all of those tendencies or (to be frank) defects at once. But the dominance of many of those tendencies in certain periods of our history and their pervasive, clinging presence even now make it absolutely necessary for us to identify that devil and vanquish it.

Because I am getting old, I resent what it does to older people as much as I resent its influence on the rest of the church. Our society is so uncomfortable with age and with the normal decline of the flesh that accompanies age that it has special need of the light and leaven of a faith community that values and venerates its aged members. All of us can profit from sharing the experience, and sometimes the wisdom, of old people who have not been shelved, hidden, or otherwise excluded from the common life. But the ecclesiastical world, instead of contesting society's fears, appears to sanction them by implying that "preparing for death" by preoccupation with church affairs is the proper business of the aged. The gospel notion that you prepare for death by living is apparently foreign to that world. If there is anything clearer in Jesus' recorded teachings than the conviction that the important moment for every one of us, no matter what our age, is the one we possess here and now, I don't know what it is.

It was a similar phenomenon in his own Jewish faith community that Jesus attacked with all his might. The same kind of closed, self-sufficient, professional religiosity. Little wonder that when we choose that world, when we make that world our home, we forfeit not only a lot of problems but also the abundant life Christ offers. No wonder that the liturgical celebrations of a Sunday assembly whose leaders have made that kind of choice look and feel and taste and smell as they still do.

Liturgical renewal demands far more than the appropriate studies and techniques. It asks all of us who would contribute to it and be a part of it just where we hang our hats, just what we have made our abode, just which world we have chosen to live (and worship) in.

Because a church that rejects self-sufficiency and self-service, that accepts the covenant, that initiates new members and re-initiates old ones not into a culture, or a shelter, or a total life system, but into a worship and support group whose life and mission is the real world's arena — such a church needs a Sunday assembly that is not commonplace but remarkable, not ordinary but festive, not a daily portion but an occasional excess, not a maintenance procedure but an inspiration. Clerics whose world is the ecclesiastical island, and who are therefore drained by its inconsequential demands, consumed by its spiritual narcissism, breathless from its ritual busy work, will never be able to preside in (or even to understand) the Sunday assembly which such a faith community must have for its survival.

26

Cultural Adaptation and
the Ministry of Reconciliation*

The fact that "it all goes together" is both a witness to the grace
and orthodoxy of conciliar reform and renewal efforts in the
church and a source of great frustration and annoyance. The frustration and annoyance make perseverance in a reform commitment
extremely difficult. I think we have all experienced this in one
way or another during these last two decades. Every time we
think that a particular faith community has got itself together sufficiently to make a tentative step forward, we find that some practice or habit momentarily out of our purview has caused our foot
to falter, or even dragged us back.

On the one hand, all this is very reassuring. The good news is a
way of life, and the renewal of the church that is its witness and
proclaimer, is jeopardized by overlooking any basic aspect of ecclesial life, as our experience testifies. A liturgical track remains only
a liturgical track unless it is consciously part of an integrated way
of life that, without the aid of a computer, encompasses the world
and humanity, conversion, the initiation process, community
building and adult education, liturgical celebration, the mission
and ministry of reconciliation, the economics and property of the
faith community, its ministries of service and organization. And all
these areas have their own problems. They resist integration, and
they will not move forward in any uniform fashion. They have to
be coaxed and wooed and babied and challenged and reassured —
all of them, all the time.

So, on the other hand, let any one of these parts escape attention or get lost in the shuffle, and our so-called "step forward"

*Worship, May 1984

proves to be illusory. And we have to start all over again — this time trying to keep everything in mind at once. That's where the frustration, annoyance, exasperation come in, and where a lot of us quit. Even though we know we're on the right track, it just takes too much attention. It's too much of a strain. You've got to have eyes in the back of your head and your feelers stretching out in all directions.

As it actually happens, or is made to happen, therefore, the work of ecclesial renewal is terribly messy and spotty and uneven: a little movement here or there which eventually may have repercussions in the other areas, one or two at a time, until finally the *corpus ecclesiae* moves. Our temptation, of course, is to claim a step before it has been thoroughly negotiated.

Sometimes I wonder to what extent certain efforts, ostensibly in the direction of "cultural adaptation," are really that, and to what extent they are (perhaps unconsciously) a bolstering of the status quo against the gospel claim of God's dominion. I don't know. I have more questions than answers about the examples I will discuss, but I think they are questions we should be asking ourselves.

We boast, for example, that we have "cultural adaptation" of liturgical celebration because the eucharistic liturgy is celebrated on Sunday in ten, twenty, thirty, forty languages, sometimes (although more rarely) with corresponding music, and because a few "black churches" have gospel choirs. On the surface this sounds wonderful. I love the babel of different languages in the city, and I love gospel song in the liturgy. In my opinion, gospel song is the greatest single American contribution to liturgical celebration.

The conciliar Constitution on the Sacred Liturgy had taught: "Even in the liturgy, the Church has no wish to impose a rigid uniformity in matters which do not implicate the faith or the good of the whole community; rather does she respect and foster the genius and talents of the various races and peoples. Anything in these peoples' way of life which is not indissolubly bound up with superstition and error she studies with sympathy and, if possible, preserves intact. Sometimes in fact she admits such things into the liturgy itself, so long as they harmonize with its true and authentic spirit" (no. 37).

The questions I want to raise have to do with the church in the United States, in urban and rural areas that have mixed ethnic populations. They concern that very mixture and the church's ministry of reconciliation in an admittedly diseased society, sick with racism and sexism and worsening conditions of economic extremes. And they are addressed principally to the dominant groups and the dominant church structures in these dioceses.

Clearly the pastors and pastoral teams of minority ethnic parishes in this country have worked valiantly and unselfishly to help regain their communities' pride in themselves and in their gifts — usually in the face of an overwhelming white, anglo, bourgeois tide. That this service has been crowned by an increasing respect for and use of a variety of tongues and of musical idioms, including the indisputably great American black gospel song tradition, is a beautiful development and a blessing.

And yet, the questions I referred to above, which challenge the whole church and its meaning and mission in this society remain.

"Cultural adaptation" is a two-edged sword in the liturgical life of the churches. If it means that liturgy is the work of a concrete faith community in a particular time and place, and, therefore, that it cannot be celebrated except in the context and out of the stuff of that church's life and experience, it is simply a requisite of true public worship. If, however, it should become, by some jaded process in the corporate psyche of the local church, an excuse for capitulating to inimical aspects of the culture of the time and place, then it is devilish indeed. Then it becomes an excuse for avoiding the gospel call to reconcile, to liberate and unify the human family, to witness to and work for the reign of God.

The choices with which these questions are concerned are between different goods, not between good and evil. They have to do with priorities. And priorities tend to get mixed up in a church scene that is constantly torn between faithfulness and accommodation, between commitment to the justice, peace, reconciliation of the reign of God and commitment to the soil of its gospel seed — a human family conditioned by cultures that remain in many ways divisive and oppressive.

The only easy answer (and the favorite of our history) is a retreat from public, political, economic, social responsibility into a narcissistic and self-indulgent ecclesial posture that tends its own fires and pursues its own "interior" life. The depressing effects of that retreat are evident in the strange combination of private commitment and public apathy that still marks the Christian community as a whole and that makes the church such an easy prey for the powers-that-be and such a staunch ally of whatever status quo may dominate at any particular moment.

That sad picture is being slowly changed by reform and renewal elements in the church. We are close to understanding how that "politically neutral" stance of the faith community is not neutral at all. Life in the real world excludes the possibility of the kind of neutrality of which we have boasted. Individual or corporate body, if you exist in this world your options are limited: either seek to change the structures and institutions of society or allow yourself to be a bulwark for those whose interests are served by keeping things as they are. The churches' famous "neutrality" has correctly imaged them in the modern world as the allies of the rich and powerful.

While that may be the image, the reality is different. Orthodox believers are saved from the media image by the symbols which are our true sources — biblical word and ecclesial sacrament. The word proclaims and the sacrament celebrates the good news that all of us are free and one in God. The common table, symbolizing both liberation and solidarity, stands at the heart and center of the church, unyielding and insistent, indifferent to the fancies and fashions of our cultural accommodations, calling us to conversion . . . and to mission.

Such a ministry of reconciliation (of all excluded, spurned, neglected, oppressed persons and groups) clearly cannot afford to accommodate itself to the divisive and oppressive aspects of a culture — the very aspects which God's reign summons us to combat. "Your kingdom come on earth." The good news is that the reign of God is at hand and that church serves world by living it here and now and inching cultures toward its realization.

If we have, at least in our best moments, responded to that call on the level of our private lives, as individuals, why should we imagine that on the level of our corporate life as local church we can be "neutral" in the daily struggles between justice and oppression, between violence and love, between reconciliation and hate/prejudice? At long last, the consciousness of the human race has caught up with the symbols of faith. Now we possess the world-awareness and the tools to assume a genuine responsibility for the institutions and structures which have been, for most of our history, helplessly regarded as our "fate." The individual Christians who participate in this awakening are already numerous, even though they constitute a small minority of those still numbered as believers. So we should not be surprised to see bishops' conferences, here and there, and local churches beginning tentatively and cautiously to recognize their corporate responsibility for social change.

With our new awareness and tools, offering bread to the hungry and drink to the thirsty, etc., translates into political and economic responsibility, world government, and a host of other challenges to the cultures that now fragment us. So a clear priority for church structures, including the Sunday assembly, is a strong witness to the faith that in God the different gifts of different sexes, colors, classes, ethnic groups, lifestyles are reconciled in a unity of common daughters and sons, sisters and brothers, whose variety enriches all. The more the eucharistic table and the Sunday assembly, in areas where typical American cultural diversity prevails in the community, visibly and tangibly reconcile the different elements of our sick, weakened and divided culture, the more faithful and the more honest and the more winning is the witness of the parish.

Cultural adaptation without serious damage to the overall vision of biblical faith makes the resolution of dilemmas a constant challenge to our responsibility. What appears to be a good when viewed narrowly or in a specialized way sometimes shows another face to eyes less restricted in their scope. This is especially true in an abnormal situation, like that of our society with its history of sexist and racist oppression in an atmosphere of individualism, yet with strong social, economic supports for the dominant groups and powers.

And also like our church, in these times of regaining (after a long abnormal period) a reform perspective on ecclesial life that was almost lost. If we as church were in a "normal" situation, initiation would precede eucharist. So that, by the time the believer reached the banquet table and full participation in the Sunday assembly, he or she would be deeply formed in the Christ who "has made the two of us one by breaking down the barrier of hostility that kept us apart" (Eph 2:14). Even with universal implementation of RCIA (The Rite of Christian Initiation of Adults), it will be a long time before that kind of integrity and maturity marks the faith community as a whole. In that future, perhaps, ecclesial scene, the eucharistic assembly would be people who are actively pursuing the liberation and unification of the human family through all available public and private channels, political and economic as well as individual. Then (and only then) an inappropriate homogeneity in the assembly would not be as threatening and debilitating as it is now, would neither appeal to nor appear to bolster those evil genes with which our history has endowed us.

Alas, such is not the case. Initiation and its parish processes are not yet universally recognized as the primary intramural task of every parish. Initiation, the Sunday assembly, and every other important element of our renewal are all mixed up. There is no neatness, order or logic in their breakthroughs. So our Sunday assemblies, far from being gatherings of formed initiates, are peopled by believers of every degree, and the experience they offer is the only catechumenate many will ever have.

Real cultural adaptation, that takes the gospel seriously, cannot in this kind of national scene or city scene continue to boast about the way we serve language and lifestyle and sometimes even age groups in ways that maximize our human comfort and minimize the mission and ministry of reconciliation.

Most of us are aware by now that "separate but equal" in our culture is an abstraction without relevance, ruthlessly employed to maintain injustice. This is simply a fact of our social life, whether the criterion is sex or color or age or physical handicap or mental handicap or a gay or lesbian identity or any of the other distinctions that have made certain groups the scapegoats of a "society" which, as yet, hardly exists. Progressive elements in our society most concerned with healing and reconciliation (and therefore most in tune with the biblical message on the level of practice) have repudiated "separate but equal" as a fantasy cloaking vicious structures and privileges. A faithful church cannot even *appear* to be adopting its own version of "separate but equal," particularly in the Sunday assembly, that chief symbol of its faith, its conviction and its message. Not even under the warm and homespun blanket of "cultural adaptation."

The questions these considerations raise are difficult ones, to be pondered. Perhaps they will lead us to see that part of the problem is the structure of the diocese and especially of its city components. The awareness of these problems and the self-criticism in our society are among our biggest assets. Churches should be rallying points and spiritual encouragement for all these elements and movements. But we cannot be as long as parishes and properties that determine parishes are maintained on the basis of their service, say, a century ago, and as isolated kingdoms, each a world unto itself. So that, instead of seeing the city, or its humanly viable components, as the community we exist as church to serve, and instead of pastoral teams and parish representatives getting together with the bishop or the dean to determine how best to develop communities of believers which are pictures (worth a thousand words) of reconciliation and gospel solidarity . . . instead of allocating property and personnel to match these ecclesial realities . . . we have the melancholy picture of outdated structures operating virtually alone and with the less than electrifying aim of self-preservation.

27

"Money or Gifts for
the Poor and the Church"*

The appearance in recent weeks of a remarkable and wonderful
document, prepared by the National Conference of Catholic
Bishops Ad Hoc Committee on Catholic Social Teaching and the
U.S. Economy, is an appropriate occasion for a formal expression
of gratitude in this column to Archbishop Weakland, the committee and their collaborators. While the burden of this month's
column is the significance and place of money offerings in the liturgy of the Sunday assembly, reference to the first draft of the
proposed pastoral letter offers both context and sanction for such
a discussion, and places it within a broad understanding of the
church's mission.

Only an indefensible ignorance of the liturgical movement in the
United States in this century could charge it with the kind of
specialization which is narrowly ecclesiastical and oblivious to the
social-political-economic good of humanity. The glory of this
movement, which for a long time virtually coincided with The
Liturgical Conference and its annual Liturgical Weeks, has been
the breadth and integration, the holistic approach to the life and
mission of the covenant community in the world, that were evident both in the pioneering work of Virgil Michel of St John's
Abbey, and in the concerns expressed in those Liturgical Weeks
from their beginnings in 1940.

As with any movement, not all of its partisans have shared the
full breadth of its vision, but the fact that such "secular" interests
were remarkable in their time made that vision visible for anyone
who cared to look. Remarkable because it was a rare flower, it

*Worship, January 1985

was nevertheless not surprising — at least for anyone who understood that liturgical worship (including of course its proclamation and reception of the biblical word) "precedes theological reflection and subordinates it. The classic Latin patristic position that the law of worship constitutes the law of belief . . . means more than that the liturgy as a whole is one source for theology among others. . . . It does mean that the liturgy as a whole is nothing other than the Church's faith in motion both at the highest and on the most practical levels. This faith surely has other modes and levels, but these are to be evaluated finally in terms of the Church at worship rather than vice versa."[1]

The symbolic actions called liturgy, because they involve us in an acting-out of that reign of God toward which a humanity and world in process (still primitive in many ways and growing) must be moving, are much more critical of and challenging to all structures of economic and political life than are those shrill, single-issue, power-conscious ecclesiastical voices we heard so frequently during last year's political campaign. Liturgy is less newsworthy, obviously, but it is the appropriate way because it is the gospel and the godly way. The draft pastoral is entirely unlike those latter, strident voices, and is as like the way of rite and symbol as prose can be, because it begins with our biblical roots and our worship and is humble, respectful, searching, persuasive, unselfconscious. The reader is not threatened or coerced but stirred and moved by its "call for a concerted effort by the Church in its ministry to bring about a greater integration of labor and leisure and a new wholeness of work and worship."[2]

It is a plea for integration and wholeness. One of the provocative gifts of our marvelous English language is the basic relationship of the words "whole," "holy," "heal," "hale," "health." To be holy is to be integrated, undivided, and that is also to be healthy. Our destiny as revealed in the biblical covenant, the reign of God, the new Jerusalem, is the principle of such integration, such wholeness and holiness. Since we live in a world that is unfinished and developing, the draft letter pays tribute to the prog-

[1] Aidan Kavanagh, *The Shape of Baptism: The Rite of Christian Initiation* (New York: Pueblo 1978) xii.
[2] First Draft of the U.S. Bishops' Pastoral Letter on Catholic Social Teaching and the U.S. Economy (Washington, D.C.: USCC 1984) 322.

ress the United States has made toward political democracy. Pleading for a similar effort and commitment in the economic area, for integration and wholeness therefore, the draft proposes the securing of some economic rights: "We believe the time has come for a similar experiment in economic democracy: the creation of an order that guarantees the minimum conditions of human dignity in the economic sphere for every person" (no. 89).

This will be news to most Americans and even to most of the American faithful. For reasons too complex to be summarized here, the vast majority of believers and church members have chosen to be ignorant of or indifferent to the most obvious implications of the gospel for social structures and institutions. Should American Catholics find themselves confronting or listening to the teaching of this document in any serious and honest way, we can expect a general reaction of incredulous perplexity at best, anger or negation at worst, or, of course, conversion. Like the peace pastoral, these seeds will need tender care for a long time if they are to live and bear fruit.

The same reasons are closely related to the subject to which this column must now attend, the liturgical tradition and principle enunciated in the Roman Missal regarding the preparation of the altar and gifts in the celebration of the eucharist: "This is also the time to bring forward or to collect money or gifts for the poor and the Church. These are to be laid in a suitable place but not on the altar."[3]

One of the ways in which we continue to prove our lack of appreciation and understanding of earthly covenant, incarnation, God's dominion in the world (and of liturgical rite and symbol in particular) is by our typical embarrassment at and irritation with the money offerings of the Sunday assembly. This typical reaction is a symptom of the same sickness that spurns the common cup of the Lord's own Supper and recoils from the kiss of peace (or reduces it to the level of polite recognition). It illustrates our fear of the body, our ineptness in sacramental and symbolic action, our ethereal distortions of a gospel that does not disdain anything that is human, especially such basic human concerns as economics and politics.

Money is a potent and universal sign of such importance in the life of every human being that the way one deals with it, earns it,

[3] General Instruction of the Roman Missal, 49.

spends it is a dead giveaway of one's values and a revelation of one's priorities. Through the offering, at first, of materials of human sustenance and, later, of the means of exchange that took their place, persons and communities of the earthy, worldly biblical tradition have from their beginnings used these tangible signs in prayer and ritual expression of their "Here I am; send me!" When the faithful gather to celebrate their public worship and their vision of the reign of God, no sign of their ultimate allegiance has more abiding relevance and punch than the currency of the realm.

So perhaps it is not strange that this appropriateness of money offerings in and as part of liturgy gives us goose pimples. On a level that has nothing to do with "Religionspeak," it reminds us that absolutely everything in our lives has to become new and oriented to the dominion of a God who unmasks idols and pretenders by the score. It is a blunt intrusion of practical honesty and everyday reality into a "faith" scene that some of us have isolated and overprotected.

Some parishes have taken the money offerings out of their ritually prescribed place in the Sunday eucharistic celebration and thus "spiritualized" (as they feel) the entire rite. All of us do silly or damaging things sometimes with the best of intentions. But if the kind of delicacy and spiritual hygiene that is offended by the sight and sound and touch of money is to be recommended in our public worship, then we should also get rid of bread, wine, music, bodily gestures, to say nothing of the assembly and its ministers and the furnishings of the space.

Sacramental worship is symbolic action by a community of faith — body language, total engagement, different functions and types and ministries all participating in a common action which knows no dichotomy between body and soul, between now and heaven, between the evolving world and its consummation. Quite deliberately *with* all of our worldly baggage, we place ourselves in the playful context of God's reign. Because liturgy enables us to do this — the heavenly banquet — it invites us, like the parable in word, to enter into a new situation which demands new decisions. Liturgy is parable in action. It doesn't make our decisions for us, but rather invites us respectfully into an environment in which godly decisions not only are appropriate but are the only ones that make sense.

Too often in our ecclesial history we have yielded to the temptation to distort this earthy, biblical vision of the kingdom into something much more ethereal, something whose real focus is after death. Money as a sign of self-offering is a bit too grabby and a bit too grubby for extremely refined tastes. If it begins to mean something in the liturgy, it might give believers the idea that the economic systems of the world need to be scrutinized and reformed in the light of God's word. Economic and military and political powers have always had all kinds of means at their disposal for encouraging the "refinement" mentioned and for keeping the church in its "place."

And, just as we have suppressed or minimized in practice so many other aspects of liturgy's symbol language, we are responsible for having allowed the money offerings to shrink to the insignificance of a mere "collection" for local upkeep. Eating and drinking together, bathing, anointing, laying on hands — all the crucial, central symbolic acts comprising liturgy — have become neglected, desiccated, shriveled up. Renewal is beginning to open them up again and attend to them, at least in parishes attentive to the Holy Spirit, but we are only gradually acquiring some of the feel for symbolic action which will eventually enrich us again with its incomparable dynamism.

Those economic steps which should be among the first taken in any genuine reform effort are usually among the last. And so it is with the church. As we saw above, the Roman Missal clearly states that the money offerings at the preparation of the altar and gifts in the Sunday eucharist are "for the poor and the Church." In how many parishes is there even now a consensus and commitment that a certain part of each Sunday's offerings will go beyond our own parish needs to aid community and social services, groups serving poor and disadvantaged people? Yet to be unambiguously agreed and committed to a clear percentage distribution of Sunday money offerings to both the needs of the parish and to definite, named agencies and works beyond it (not just "the poor" in general) seems a minimal requirement if the liturgy's prescriptions are to be taken seriously.

As long as Catholics are convinced that the money offerings on Sunday are merely to heat our buildings and repair our plumbing and pay our ministers and serve our needs, our giving will probably remain as ungenerous and uninspired as it usually is. But we should not be so pessimistic as to discount the motivation of the assembly's planning and knowing that this giving is clearly a part of our ministry of reconciliation in the world, our mission, our discipleship and stewardship. When a parish community agrees upon a certain percentage of its money offerings (in the appropriately single collection, at the appropriate moment in the preparation of the altar and gifts, during the appropriate Sunday assembly) for such a purpose and agrees upon the causes and agencies to receive such help, it is certainly easier to be conscious that this eucharist is no island, but direction and fuel for the rest of the week.

We don't have to wait for this. It is something every parish can do to enhance both its sense of mission and its liturgical celebrations. And, if we begin this way, perhaps we will gain the vision and the energy to tackle some of the other counterproductive economic habits of the church which block renewal at every turn. For example, the custom of Mass stipends so camouflages and distorts our sacramental understanding that people simply know we can't mean what we say when we talk about the eucharist in language that makes sense today. People's attitudes are formed by what we do more than by what we say. As long as the Mass stipends are collected and the parish bulletin lists the "intentions," we can preach good sacramental theology and practice to our heart's content and be confident that no one will hear us, or, if they should happen to catch the drift, will take us seriously. Please read Francis Mannion's article in the May 1983 *Worship*.[4] If you accept his conclusion that the stipend system is "ecclesiologically and liturgically pathological," then let's raise such a storm about it that it can't be ignored any longer. This will mean more attention to the general intercessions (the true liturgical statement of our "intentions") and, above all, the kind of atmosphere in which it will not be impossible to understand the eucharist.

The same economic ineptness (or mess) affects seriously so much of our church life, especially many ministerial reforms long overdue. Because clergy and other professional servants of the churches are kept in a state of economic serfdom and dependency

[4] M. Francis Mannion, "Stipends and Eucharistic Praxis," *Worship* 57 (1983) 194–214.

on fringe benefits, sycophancy and tax evasion, discouraging the very freedom, independence and maturity we are finally beginning to desire in our ministers. And perpetuating, we may not forget, a clerical lifestyle and straitjacket of habits and expectations (far more intransigent as barriers than any "theological" problems) which effectively prohibit the enlistment of women and married persons with qualifying talents and training into the presbyterate and episcopate.

We all know that we are practiced at "theologizing" ourselves out of any hole. And we keep trying to get out of our economic hole by all means except by facing it. When we get around to dealing with our fiscal problems, I suspect most of our heavy theological argumentation in defense of current economic policies in the church will disintegrate like puffballs. Even if I am wrong about the possible extent of its effects, I know I am right in pleading for the kind of distribution of money offerings on Sunday for which the Roman Missal asks. And then the "collection" could begin with passing the basket to the presider and the other ministers, since all together are sharing with the rest of the assembly in a common mission of which this disbursement is a sign and instrument. (What a visual statement that simple change of practice would be!)

Some parishes call this parish tithing, just as individual members are expected to share a significant part of their income with the faith community and the world we serve. Whatever it is called, the practice of offering money along with bread and wine as signs of the faith community's self-oblation in Christ and with Christ is an integral part of the Sunday assembly's eucharistic liturgy, totally appropriate, potentially involving, and *demanding* (by the very nature of the church as a ministry in the world and not a self-serving entity) that it serve directly, at least in part, our ministry and mission of reconciliation.

If this means spending time and effort on stewardship campaigns and education toward appropriate giving, it is time well spent, effort overdue. It is not at all "unspiritual," nor is it in any sense alien to the gospel's call to worship God "in spirit and in truth." There is no spirit and no truth in a worship which eschews the concrete signs of our human support and our human survival and our human sense of responsibility for the common good.

28

Liturgy:
"Effective Political Action"?*

"The celebration of the risen Christ by the assembly of believers is one of the most effective political actions people can perform in this world — if it is true that this celebration, by contesting any power system which oppresses humankind, proclaims, stirs up and inaugurates a new order in the created world." Joseph Gelineau's comment, at the beginning of a new and welcome volume on liturgy and justice, surprises many Christians, confirming the fact that our liturgical renewal is still primitive. It also suggests the ordinarily unspoken but certainly cogent reason for the vehemence of the opposition.

In most churches at the present time, our engagement in and ownership of the rites has not progressed to the point where we recognize that Gelineau's statement is a truism — obvious and fundamental. What is most evident today in the lives of believers generally is not our love for one another. It is rather our chameleon-like embrace of local color, sex and class prejudices, of economic injustice and political violence. Exceptions are quite clearly such, and prove the rule.

And, except for a few writers and thinkers, we do not sufficiently reflect on the fact that the reasons usually given for opposing liturgical and other ecclesial reforms are not necessarily the basic or motivating ones. Military and financial interests may not represent the most committed members of the churches, but they have a great stake in making sure the churches stay out of their affairs. Not only schismatic groups like that of Archbishop Lefebvre, but also the power and groups opposed to reform while

*Worship, July 1989

remaining in the various churches tend to have a political and economic agenda more afraid of democratization and socialization in the world than of ordaining women for the churches' ministries.

For these and literally countless other reasons, I think all of us believers owe a debt of follow-up as well as of gratitude to J. Frank Henderson, Kathleen Quinn and Stephen Larson, Canadians who have labored over the course of several years to give us this primer, text and workbook: *Liturgy, Justice and the Reign of God: Integrating Vision and Practice* (Paulist Press 1989). It is an 8½" x 11", 132 page, $12.95 bargain. I will come back to it below.

Because liturgical celebration is both fount and summit for us believers, some questions which may appear to be unrelated to liturgy are actually basic liturgical problems. For example, people who "have it made" simply cannot do liturgy. If we fancy ourselves already free of idols and at peace with the rest of the world, we are not merely poor candidates for the Sunday assembly—we lack a candidate's essential qualifications. People who are not sinners have no need of redemption. Without corporate, conscious grounds for repentance and a consequent openness to a new and different way of life, one that involves change, letting go, liberating and reconciling deeds, we have no need of the faith community and its liturgy. That is a very important reason why the latter is merely a *pro forma* obligation for many.

I hope readers of this column (though an uncomplaining lot) are not tiring of my reiteration of the essential relationship between a justice/peace mission in this world and an engaging liturgical celebration (also in this world . . . and for it). We experience the reality and power of that relationship whenever we participate in a worship assembly predominantly black, hispanic, feminist, gay, impoverished, or of any group clearly oppressed in the particular larger society in question. Apart from relatively superficial cultural differences and when not spoiled by self-pity, most such gatherings communicate a palpable spirit informing texts, gestures and actions, and disclose an unsuspected dynamic in rite.

I am not advocating that kind of homogeneous assembly, but merely pointing out that when composed of the obviously oppressed it tends to grasp the political/economic/cultural relevance and dynamic of the gospel in a strikingly powerful way. Paradoxically, homogeneous Sunday assemblies are not to be encouraged because they have the disadvantage of not imaging the reconciliation of the reign of God. In spite of the dynamism mentioned, they image in too many ways the opposite of that liberation and reconciliation. An assembly mixed in sex, nationality, color, class, age, lifestyle, etc., is a basis, at least, for an icon of the reign of God. For the Sunday assembly is engaged in making present that reign along with ultimate justice and peace, so that its participants can live *all the time* as new persons in Christ Jesus, engaged in making liberation and reconciliation happen in this world, as much as possible in this time, this place. In such happily mixed assemblies, the patently oppressed have a critically important role and should be visible in leadership tasks as elsewhere: to bring the sensitivity and other gifts of their condition to the celebration and to conscientize the rest into an awareness of the more subtle oppressions which bear upon us all.

The entire symbol — biblical word and sacramental gesture and deed — comes alive when participation is full, conscious and active, and when there is general recognition that the God we worship is the one true God who frees us from all our idols, pretenders-to-allegiance, habits and ruts, and who reconciles us, not by eliminating our differences, but by moving each to value the other. The God we worship calls us beyond any status quo, however much improved it might be over any former state. To that God's Word we always pray, "Come!" and we always receive the reply, "I am coming soon."

One of the troubles is that our churches are now well organized. It is not an evil phenomenon, but it is one that is dangerous for a human race given to the manufacture of idols. Our achievements in ecclesial organization can become objects of idolatry so noiselessly and slyly. We have "departments" of worship and "departments" of justice and peace. What begins as a necessary facilitation for practical accomplishment is quietly appropriated and used by our habitual desire to be "numbered among the King's Friends, and . . . enriched with silver and gold and many gifts" (1 Mc 2:18).

Former President Eisenhower's valedictory warning made a brief splash (it was such a surprise from that source) — about the threat of the military–industrial complex in our society. But it is a truism too painful and too demanding for a country which regards itself as having achieved the very best forms of political and economic organization. Who wouldn't rather glory in past accomplishments than respond to the challenge of work that lies at hand? So, too, the churches, whose job it is to contest that self-satisfaction and to motivate change with the vision of God's reign, corporately defy our prophets and our small voices again and again, and always with pious reasons — never a hint of the money-power always at work to preserve the status quo. We are its servant, clouding or postponing the vision, imagining that what we are about is not the way of Jesus but rather a perfect ecclesiastical system, no longer pilgrims, no longer in the process to which the Spirit, Bible and sacraments testify.

The last column in this space, the one before that, and many others in the course of the last seven years have commented on the tension we can always expect between pastoral/prophetic and administrative aspects of our life as churches. Nothing surprising about that. Nothing wrong with it, although it is certainly uncomfortable most of the time. But when tension is removed, small voices smothered, prophets silenced, we are all spiritually impoverished. The thirst for liberation/reconciliation fostered on Sunday at the assembly's table of word and sacrament is not only for those hardy souls who have a sense of humor about officialdom. It is for all of us, including the humorless. It wants to be the corporate thirst of the body of Christ for a better day, a better world, a better life.

No doubt our sources at that table should be enough. But our faith is a common faith and our life as church is a common life and we need the visible and tangible support of joined hands. The authors and publisher of the book I cited at the beginning of this column have offered all of us Christians and our leaders not an exhaustive treatment of so immense a subject, but some very faithful and capable hands. I can't think of anything that most of us believers need more than to join them. Listen to part of their Introduction:

". . . we believe that the relationship between social justice and liturgy is not artificial, contrived, secondary, or imposed, but rather is completely intrinsic to the very nature of both these facets of Christian life . . . . Our aims in this handbook are threefold:

"1. To provide a practical study guide to help people discover the connections between liturgy and social justice;

"2. To provide a practical aid to improve liturgical practice so that the intrinsic connections which exist between liturgy and social justice will be better expressed within the liturgical celebration;

"3. To provide an aid for communication among liturgists, social justice people and religious educators, especially with a concern toward bridging the gap between theory and practice in the parish regarding liturgy and social justice.

"This manual is intended to be accessible to an ecumenical audience whose basic pattern of worship is word and sacrament, with baptism at Sunday worship on occasion . . ." (pp. 2–3).

Beginning with three basic sections — Introduction; Liturgy's Call to Social Justice; Principles of Liturgy and Social Justice — the manual's next five sections follow the structure of liturgy — The Gathering of God's People; The Liturgy of the Word; The Liturgy of Baptism; The Liturgy of the Eucharist; The Sending Forth of God's People — and concludes with bibliography and notes. The Lutheran and Roman Catholic authors gathered criticisms and suggestions representing particular concerns of other confessions in their careful preparation and testing of material first assembled in another arrangement several years ago. Along with essay treatment of each topic, they include quotations from helpful sources, questions for reflection, action and evaluation suggestions, and attention to verbal and nonverbal dimensions of each part of the liturgy.

They conclude their introduction with four pages which begin: "We are very much concerned that the use of this study guide lead to concrete action in your own local congregation . . ." (p. 8). In that appeal, they elicit the first "Amen" in the history of *The Amen Corner.*

29

Singing Up the Steps to Freedom*

. . . Diversity and difference in creation, among human beings as well as other creatures, is one of the most obvious facts in our experience. All that we have in common cannot obscure the fact that each of us is different from all the others. Even the natural groupings of family, tribe, area, or other identifiable social categories are differentiating factors. They assert a certain commonness in my group and at the same time its difference from every other group. It is amazing that we should have such a hard time coming to terms with so basic a fact about humanity and the world. We are still primitives in this matter. We may brag about our diversity at times. We may in a lucid moment even recognize how important that diversity is to our own growth and to the evolution of the human race. But our barbaric fears and suspicions of the "other," the different, are never far below the surface.

Musicians have to deal with more than the striving for excellence in their profession and the artistic development and achievement the profession demands. For terms like "excellence," "development," "achievement" are defined, like other words, in a certain social context. And, because we are a sinful lot, needing repentance all the time, we humans tend to regard the particular cultural context in which each of us or each group of us was brought up and lives as the norm for all the others. *We* are not "different." It is the others who are "different." It is never *we* who are odd. It is all those others. Even when we are able to discern some of the differences of the "other" as gifts, as "pluses," as teaching and enriching us, we cannot help, it seems, but judge them by the "standard," the "norm" of our own gifts and ways

*Worship, September 1989

— as better or worse, higher or lower, generally, of course, the latter in each case. The truth that comes from one God, one Source, one Ground of all our beings seems quite beyond our grasp. Although it finds occasional contemporary expression, as in Pope Paul VI's address to the United Nations in 1965: "Let no one . . . be superior to others. Never the one above the other . . . Never again the one against the other . . . ."

Each of us sets self up as judge and norm. This is true of us as individuals dealing with each other. It is true of us as families, tribes, nations, faith communities, in every group we identify with. It is true of us as cultures (whatever that means) dealing with other cultures. It might be funny if it were not so tragic. If our history were not a story of almost constant hostilities, prejudices, discrimination, oppression, slaveries, wars, pogroms, even attempted genocides. To talk about our differences and diversity, cultural or other, without facing the ugly facts of our life and our experience, would be totally irresponsible.

With this background, and with our experience in the Reagan-Bush era of reversing our hardwon progress in civil rights and of tolerating increasingly open manifestations of anti-semitism and racism, we cannot ignore the paradox of our subject here. With a special sadness, I confess it seems to me as evident in the church at present as it is in the rest of our society. We witness leaders and groups in ascendancy in the Roman Church and in the churches in communion with it who would impose a monolithic "party line," a single interpretation of our Jewish and Christian sources, on all believers everywhere. Instead of valuing our variety and listening, as pastors should, to all of the many ways in which this variety of God's people both hears the word of God and contributes, as the body of Christ, the community of the Spirit, to its interpretation.

It is a hopeless project, thank God!, to try to solve the "problem" we have created out of innocent diversity by a forced conformity and uniformity. We must confess and *feel* that it is the way we view diversity and difference that is the problem, not the fact itself. Jesus made this central in his public ministry, in parable and in action. He welcomed women as partners in spiritual dialogue at a time when those matters were thought to be exclusively the province of the male. And continually the Lord sought out the excluded, the "other," those rejected by most because they were "different," in order to bring them into the common life, to give them a place. The alien, the handicapped, the impoverished. . . .

Since then our technology and science have changed the world (not without the goading help of liturgy — Bible and sacrament), made it small and one. But our morality has not kept pace. It is so hard for us to give up the narcissism, the self- or group-centeredness, the idolatry of competition, the notion that the only way we can be proud of ourselves is by putting down everybody else. Even when we congratulate ourselves for not being vicious, we are patronising. I alone, or my group, continue to act as judge, as norm, as standard for all. This is not merely the sickness of some, it is in all of us and in our leaders. It is part of what we mean by that strange phrase, "original sin." The point of such a common sense reflection is not to make us feel bad, or guilty. The point is to encourage us to get into the biblical business of repenting, that is, not being stuck in a rut, opening ourselves up to growth, to the word of God that is always beckoning us onward, to allowing ourselves to be made free and one by the one true God. . . .

None of us can do this alone: this repentance, this opening up, this identification with *all* "others." Biblical faith, Judaism, the churches and their liturgy offer a common way. We do not have to do it alone. Particularly in our conciliar reform and renewal, two instrumentalities of this grace are ours. One is the recovery of catechumenate and initiation as the very life of the local church, converting regularly with the help of annual cycles, us old timers as well as newcomers. And its partner, the full, conscious, active participation of all the baptized in the Sunday celebration — the celebration you serve with your musical gifts.

Scripture says the love of God is like the love of one another and vice versa. It does not say "belief in," it says "love of," and we know well how elusive love is — in the churches as well as elsewhere (but with less excuse). So we are here to pray and think about love in connection with both our cultural diversity and the music that serve liturgical celebration. And about how cultural diversity, like all of our other diversities, is a gift of the one God who *alone* is judge and whose word is the only norm. And about how faith saves us from idolatry, from absolutizing our own limits (the limits of our selves, our many groups, and *all* of our leaders), frees us from the prison of those limits so that we can learn from and be enriched by others.

Most of us here are graced with an acceptance not only of the gift of Christian initiation, the priesthood of believers, but also of the gift of a specialized ministry (within the common ministry of the entire body of Christ) dealing with the heart and center of the churches' life: worship, primary theology, "the primary and indispensable source," in which Bible and sacrament offer the promise and communicate the experience of the reign of God. The reign of God not merely as the afterlife, but as the world's business, the world's vocation — liberation and reconciliation for every individual and every group, including especially those we think of as "the least."

As commentators have pointed out, the liturgy is in total story-and-action what the parables of Jesus are in stories alone. They form us not by arguing from where we are to where God wills us to be, but by creating a scene that shocks us with the necessity of making a personal decision. Parable and liturgy are not rational exercises, after the manner of the local teacher or professor. They put us in unfamiliar territory, deprive us of all our excuses and supports, and leave us no alternative but to take sides in a struggle. They do not give us little lists of DOs and DON'Ts — no matter how urgently we demand them or pretend them. They do not give us the "answers" — no, they ask us to grow up and develop a conscience of our own and figure out with the rest of the human race the concrete, little, tiny steps we can make here and now toward that reign of God, that justice and peace, that liberation/solidarity. They create a scene even more disturbing than our private efforts. And in that scene, problems become evident, discrepancies between the biblical-sacramental experience of God's reign and our status quo, so that active, conscious participants are moved to an "amen" in deeds as well as words.

So the liturgy with its biblical stories and its simulation-in-action of a social scene in which yokes of oppression crumble into dust and diversity is not obliterated but appreciated and reconciled — that liturgy assumes and therefore demands that barriers of hate, prejudice, "superiority" are laid low and that all of our idols (including the flag, in the tiresome tizzy we experienced this past summer), all the powers and principalities which claim the kind of dominion over us that belongs to God alone, are relativized, deprived of their pedestals, seen as the creatures they are. It graces our status quo with the vision of where we are supposed to be going. We act out the reign of God, where we are without distinction equally loved, equally invited to make our own the revealed truth of God's words, equally reverenced and honored with water and incense and kisses and touches, equally sharing the holy plate and the holy cup. In other words, liturgy is where on that holy day we experience the liberation and reconciliation in God which are also our mission in this world of ours. To add a dimension to the author's probable meaning in the Epistle to the Hebrews: "All of these died in faith. They did not obtain what had been promised, but saw and saluted it from afar . . . they did not obtain what had been promised. God had made a better plan, one which includes us . . . " (11:13, 39-40). We see and we salute from afar.

How can we keep from singing when we not only experience with our sister and brother believers the kind of world we hope for, but also and even share a specialized ministry crucial to making that experience as involving and moving and glorious as it should be? Music is of the essence of a human and social celebration, whose nonverbal, symbolic communication is the more adequate expression of the mystery and the vision! Where the celebration is an experience, that is its content. Because it is so different from our various and partial situations and beings, in any given time and place, it always exceeds our grasp. So it keeps us pilgrims, on a journey, in process, all the time. But every little step we make in our individual lives and in our political-economic-cultural lives is a holy and God-like work, a making straight the way of the Lord, a smoothing of the rough places, a leveling of the hills, a filling-up of the valleys. "How beautiful upon the mountains are the feet of those who bring glad tidings" (Is 52:7). Or, as Paul quotes and interprets the prophet Hosea: "Those who were not my people I will call 'my people,' and those who were not loved I will call 'beloved'" (Rom 9:25).

How can we keep from singing when, with all of our limits and our sins, our different cultures and ways, our warts and handicaps, our weaknesses and discouragements, we are so invited and charged to be a small part of such a process, such a pilgrimage . . . and to be dealing with such dynamite? Of course, you know as well as I do that this picture is pretty idealized, is not your average Sunday experience. Partly because its participants (ministers included) do not yet believe and agree and desire and labor that it should be. Partly because the well-established custom of finding it all "in the book" is still very much with us and with our clergy. Partly because we do not yet take music, the other arts, gesture, movement, signs as seriously as a true body language must. Partly because liturgical reform gets lip service but not yet the money, competence, time, energy, commitment it requires . . . .

I emphasize what I think are basic principles for all our local efforts — attitudes and norms to guide our local efforts. Our modesty as fragments, partial creatures, our liberation from feelings of superiority, from any and every patronizing attitude, is a rock-bottom basic. We cannot do anything right in our ministries if we are still carrying around the burdens of sexism, racism, anti-semitism, homophobia, and other manifestations of the tendency to make one's self, one's group, one's culture the "norm," the "standard" that measures all the others. While it is true that life has laid these burdens on every single one of us (none has escaped), it is also true that God can and does liberate us.

So when we plan and celebrate in our local assemblies, we are modest about our own gifts, for most of us are limited to one musical tradition, and we recognize that every distinct cultural group in that assembly needs some liturgical musical experience in its own idiom for the sake of the "full, conscious, active participation of all." "Let no one be superior to the others. Never the one above the other . . . Never the one against the other." All enrich and teach each other if our fears and suspicions, our self-centeredness and self-aggrandizement do not cut us off in isolation.

How can we keep from singing when we repent and open up and discover the many hues and colors, the strange and wonderful experiences, the interesting approaches and insights, the special gifts which no fragment of the human family lacks . . . of all those "others," those "different" ones, those "odd" ones, those "perverts," those "aliens," those "strangers"? That is why no individual believer can stand alone and no local church (not even the Roman Church) can stand alone. All believing communities are miserable signs of a reign of God that explodes into our scene when we assemble on Sunday and both liberates and reconciles all of God's created variety, not in competition but in harmony, not as higher or lower but as equals, not as majority or minority but as testament to the wondrous and multiform beauty of a human race, finally, with God's grace, beginning to understand itself.

LITURGY AND THE ARTS

30

The Vesting of Liturgical Ministers*

In a speech accepting the 1970 Nobel Prize for Literature which he
wrote but could not deliver, Alexander Solzhenitsyn boldly
proclaimed the belief that "falsehood can hold out against much
in this world, but not against art." Some of what he wrote for
that occasion should be held in the memory of all Christians who
take public worship seriously, especially those with responsibilities
for planning or conducting the same: "So perhaps that ancient
trinity of truth, goodness and beauty is not simply an empty,
faded formula as we thought in the days of our self-confident,
materialistic youth? If the tops of these three trees converge, as
the scholars maintained, but the too blatant, too direct stems of
truth and goodness are crushed, cut down, not allowed through
— then perhaps the fantastic, unpredictable, unexpected stems of
beauty will push through and soar to that very same place, and in
so doing will fulfill the work of all three. In that case,
Dostoyevsky's remark, 'Beauty will save the world,' was not a
careless phrase, but a prophecy?"[1]
   One of the curiosities of these otherwise encouraging first decades of our broad, profound and soundly based twentieth century
church reform is the obvious fact that beauty and the arts still fare
so badly. As the editor of *Worship* wrote in last November's
Chronicle,[2] beauty and the arts remain low, if mentioned at all, in
the lists of priorities, interests, commitments of both present and
future leaders of the faith communities. I do not think it is a case
merely of our capitulation to a culture whose orientation is

Worship, March 1980

   [1] *Washington Post* (27 August 1972) B1, B4.
   [2] *Worship* 53 (November 1979) 550.

capitalistic and militaristic and whose ways are scientific, technological, pragmatic — a culture, therefore, that is in dominant ways
anti-Christian, anti-play, anti-feast and anti-fantasy. Because some
facets and strains of our reform have moved us to brave and
forthright challenges to that same culture's domination, we are
capable of serious criticism. We have proved ourselves willing to
suffer the crowd's disapproval. For freedom, for justice, for peace,
for important things . . . but never for beauty and the arts, never
for play, never for the festivity that belongs to liturgical celebration. Never for those arts that theologian Joseph Sittler called "the
supreme record of all that gladdens and saddens and maddens
human beings."[3]

It is no reflection on the great Second Vatican Council nor on
the renewal movement generally to point out its still fairly narrow
character and to pray (not for a return to the tidy and unreal
preconciliar ecclesiastical ghetto) for the broadening of its vision
and the intensification of its efforts.

I wonder whether the reactionary and counter-reformation activity evident in the current papacy and in recent actions of the
Congregation for the Doctrine of the Faith would be possible at
this early date in perhaps the most thorough and best-equipped
reform the Church has ever undertaken if it were not for our
preoccupation with the cerebral and the verbal? If it were not for
the fact that the only life we look for, want, or are capable of appreciating is that of the mind? And the horror with which we
view such narrow and repressive measures is increased because
we have so little else, we are so alienated and estranged from our
rich tradition of symbolic act, we are so bereft of those "stems of
beauty" which could "push through and soar to that very same
place."

Because liturgical celebration — and the arts which make it an
experience of beauty as well as of faith and prayer — is not yet in
the running. Biblical studies have achieved an appropriate and
basic place in the formation and education of candidates for
specialized ministries, but with an approach that tends to be too
limited and scientific to do justice to the liturgical character of the
books. So liturgy remains on the outside, at the tail end, unrecog-

[3] Address by Joseph Sittler, Lutheran School of Theology at Chicago, 29
April 1979.

nized, on the level of luxury rather than of necessity — even though it is an indispensable and major source of all theology, and the constitution, the symbolic expression and the major actual gathering of the Church now as always.

In his address last June at a conference on "Environment and Art in Catholic Worship," the archbishop of Milwaukee, Rembert Weakland, said that whenever someone asks him how to become a church musician he replies, "First become a musician."[4]

But that kind of fundamental, common sense respect for the arts of the human family is disastrously rare in the life of today's church. One fears to speculate about the time it will take before pastoral teams and liturgy committees begin to counsel prospective donors of materials for liturgical celebration and prospective ministers in the same way: "First become an artist." Or, appropriately and reasonably for donors: "First search out an artist who is attuned to the liturgy to create the object or to help select it." (Whether "it" is a space and its basic furnishings, or music, or a vestment, or a vessel, or a cross, or candlesticks, or a liturgical book, or a banner, or whatever.)

Such a respect for competency in the arts connected with liturgy is a right of the church, a right of the people of God. And clergy or liturgy committees who spend the church's money without consulting competent artists in the provision of liturgical spaces and the purchase of liturgical materials are unjustly trampling on the rights of the church.

Beauty is a human need that does not respect sex or color or class. Beauty is a human need more keenly felt as one's humanity is less encumbered by luxury and excess. It is true that we have tried to put beauty and the human arts in the class of "things" purchasable only by the very rich. But we have not entirely succeeded, even in the U.S.A., nor will we. Not only are the senses of the very rich so cloyed that they can scarcely take advantage of their economic power with artists and the arts, but also the latter are not always nor even mainly the sycophants that would enable them to do so. And the economically poor, the depressed and oppressed groups, in witness to an irrepressible and marvelous human instinct and capacity as much as to their aversion from the

---

[4] Marquette University, Milwaukee (4 June 1979).

inhuman ugliness of their urban environments, are frequently precisely the ones who can show the rich how to celebrate, how to have a feast, how to care about beauty and the arts, how to go "all out" for an occasion.

My subject in this article is the vesting of liturgical ministers (the term is plural) for purposes of public celebration. I cannot attend to that subject, however, without further preliminary but extremely relevant remarks. In our culture one is expected to offer an apology before one presumes to divert the attention of even a small segment of the citizenry to any question of environment, or art, or beauty, or symbolic action; especially if the purpose of the diversion exceeds established limits (like the cleaning up of the earth's atmosphere) and ventures to fantasize about the creation of an atmosphere-environment that enables people to have certain kinds of feelings about themselves, about their dignity, their beauty, their mystery, their deep-down freedom and oneness through their relation to God.

One is permitted, of course, even in our culture, to have an anthropological interest in human ritual action and to be tolerant of its persistence in such otherwise admirable faith communities as those of Jewish and Christian persuasion. As everyone knows, those synagogues and churches are redeemed by their ethical preoccupations . . . which quite certainly are as unrelated to their rites as they are invisible in the concrete economic life of the world.

To talk about liturgical vesture in this kind of scene is like proposing the value of clowns at a meeting of the American Medical Association or the National Association of Manufacturers or the Joint Chiefs of Staff. Very like it. Not only because our church gatherings apart from liturgy bear striking resemblances to those of the Pentagon, the AMA, and the NAM, but also because what we are proposing when we talk about liturgical vesture in a traditional way is both beauty of form, color, texture, and the value of clowns — the great value, the inestimable value, the transcendental value of clowns. We are talking about the first of the "three essential ingredients" which Harvey Cox says a festive occasion (like liturgical celebration) must have: "1) conscious excess, 2) celebrative affirmation, 3) juxtaposition."[5] Part of the liturgical minister's

[5] *The Feast of Fools* (Cambridge: Harvard University Press 1969) 22.

service to the rest of the assembly is, like that of the clown, to incarnate some of this *conscious excess* of festivity. Dressing up in an uncommonly beautiful and colorful way is part of that service. Gesturing in uncommonly broad and public ways is another part. Occupying with graceful movement the assembly's ministerial chairs and ambos and tables and the rest in a way uncommonly assertive of divine grace and human dignity is another part. I could go on.

But we cannot understand this service unless we understand ministerial functions in a church in which the sacraments of initiation (baptism-confirmation-eucharist) constitute the fundamental ministerial delegation. Those sacraments at the climax of an initiation process constitute the church as covenant community, all of whose members have been baptized into the priesthood of Jesus Christ, baptized into the mission of a ministering people. Once we get a few things straight again about initiation, about our all being part (clergy and religious, too) of one church, the basic meaning of which is the joining of hands in common discipleship with a common dignity, a common mission, a common struggle — then and only then will we have a chance of recovering some clear sense of the specialized ministries (full-time or part-time, professional or amateur, stipendiary or nonstipendiary) which that church-of-the-baptized calls, trains, and ordains or commissions according to its needs at particular times and in particular places.

Such a sense of the particular specialized ministries begins with their subordination and service to the church as a whole. Far from diminishing the traditional roles of bishop (including the pope), presbyter, deacon and other ministries that have been found serviceable through all or at least great parts of our history, this sense of their subordination and service to the community of sister and brother believers offers the firmest foundation for appreciating them, understanding them and valuing their offices. "Different ministries in such an assembly do not imply 'superiority' or 'inferiority.' Different functions are necessary in the liturgy as they are in any human, social activity."[6]

Certainly the priority that the churches in communion with the Roman church have given to the maintenance of unity, to joined

[6] *Environment and Art in Catholic Worship* (U.S. Bishops' Committee on the Liturgy 1978) 23, n. 37.

hands not only within the local church but also among the churches, has been well served by the collegial character of the episcopal office, with the bishop of Rome as head, and by the same character in the presbyteral office in each area with the local bishop as head. Such personal bonds of unity among the churches, in addition to creeds and codes and sacraments, are neither irrelevant nor inappropriate for churches of personalist faith. Flesh and blood bonds for an earthy communion, a joining of hands, even when the hands are, as they always are, dirty. To begin to see these two colleges of ordained ministers in terms of communion, rather than simply in the turgid and legal language of jurisdiction and stepladder authority, is to begin to understand the Church as sacramental reality.

It is also to begin to see why it is so important for Catholics (and not, understandably, for those whose ecclesial priorities are more cerebral and dogmatic or more spiritual and ethereal) to celebrate the eucharist, the great central sacrament of the church, with the presiding ministry of a bishop or presbyter in collegial relationship with the other churches. That kind of relational context of eucharistic celebration is not merely a matter of satisfying some obscure legal requirements, not merely a matter of "validity" or "liceity" (assuming that we know what those terms, so alien to the symbolic sphere, mean). The presiding action of bishop or priest incarnates, makes tangible, the communion, the joined hands, of all the churches . . . or as many as we can get together in hard times. It is a dramatic illustration of the fact that one does not destroy but rather restores the specialized ministries of bishop and priest when one relocates them in and of the church, instead of dangling somewhere up above.

The restoration of the episcopate and presbyterate, practically speaking, to the church, as essential services in the local community and bonds with the other churches, is the companion of another ministerial rediscovery close to the heart of current reform efforts. The community of faith, if it is living and exercising its mission, needs a variety of specialized ministerial services, none of which are exclusively liturgical and all of which have a liturgical component and climax. In addition to bishops and priests, who have been visible all along, we now see permanent deacons, vocal and instrumental musicians, readers, acolytes, ministers of communion, ushers, and so on. (Soon we must stop ordaining candidates for the presbyterate to a "diaconal" ministry — a stepping-stone "diaconate" — incompatible with the restored and important permanent diaconate.)

Although the liturgical function of each ministry is the climax rather than the fulfillment of its service in the ministering Church, this recognition of a variety of gifts as well as of needs in the local community assumes a corporate visibility in liturgical celebration. No longer does the priest stand alone facing a congregation — at *any* liturgical celebration. Many ministries should be in evidence, each acting appropriately, beginning with the ministry of the assembly. The effective functioning of women in these roles will certainly mean the end of male hegemony in the ordained ministries also. In fact, all that I have noted thus far will, I think, force us to drop the irrelevant qualifications which have mesmerized us since the days when monasticism became the clerical model. Then we can adopt qualifications for each specialized ministry which are scrupulously relevant to the function in question.

With these preliminary and critically relevant developments before us, we can proceed to discuss the vesting of specialized ministers for liturgical celebration. Like so many sense experiences which rationalist types dismiss as trivial, liturgical vesture has a considerable impact on the feelings of the assembly as a whole as well as on those exercising a particular role of leadership. Anyone who, contrary to the most elementary human experience, persists in the stubborn conviction that ideas, points, arguments are the stuff that move human beings, is natively unfit for liturgical leadership, if not for liturgical life. Even the homiletic moment of celebration is being scrutinized anew by many of those whose tradition makes much more of it than Catholic tradition does. Don M. Wardlaw, professor of preaching and worship at McCormick (Presbyterian) Theological Seminary in Chicago, reminds his students that people change when their imaginations "are captured by new visions, when they receive images of new possibilities in grace":[7] "Preaching that reenacts God's saving events in scripture, therefore, is necessarily grounded in the narrative genre. If form is to arise from content, if sermon shape is to participate in

[7] *Eventful Sermon Shapes*, address, McCormick Theological Seminary, Chicago, 17 May 1979, p. 15.

God's word in scripture, then the sermon will be structured on narrative lines. The basic movement of the sermon will be eventful more than argumentative, dramatic more than discursive."[8]

There is a modest and essential place in every liturgical celebration for human rhetoric, but it is a modest place, subordinate to the proclamation of the word of God in Scripture, subordinate to the symbolic action of the whole assembly. Implied in all this is the conviction that what is most important about public worship is that we gather the sisters and brothers together for a festival, a special occasion, a celebration of the reign of God (not yet terribly evident in daily life nor in the institutions of society), that helps all of us feel so good about ourselves, so important, so dignified, so precious, so free, so much at one . . . not as escape, not merely in distinction to daily routine, but in judgment, in the Lord's judgment on those ways and institutions. A celebration of the reign of God that goes way beyond the tight little, drab, rationalistic, verbose, pedagogical exercises we sometimes try to make of it — all those dreadful "themes" that we love — into a large, broad, fully human landscape, where Jesus is truly the first-born of a new humanity, and where our other liturgical tools (festival excess and colors and tastes and textures and odors and forms and touches) penetrate the Babel of our words and points and arguments to heal the human spirit and to raise it up in the covenant community's vision of new possibilities. Good liturgical celebration, like a parable, takes us by the hair of our heads, lifts us momentarily out of the cesspool of injustice we call home, puts us in the promised and challenging reign of God, where we are treated like we have never been treated anywhere else . . . where we are bowed to and sprinkled and censed and kissed and touched and where we share equally among all a holy food and drink.

"The vesture of the officiating ministers and their assistants is one of those factors [making up the totality of the liturgical act], secondary in themselves, which contribute to the total effect of the celebration, and is therefore deserving of serious attention . . . any move toward the abandonment of distinctive liturgical vesture (except in extraordinary circumstances in which other considerations may take precedence) is folly. Functionally, it can only create

[8] *Eventful Sermon Shapes*, 8.

confusion; theologically and historically, it can only suggest a contempt for the continuity of the Christian worshiping tradition which is pastorally intolerable; aesthetically, the 'ordinary dress' of the western and westernized societies of our time, whether formal or informal, must surely rank among the least attractive forms of clothing which the human race has ever devised.''[9]

I think it is fair to say that the rich and the comfortable feel the kinds of liturgical needs I am discussing at this point the least. People who know they are oppressed, who have to struggle for survival, are much more likely to appreciate the need for an outrageous feast in the midst of obvious famine. It is no accident that the choirs of black inner city churches are festively vested, while those of middle-to-upper congregations look as drab on Sunday as they do in their supermarkets or their offices. Nor does the hispanic fiesta feel a moral obligation to duplicate in its celebration the miserable conditions of everyday life which so many of its celebrants are forced to endure. It takes the grim, pursed lips and the non-sequitur thinking of an Anglo type to come up with and publicly articulate the notion that if excess and ''waste'' and frivolity are eliminated from liturgical celebration it will somehow contribute to a reconstruction of the social order. (''Order,'' of course, is in this use a euphemism.) In T. S. Eliot's words, ''You must not deny the body.''[10]

The U.S. Bishops' statement referred to above has a simple and straightforward explanation of the purpose of liturgical vesture: ''The wearing of ritual vestments by those charged with leadership in a ritual action is an appropriate symbol of their service as well as a helpful aesthetic component of the rite. That service is a function which demands attention from the assembly and which operates in the focal area of the assembly's liturgical action. The color and form of the vestments and their difference from everyday clothing invite an appropriate attention and are part of the ritual experience essential to the festive character of a liturgical celebration. . . . The more these vestments fulfill their function by their color, design and enveloping form, the less they will need

[9] W. Jardine Grisbrooke, in *The Study of Liturgy* (New York: Oxford 1978) 488, 492.

[10] *The Complete Poems and Plays, 1909–1950* (New York: Harcourt, Brace & World 1971) 111.

the signs, slogans and symbols which an unkind history has fastened on them. The tendency to place symbols upon symbols seems to accompany the symbolic deterioration and diminution already discussed."[11]

Aidan Kavanagh is helpfully more specific about the character of liturgical vesture: "The General Instruction of the Roman Missal is categorical in stating that the beauty and symbolic value of the vestment must derive from its material and form rather than from its ornamentation. The vestment is a garment, not a costume. Its sacredness in turn derives from the nature of the events in which it is worn. Since these events are not trivial, neither can the sacred garment afford to be trivial. . . . Vestments that are trivial by the standards of the culture that uses them, or vestments that are serious according to norms other than those to which the act of worship itself gives rise, not only transgress the authentic sentiments of the community but comment on a shift of Christian sentiment into areas foreign to the basic purposes of Christian worship — areas such as aestheticism, triumphalism, saccharine emotionalism, or cheap tastelessness. The liturgical garment then becomes less than sacred, a mere vehicle for applied 'symbolism' chosen at whim; less than a garment, a mere costume, overly ornamented and ignoble in form; a billboard whose purpose is to shout ideologies instead of clothing a creature in beauty."[12]

Perhaps it needs to be said that the subject of this article has absolutely nothing to do with the question of a special or distinguishing dress for ministers outside of liturgical celebration. The fact that the two unrelated issues are sometimes confused has damaged and is damaging the celebration of common prayer wherever clergy and others have become convinced that the abandonment or radical transformation of traditional ritual vesture is an effective way to attack the disease of clericalism. Like the presider's chair, liturgical vesture has become an innocent victim of those whose anticlericalist intentions are far superior to their common sense regarding human social activities.

Ironically, those faith communities that have confused these issues generally seem to end up with a "solution" that involves a

[11] *Environment and Art in Catholic Worship*, p. 46, nn. 93, 94.

[12] Aidan Kavanagh, in *Raiment for the Lord's Service*, ed. Christa C. Mayer-Thurman (The Art Institute of Chicago 1975) 14–15.

sole vested minister (naturally, the bishop or presbyter) and all other functioning ministers in ordinary dress. Compounding the irony, the chasuble (and its garment function) frequently is thrown aside in favor of a stole (which has never been anything but a status symbol). That these "developments" could be regarded as a blow against clericalism boggles the mind.

I would be happy to see clerical garb in daily life and work go, because I think its minuses far outweigh its pluses (taking into account, as we must, our history of clericalism and the needs of a reform already sufficiently discussed here). The issue is debatable and can be debated elsewhere.

These pages, therefore, are concerned *only* with the use of traditional vesture for leaders (all leaders) in the public worship of the church. Aidan Kavanagh describes the function of liturgical vesture as twofold: "to act as insignia designating the diversity of liturgical ministries, and to contribute to the dignity of the rite itself."[13] Clearly, vesture in this traditional view is a part of one's ministerial service in the assembly. A combination of capitalist, competitive individualism and an almost total lack of collective consciousness have contrived to see in liturgical vesture a minister's self-assertion, but that curious "explanation" would be incomprehensible in other cultural circumstances.

Perhaps the churches in communion with Rome can learn from the experience of an earlier reformation that one's first thoughts about such matters are not always best. Presbyterian Horace Allen talks about the continuing "temptation to vest" among Protestants and, although writing in terms of one presider rather than a diversity of ministers, comes back to a profoundly traditional view: "With reference to the role of sacred garment, this theological proposal would shift the significance and functioning of these sacramentals from their reference to the wearer to the definition of corporate occasion. In just such a sense a Catholic author very recently declared that 'the most important visual aspect of worship is the gathered congregation' and further, that 'picture' inevitably includes the leader or president as a visible focus. His or her garments are 'sacred' therefore, not by association with himself or

[13] *Raiment for the Lord's Service*, 13.

herself, but with his or her function within the community and the garments' functioning for the whole community."[14]

Catholic tradition in this matter, although distorted by the same history that shriveled up symbolic action in general and made its current restoration and "opening up" so difficult, is quite consistent and of long standing: the two basic liturgical garments common in the West today — the alb and the chasuble — were the ordinary dress of at least many people (male and female) in the dominant cultures of the first few centuries of Christianity. They were retained by the church for liturgical use when they passed (gradually) out of secular fashion during and after the barbarian invasions. Grisbrooke points out, however, that even while they were still ordinary secular attire very special ones seem to have been used for liturgical celebration, since a fourth century emperor, Julian "the Apostate," charged Christians with dressing up in special clothes to worship God.[15]

Christa C. Mayer-Thurman says plainly: "The vestments of earliest Christendom were a second set of clean secular clothing."[16] Just whose clothing they were is still debated. Cyril E. Pocknee says one thing: "We may say that the garments now hallowed by long usage as the ceremonial dress of the Christian minister at the Holy Communion are derived from the dress worn by the Roman citizen, both male and female, in the first centuries of the Christian era."[17] While Peter F. Anson says another: " . . . in its [the chasuble's] original form it was nothing more than a large semicircular cloak, covering the whole body, with a hole in the top for the head to pass through. . . . Cloaks of this type were worn by the middle and poorer classes who were not legally Roman citizens. . . . It was known as *phenolion* in Greek and *paenula*, or *planeta*, in Latin. [It was] invariably bell-shaped, i.e., rather like a cope with the front edges joined. In fact, the two garments were in origin the same. . . . The chasuble would have been made out of a semicircle of cloth with the straight edge folded over in the middle and the two borders sewn together."[18]

[14] *Raiment for the Lord's Service*, 23.
[15] *The Study of Liturgy* (n. 9 above) 489.
[16] *Raiment for the Lord's Service*, 43.
[17] *Liturgical Vesture* (Westminster, Md.: Canterbury 1961) 13.
[18] *Churches: Their Plan and Furnishing* (Milwaukee: Bruce 1948) 189–90.

There is not space here to review all known subsequent developments in and additions to this basic liturgical wardrobe. Obviously
the chasuble, at first common "to all liturgical ministers,"[19] was in
time reserved to the exclusive use of the presiding minister at the
eucharist, the bishop or presbyter. Then the alb ceased to be
merely an undergarment, so that we now have two distinct types
of alb use — one as undergarment, another as *the* vestment — and
should therefore have two distinct types of albs. Two types are
available, but, unfortunately, many parishes seem to prefer using
the undergarment as outer garment, thus unnecessarily adding to
the visual disappointment if not dismay they regularly inflict upon
their assemblies. The undergarment type alb is easily distinguish-
able: cheap material, partly open in front, tied with strings at the
neck, made without reference to the size of the wearer so that it
must be hitched up with a cincture in use. An alb used as outer
garment (as by acolytes, readers, ministers of communion, and so
on) should be of sturdy material, cut for the wearer (no cincture),
hanging in folds, with ample sleeves, and buttons or zippers to
eliminate gaps.

The chasuble is the principal eucharistic vestment, the outer garment, the one whose design and form and texture helps to focus
the action of the assembly and whose massive color relates to
feast and season and festive celebration. The traditional pattern,
described above, produces horizontal folds when the arms of the
presider are raised. Newer patterns with even more ample use of
cloth produce vertical folds. In either case, the chasuble is the garment that covers the body entirely, from neck to foot. Neither bib
nor apron, the chasuble should help the wearer feel that he or she
is wearing something important, something that urges grace and
dignity in movement, something that serves the festival excess
and the clown function of liturgical ministry. If the design of the
chasuble is convenient for the most efficient movement and frail
enough for comfort in the hottest climate, it is probably entirely
unsuited for liturgical celebration. A chasuble sufficiently reduced
in size and quality to meet these criteria (as happened in the medieval period and still characterizes most vestments sold and used)
will lack the dignity and visual impact necessary for its corporate
and celebrational function.

[19] Kavanagh, in *Raiment for the Lord's Service*, 13.

The happy fact that both alb and chasuble were originally unisex garments is an encouraging if less than decisive stimulus to the hopes and struggles of many of us for a universal recognition in the churches that we need the services of women also, appropriately gifted, trained and called, in *all* specialized ministries, rather than in just a few. Our traditional vesture for the liturgical functions of all ministries presents no obstacle to the ordination of women. Admittedly, this is a small consolation in view of the heavy weight of our cultural sexism, but it is worth noting.

The Art Institute of Chicago's 1975 exhibition, with the same title as the book that it produced, drew attention to the historical vicissitudes of this and other liturgical garments: " . . . vestments have gone the full cycle, from very simple, generously cut robes, made of silk, linen, or wool, to the rich, elaborate but most distracting achievements of the later centuries, to contemporary re-introduction of early Christian simplicity in purpose, form and function."[20] This is true, but our self-congratulations should be tempered until the "contemporary re-introduction" is more successful and general than it has yet become. Current neglect of the arts and of any real concern for beauty in worship is evident in vesture as in all other aspects of public worship today. I suspect it was a commercial entrepreneur earlier in this century who decided that if he or she could somehow make the stole the principal vestment and the high-priced item, he or she could make a killing. At any rate, it happened. And our American pragmatism and efficiency (both natural enemies of liturgical celebration, with its excess, its lack of "purpose," its reluctance to hurry, its clear preference for idle play over productive labor) clasped the barbarism to its bosom.

At first, the fad merely faded the chasuble into insignificance, reducing it from a strong, colorful, textured garment to a drab and neutral insipidity, worn according to the rules but now *under* the stole. The latter, therefore, became the sole focus of color, which it had never been before in its history: broad, ornate, lending itself to the talents of volunteers and amateurs who could never have tackled a chasuble . . . and even to ecclesiastical graffiti. Stoles were easy to make, required less cloth, were lightweight (in

[20] *Raiment for the Lord's Service*, 11.

more ways than one). And in this dispensation, the chasuble no longer mattered. It was half hidden anyway. If it had any form, any folds (vertical or horizontal), it was so obscured by the stole's pretensions that it was lost. That kind of chasuble could be made with one's eyes closed, run off the assembly line like Fords . . . or Edsels.

Of course, one no longer has anything like the focus of form and color and texture that the chasuble at its best had offered to the assembly and the celebration, but the parish has probably saved enough cash for an extra toilet. There is nothing new about "developments" like this. We have had these experts with us in the church from the beginning. They led us from the breaking of the bread and all that inefficiency and cost and mess right on up to the practical and "pastoral" (and cheap) little wafer that we know and love today. They showed us how to take that clumsy old baptismal bath and hone it right down to a practical and "pastoral" size — a trickle of water across the forehead. Under their aegis, at various times in our ecclesial history, we have systematically removed the guts from almost everything we do in sacramental worship . . . until the twentieth century Vatican II reform we almost had, or are almost having, begun to recall the dangerous and powerful language of symbol, began to open up those old symbolic acts and their materials and let them speak the inimitable tongue of dreams, imagination, senses and the heart.

It was only a small step further to the abandonment of the chasuble altogether, an accomplished fact in many American parishes and other faith communities. So one sees the alb, usually the undergarment type, festooned with this band of color and ornament, and one wonders when the Geneva gown will sweep our clearly commercial market, imposing on the faithful an appropriate sobriety and ridding liturgical celebration of this last vestment, this last vestige of festivity and fun.

I would find it hard to regard the disappearance of the stole as a great loss. It belongs to those vestments that came into use considerably later than the alb and chasuble: dalmatic, stole, cope, bishop's mitre and pastoral staff, archbishop's pallium. Most authorities see the stole originating in an ensign worn by Roman consular officials.[21] Peter Anson has a more vivid story, worth

[21] *Raiment for the Lord's Service*, 35; *Liturgical Vesture*, 21.

repeating even if it has been largely discredited: "The stole was originally a large linen handkerchief thrown over the left shoulder by the deacon at mass — rather in the same manner as a waiter carries a napkin when serving a meal. It was used to cleanse the sacred vessels. As time went on, linen cloths — now reduced in size and known as purificators — came into use, the deacon's stole ceased to have any practical purpose and became a mere ornament."[22]

That's the trouble with the stole. Whether its origin is a senatorial or consular status symbol or as Anson describes, it ends up being "a mere ornament." Whereas the alb and chasuble are garments for clothing the human body in a way that serves one's neighbors by pleasing them. Estimates vary widely as to when deacons generally began to use the stole and when bishops and priests adopted it as a part of their vesture, under the chasuble, under the cope (which was simply the chasuble form with an opening down the front, for processions, or the hours, or other services or ministries), or simply atop the alb. Like the no-longer-existing maniple, the stole seems to lack both a clear function and a strong claim. Originally a narrow scarf, it could have been worn on the outside of chasuble or dalmatic at times, but never in such a manner or of such a size as to hide or displace or obscure the chasuble's function.

Whatever one concludes about other vestments — whether those that came into and passed out of existence in our history or those still in use — Anglican Pocknee's verdict is sound, clear, and probably more hopeful than accurate: "By common consent throughout the whole of Christendom, it is the chasuble and alb that are the proper vesture for the Holy Communion."[23]

He means for the presiding minister, of course. In the centuries of relatively rigid, frozen and unadapted liturgical celebration, there was a redeeming common feeling that everyone (clergy, religious and parish pets included) was under the same liturgical discipline, and that the rites *belonged* to the whole community. Among all the good things that have happened to that rigidity and formalism since the Council, it would be tragic if people otherwise well disposed to necessary reform and the newness al-

[22] *Churches: Their Plan and Furnishing*, 186.
[23] *Liturgical Vesture*, 17.

ways required of the disciples of Jesus were to be made to feel that the assembly is governed by the whim of a minister rather than by the tradition of the church. Pastoral adaptation is as delicate and difficult as it is essential in the life of a faith community. It is a collegial operation precisely because it would be such a liturgical and ecclesial disaster if people were to feel that their ministers are free of the ritual discipline which the rest of the church has accepted. The obvious visual impact of liturgical vesture means, at least, that there must be evident, clear and strong pastoral reasons for basic alterations. Departure from the colors which have been traditional for the different feasts and seasons since the thirteenth century or so is another matter, of lesser consequence, but even in that area the colors associated with Lent and Advent and with the great feasts seem to me to merit a general adherence, depending on local custom.

If a greater variety of liturgical celebrations, in addition to the eucharist, becomes common in the prayer life of the church, then the cope (an adaptation of the chasuble without its eucharistic associations) might well become more common as the presider's garb — for morning or evening prayer, reconciliation services, communal anointings of sick or aged persons, and similar functions. But these are not apt to become popular as long as the eucharist is celebrated as frequently — daily and, in some churches, several times a day — as it now is.

Meanwhile, we have the gratifying and rapidly spreading employment of many other active, functioning, specialized ministers, especially in Sunday eucharistic celebrations: instrumental and vocal musicians, acolytes, deacons, readers, ministers of communion, ushers (all of whom are more or less regularly functioning and visible in very many urban parishes), as well as guest preachers, audiovisual experts, mimists, actors, dancers (less frequently seen and in a smaller number of parishes where trained talents are available).

Ideally, of course, all of the variety of functions of leadership in liturgical celebration should be done by ministers who have been selected by the community because of talents related to the function, who have been trained for the function, and who are actively involved in other (not exclusively liturgical) ministerial activity in the local church (for example, in parish administration, work with sick people, with old people, with religious education, with youth, with social action, with ecumenism, with poor people, with minority and/or oppressed groups). I referred above to the principle that any office of specialized ministry in the faith community is 1) not exclusively liturgical, 2) ordinarily climaxed and celebrated in a liturgical role, frequently one of active leadership, in any case one of active participation in the Sunday assembly. Normally also, since these are all roles of leadership, they are appropriately filled by adults.

The parishes of the United States (or anywhere) where these roles are visible in their variety and multiplicity in Sunday celebration merit unqualified congratulations. Given our background of several centuries, with its quite ordinary pattern of solitary priest facing a congregation, the speed with which we have responded to the Council's call for recognition of different gifts among us and our need of one another is remarkable. It is also salutary in the deepest sense, because this recovery of a variety of ministries enables all kinds of other recoveries which are part of our reform and renewal effort. Women's rights in the church; minority rights in the church; a pattern of clericalism which had isolated bishop and priest; a language and attitude about ordinary Christians that assumed passivity and disinterest — all these questions and more are decisively moved toward solutions by the rapid emergence of these nonclerical, nonordained ministries.

Before I discuss their place in the assembly on Sunday, when they are functioning as leaders, and the matter of their vesture for those functions, let me mention another of the ordained clergy: the deacon. I mean the permanent deacon, of course, since I do not understand the other kind.

The deacon has a traditional outer garment, the dalmatic, worn over alb and stole. Apart from the complicated question of its origins, the dalmatic can be urged as festive garb (for the same reasons by which I advocated the chasuble for the presider), especially since several of the other ministers may well be wearing the alb also. The dalmatic invites an appropriate liturgical attention to the deacon's critical ministry in the community, focusing the community's care for women, minorities, poor people, groups that are oppressed, exploited, or despised — all the gospel's favorites. When the deacon reads the words of the gospel or the intentions in the general intercessions, the whole assembly can use the visual aid of his or her vesture to help feel its own responsibility for and involvement in diaconal ministry.

With regard to other liturgical ministries, ordinarily undertaken by adult members of the community who are not bishops, presbyters or deacons, but who are normally chosen, trained and commissioned by the local church (the Sunday assembly): current practices regarding their physical place in the assembly and their vesture or lack of same convince me that they could do with a bit of examination and reflection. Some of those practices are becoming popular simply because some parish started them and nobody has had time to train a critical eye in their direction.

It is very difficult to be consistent in a period of reform and renewal. In one aspect we move ahead, in another we lag behind, in one area we begin to see more clearly, in another our ingrained habits cramp our vision. In talking about the place and vesture of ministers, I must assume that we have renovated the liturgical space as a whole, so that we have one space (not a series of spaces: nave, choir, sanctuary) with the assembly seated for maximum visibility, audibility, eye contact and active participation. The presider's chair is in a place that enables him or her to have frequent eye contact with the other ministers and the entire assembly. Chairs for the other ministers who are actively involved in the leadership of the act of public worship are in places convenient for their function(s). This includes the musicians who must be in the best place for their twofold task: leading the assembly in song and singing to the assembly.

With this kind of physical environment and arrangement, we should be free of the old clericalist assumption that a ministerial chair stands for separation from the assembly. Just the opposite, it stands for service to the assembly. So there is nothing to be gained and much to be lost by the well-intentioned but essentially destructive practice of having ministers sit unvested in inconvenient places in the assembly only to pop up and privately process when their time comes. For a time, people can be very patient with this kind of labored point-making, but it rapidly wears thin. All of the ministers in a given celebration, whether it is Sunday mass or any other rite, are supposedly functioning as a team of leaders, to facilitate, to enable, to make things as smooth as possible, as conducive to prayer, to beauty, to dignity, to gospel. We are not there to make things difficult in order to make a point, or to make things as clumsy and ugly as possible, to prove our "spiritual" superiority to sacramental worship. One has to take oneself a bit more seriously than any good liturgical minister should if one has to make even one's seat in the assembly a manifesto. A good clown has to dress up and act differently from the people he or she loves in order to please them, in order to serve them, in order to image them. A good liturgical minister has to do a bit of the same, dressing up, performing a choreographed function with other ministers and the whole assembly, to enable the kind of experience people have a right to seek in worship.

Let's not make a big deal then out of appropriate places to sit and appropriate vesture to please the eye for the whole team of specialized ministers at the assembly's celebration. Both are as natural as apple pie. It would help if we would all think a little more about our service in the assembly and a little less about ourselves and our antisacramental prejudices. We will get over the latter a lot sooner if we stop coveting them as "virtues."

Exceptions, of course, would be the ushers or hosts, whose place is not in reference to altar, ambo and presider's chair. Another possible exception would be the ministers of communion where there are very many (since we now need two cup bearers for each plate) and who may choose to approach the altar only after the Lord's Prayer, returning to their places after holy communion.

But certainly deacon, acolytes, readers should be seated formally and ministerially to face at least part of the assembly, the presider, and to be proximate to the places where they function. If they do not wish to cast a frowsy pall on the entire celebration they should be vested, at least in an alb (the outer garment type). On special occasions they might use copes as well. Everything I have said above about vesting for liturgical leadership applies to all of them as well as to the presider. The beauty, the choreography of movement, the festival and celebrational feeling of the act of common prayer, the worship event, depends on the willingness and ability of all the leaders (the team of specialized ministers) to accept and fulfill their roles. That means looking and acting as if you are doing what you are, in fact, doing: not trying to duplicate the status quo of the planet's life, but facilitating the creation of a whole new scene, a scene of the reign of God, where momentarily we are out of the clutches of the military-industrial complex and its uniforms (which are our ordinary clothes). If everyone in the eucharistic assembly could be vested in traditional liturgical garments, that too would be appropriate, but it is clearly out of the question. The assembly that gathers to nourish its fighting strength with an experience of the reign of God has a right to ask this much of those it calls to leadership roles of service.

Instrumental and vocal musicians, if they have a front and visible place, should also consider vesture — choir robes. And all specialized ministers and ministries should be part of the worshiping assembly from the beginning of the service to its end. We want no ministers who simply drop in for their moment of leadership and then retire. A Christian rite is an act of common prayer that has a beginning and a middle and an end, and that we all do together in its entirety. . . .

31

There's Nothing Like a Professional Musician!*

The difference between the professional and the amateur in any art or craft or other human skill is not in sincerity or native talent or (as the word "amateur" suggests) love of the work. In the field of instrumental and vocal performance, both professional and amateur may be sincere, talented, and in love with music. We need both in liturgical celebration, and we have not been sufficiently conscious that we need the former. The difference, it seems to me, is that the professional has put *all* of his or her eggs into the one basket: has undergone training which tests both talent and application and which offers a basis for a continuing, undivided development of the art and has entrusted the vital matter of livelihood to its fragile bark. There is a faith and trust here that involves a deep and many-faceted personal commitment. It distinguishes professionals quite clearly from even the most gifted amateurs and volunteers. It is perhaps hard to describe but easy to experience.

Prophets, pioneers, the liturgical movement and the General Council in the '60s have made the churches in our time again keenly aware of a variety of specialized ministries within the common ministry of the baptized, a distinction of roles in liturgical celebration as elsewhere. But the period immediately past (and still gnawing at our vitals) had succeeded, with the aid of the printing press, in overwhelming the spatial, visual, sonic and body language of liturgy with its almost exclusive book and textual concern. Regaining our balance is a slow and painful healing and it is not surprising that the arts (even that primary liturgical

*Worship, September 1986

234

art of music, called "necessary" and "integral" to the liturgy by the documents of reform) were not the first remedies to be sought.

Lately there are encouraging signs that churches which have long ignored our patently desperate need of the ministry of professional musicians are beginning to seek it, to budget for it, and to employ and pay such ministers. Not only the liturgical principles I espouse but my lifetime's experiences in the Sunday assembly *convince* me that this awakening, this awareness of our need of gifts we have slighted for so long, is critical for the kind of liturgical celebration that will enable and encourage the living, moving, deep experience of word and sacrament to which the assembly has a right. *Significando causant.*

Recently, a reputable school of church music noted a growing number of inquiries and applications from people desiring to prepare for music ministry in Catholic churches. Since, at least in this country, the churches in communion with the Roman church have been the slowest of the major Christian communions to enlist the aid of professional musicians, this is good news. The same school sponsored this summer, for the first time in its history, a week-long session specifically on Catholic liturgy and music.

It is the parish budget, of course, that indicates where our real priorities are. In this connection, a friend in the St Paul-Minneapolis archdiocese sent the results of a long-range budget survey in one of the parishes there: "Respondents ranked seven operating budget priorities on a scale of one to seven — one being the highest, seven the lowest priority. The results were: Liturgy and worship was given the highest priority by parishioners with a ranking of 1.52."[1] . . .

The appearance of *Worship III*, the new hymnal from the Gregorian Institute of America, is for me another happy sign. Musician friends tell me it is an improvement on *Worship II*, which was our chief resource for the assembly as a whole during my last five and a half years of parish work, in the best liturgical music situation I have ever known. It was a relatively small (with the Sunday assembly appropriate to the 150-year-old space) urban parish. Its budget commitment not only put good hymnals in the

[1] *Crossroads*, Nativity of Mary Church, Bloomington, Minn. (February 1986) 4.

hands of the assembly and a rich and varied repertoire in the hands of organists and its two choirs but also sought, hired and paid professional musicians: a full-time choir director/organist and a part-time assistant; two part-time cantors; and several members of a mixed volunteer/professional choir for the principal Sunday celebration. As a consequence, the congregation sang its parts with a thrilling confidence and strength. In my judgment, that concern, respect and love for the art of music in the liturgy — in concrete terms, that budget — was a principal cause of the general participation in those assemblies, of their beauty and their experiential quality.

The conciliar Constitution on the Liturgy and its implementing documents have asserted the same thing in their way, but they remain largely unheard. Experience, when we are fortunate enough to find it, teaches as nothing else can. Even the ruefulness which this experience of recent years makes me feel about my own past ignorance and omissions, while unpleasant, is a plus. Like the Jewish and Christian constant biblical refrain of repentance, the regret we feel when experience reveals our past shortsightedness is less a burden of guilt than a newness, an opening up to growth, progress, evolution. Its focus is not the past but the newly realized possibilities of the present. At any rate, it is a fairly common experience for me, probably because I write out homilies and addresses and tend to keep them too long. We do grow, in spite of ourselves, and to be open to that process, to change, is one of God's great gifts.

It is not the fact that music is a specialized ministry in liturgical celebration which demands the leadership, help, support and strength of professionals. Many specialized ministries are handled well by volunteers, because they concern themselves simply with the proper and effective rendering of what is given them — a function, a text, a pattern of action. The demands of the art of music in our rites exceed immeasurably the demand of other specialized ministries, excepting only that of the presiding minister and preacher (where we also rely on professional commitment). A living church with a living liturgy employing living arts desires and needs, from at least some of its musicians, much more than mere vocal or instrumental competency.

Theologian Joseph Sittler called art "the supreme record of all that gladdens and maddens and saddens human beings." It is a record that opens our world and culture to us all. Art is one of the ways we reveal ourselves and our world to ourselves. In large measure we may be the products of our environment and education, etc., but when art's creative process seizes us we become more than we are, mysteriously more than there is any explanation for. And somehow our slender, fragile talents can reach beyond the limits of ourselves, our time, our place, to illumine in some way the human journey. Art enables a lifting of our hearts. Whenever they settle down and get sluggish, art touches the imagination and moves us again to the quest, search, pilgrimage, to the path of change and growth. The arts repeat in action the words that Samuel Beckett's *Rockaby* has that old woman dying in her rocking chair utter over and over again: "more . . . more . . . more. . . ."

The arts serve us, not by reflecting the popular will, not by getting stuck in any particular historical stage of their development, but by reverencing the tradition so much that we carry it on — by envisioning all the possibilities of the present, putting where we have been together with where we are and then letting the interior gifts of the artist blaze a trail. Like every art, music sees nature, the world, humanity, everything not as inert, static, fully developed accomplishments of the past, but as en route, on a journey, full of promise and as of yet unrealized possibilities.

Liturgy is symbol, is full of what has been called "the inaudible language of the heart." The choreography and the gestures of worship communicate a valuing and a caring that defy verbal definition. But there is an audible language of the heart, also, that likewise exceeds our words. And that is the language of music. That is why music is indispensable in the Sunday assembly of the believing community. We cannot allow our celebration of God's epiphany in the world, creation, covenant, law, prophets, and in the Christ, our celebration of meaning and purpose in life, to be deprived of this language of the heart. Our celebration is stripped bare and made lifeless without music. Not only must certain texts of the rite be sung, because they are songs — and, unlike Bob and Ray, we do not say songs — but the symbolic act in its entirety is a realization in the raiment of all the talents of the community of that reign of God which Jesus enfleshed and demonstrated. *All* the talents! Not merely our little cerebral points one, two and three. Before God we can be, must be, whole, together in ourselves, as well as commonly one with our sisters and brothers.

"Give to Caesar what is Caesar's, and to God what is God's." We can be, perhaps must be, divided in the sphere of our daily roles and functions, lesser loyalties and obligations. But that must always be within the sphere of wholeness, where we are fundamentally undivided and before God. That is why liturgy is anticipation of the full realization of God's reign, because all the oppression and division of the status quo is reduced by a unique and social (ecclesial) intentionality to creature-size and totally subsumed into the sphere of wholeness.

We cannot be whole without music. Music is not a decoration applied to the liturgy, like icing on a cake. Music is not an ornament on a liturgy that is substantially intact without it. Music is an integral part of liturgical celebration because it is an integral part of a whole human communication, of a full, rich human celebration.

What the liturgical assembly asks of the professional musician is, first of all, to be an artist and to contribute to the life of the community of faith the historical appreciation, the imagination, the vision and the technical skills of the artist — not as an alien or from "above" (like the old clericalism), but as an important and critical ministry, among the variety of ministries and gifts which all the members of the assembly contribute to its communal existence. When one forgets the art one is dealing with and trying to achieve excellence in, then one can talk forever about ministry and it means nothing because one has nothing to contribute. The ministry, the service of the musician depends equally on mastery of the art (a continuing process) and on identification, at least in basic biblical faith, with the assembly.

Then, whether one's art is vocal or instrumental, one approaches the task of music ministry in the Sunday assembly as a participant, attending to every part of the rite (not only to those parts which involve music), standing together with all the others before the mystery of the Holy. No human strutting or swaggering, no status-consciousness or self-assertion is appropriate. That is basic.

It's a neat trick (but also a *sine qua non* of service in liturgical celebration) to take one's art, one's special gift, with seriousness, love, commitment, and yet to assert the priority of our utterly common situation with all the other members of the assembly before the Holy One. The clergy fail in this so frequently that we dare not be too hard on musicians. But striving for it is crucial. All different, all equal, all needing each other's gifts.

What the liturgical assembly asks of the art of music is as complicated as it is hard to define in practical terms: quality and appropriateness. Quality — competence in the art — an experience of such beauty and elevation of the human spirit as will facilitate an almost tangible sense of the Holy, the Other, the Beyond . . . God. Quality that only good musicians can create. Quality that makes the liturgical celebration an expression of the very best that this time, this place, this community has to offer.

And appropriateness. Which means that musicians need to have a feel for liturgy, for the action, the movement, the rhythm of the rite, for its feasts and seasons and the scriptural word proclaimed, as well as the supper shared. We need professional musicians, musical specialists, but we also need them to be fully human, sharing human concerns, including worship, and especially sensitive to our need of an experiential Sunday assembly.

I do not mean the kind of soupy, self-centered, sentimental experience which so much of the trivial music available supplies in abundance (and which so many believers mistake for progress). I mean an experience that is awesome, full of wonder, worshipful, even stunning. The rejection of autocratic methods and decisions (which in their long reign guaranteed neither quality nor appropriateness) should never mean a lowering of standards. Collegiality does not mean reducing everything to the most ordinary, the most common denominator. Collegiality is a return to a more ancient and genuine tradition of communitarian and consensual decision making. It means respecting each other and each other's competencies. If the new committee acts like the old autocrat, we will get the same unfortunate results. We must stay within our various competencies and operate out of them. So the committee should be the seeker of professional help, not its pretender.

Our need of professional musicians, who earn their livelihood by their total commitment to music, in no way suggests that we do not need the thousands and tens of thousands of volunteer and amateur musicians who have served and are serving our public worship everywhere. The latter, more than any of the rest of us, know how much we need expert leadership, how much the ministry in which they have been engaged and to which they have been dedicated is improved when its cantors, choirs and instrumentalists enjoy the leadership, the added strength, techniques, repertoire and vision of the professional. Far from opposing each other, they are complements.

Epilogue: Response to the Berakah Award*

Thank you, sisters and brothers. I do not feel I merit this award, but that's all right. Awards are gifts, and this crowd has some experience of grace. So I am glad to have my feelings overruled. Although age has tempered the desperation of my perennial search for approval, it has done nothing at all to slake the thirst. You will be relieved to learn that I do not interpret the Berakah Award as an endorsement of any of the stubborn and sometimes singular views I hold (and I do hold many, and I hold them dearly!). However, the fact that it comes from you whose work it has been my pleasure to attempt to interpret, as well as from you other interpreters, gilds the lily of this honor.

More important than my private delight is the salute to the improbable existence of The Liturgical Conference which I — and I hope many of you — see as implicit in this event. It seems to me that only The Liturgical Conference — with its sound Benedictine roots, its voluntary membership, its unofficial status, its innocence of the economic determination of almost everything, its remarkable corporate freedom from self-seeking, and, since the '60s, its ecumenical character — could offer a focus orthodox and innovative, traditional and pastoral, to a movement threatened by sudden exposure to unprepared reaches of the Churches, by fads and fancies and the fast buck. If I have done anything that merits your recognition, it is because that association enabled it . . . in every way.

The North American Academy of Liturgy, from its genesis in the Scottsdale meeting organized by John Gallen and the Franciscan Renewal Center in 1973, also has resisted the predictable professional temptation to narrow its scope to comfortable dimensions,

*Worship, July 1982

carefully abstracted from the web of life. It has demonstrated breadth and catholicity of concern, a welcoming of inconvenient relevancies — qualities inviting and endearing to eclectic amateurs like me. (One of the memories that has sustained me is that of Boone Porter's description of an amateur, in one of his pieces on ministries, as one who loves what he or she is doing. It should be obvious why I am partial to Porter's definition.)

Three years ago on this occasion, Horton Davies quoted the reply of Dean Inge to a question about his background. Asked whether he had ever studied liturgiology, the dean replied, "No; nor do I collect foreign postage stamps."[1] Like the dean, I have not studied liturgiology in any systematic or adequate way. Unlike the dean, I regret the fact, even though it probably is responsible for a certain lack of inhibition which has proved helpful almost as often as it has proved disastrous. Nor can I claim ecclesiastical status of any consequence. Currently, I am a temporary assistant priest at St Joseph's Church in Greenwich Village, Manhattan — a situation which I consider happy, and a veritable mini-academy with Bob Lott on the staff and Bob Rambusch an active parish leader . . . but which, at my age of sixty-one, hardly can be considered a notable achievement.

So I have had Georgia on my mind ever since President Don Saliers' call last October: wondering what the citation might say, speculating about the kind of mood that must have swept over that meeting of the Academy Committee — devil-may-care? . . . festival excess? . . . a yielding to chance prompted by a dart board in the local pub? It is fortunate that no one receives this honor while still young enough to be intoxicated by it.

There were some giddy moments. Some of you must remember the "Dreams of Glory" cartoons by Steig in *The New Yorker* of the '50s. The old favorites danced in my head — a phenomenon which may interest those with the psychological bent that seems to preoccupy an excessive number of the clergy in our time. Each cartoon in that series portrayed a crisis scene, with a child-hero in a posture of complete command of the situation, and all of the other characters in total disarray. Mr Steig produced them by the score. One was captioned "Getting the Serum Through to the

[1] *Worship* 53 (1979) 371.

Stricken Settlement"; another, "The Catch that Saved the Series";
"Thirty-eight Days at Sea," and so on.

Fortunately, my annual holiday depression took care of those
brief fantasies. By the time I got around to preparing remarks for
this banquet and festive occasion last week, its full, morose weight
was lying heavily upon me. So you are getting the real me: a
genuine Scandinavian melancholic, happily startled by the slightest suggestion of light amid the encircling gloom. When one has
been sixty-one years at sea, Steig's thirty-eight days sound trivial.

And, somehow, the more I hear of all the definitive judgments
of all the stars with whom our culture is mesmerized, the more
"at sea" seems like a damned good place to be. Our star syndrome (not only in the entertainment industry but also in ecclesiastical and civil affairs and roles of leadership), the product of
a technology that far outstrips our general evolution, reduces us
all to the level of observers and consumers of the star's reaction,
the star's judgment, the star's opinion. One thinks nostalgically of
the day when popular leaders — even bishops of Rome and elsewhere — communicated in a less immediate and overwhelming
manner . . . when an event or a problem would come to our attention long before the star's judgment, so that we had to turn to
our scriptural and liturgical resources (just imagine!) and assume
the human responsibility of forming an opinion . . . when there
was time for the Spirit and us — all of us so inclined — to make
this kind of contribution to the *sensus ecclesiae.*

I wouldn't be going to the corner every night at eleven for the
early edition of the paper, or jealous of opportunities to watch the
TV news, if I were not grateful for contemporary technology in
communications. But its dangers for the human community in
general and for the community of faith in particular are evident.
The judgment comes with, or even before, the fact, with the
speed of greased lightning. Oh, to be at sea again, and to let our
resources in Scripture and liturgy have a chance in the Sunday assembly to get beneath our preconceptions! To let the Epiphany star
eclipse all the glittery media prefab commentary! To be encouraged
to make the human journey from data and problem to judgment
and conviction! How much easier it must have been, before the
Vatican and the local chancery vied for the evening tube, to see
the bishop as personal symbol of our oneness and communion,

rather than star, or substitute for our resources, or even antagonist!

As I said before, I consider my gifts and contribution to our common enterprise to be chiefly in the realm of interpretation. At the risk of boring you, I cannot go on without saying something about my youth and the thanks I owe to persons and institutions who have fed and enabled me at every turn. The text that comes to mind for this is from a country music lyric: "I borrowed the shoes, but the holes are mine." Interpreters have a way of bending their borrowed shoes all out of shape and leaving them full of holes, but without those shoes we would be confined to the straitened circumstances of our own limits, and that would be intolerable! Time is short, so I can touch only a few highpoints.

Since I have been known to complain about the covenant community, I had better begin this hymn of praise and thanks with a general and overarching expression of gratitude to the church. And that means what lovers of tautology call "the institutional Church," since there ain't no other kind. Long before I knew anything about Christian initiation, the conditions of my childhood made church my foster home. In the space of my first twenty-four years, Lutheran, Methodist, Anglican and Roman Church homes nurtured and sustained me — in a way that made their commonness much more impressive than their coveted distinctions. I don't mean to imply that the commonness was always a *plus*, but it was always there.

Even though my parents were estranged from church, more or less, they saw to it that I had a Christian catechetical formation and my first liturgical experiences in Minnehaha Norwegian Evangelical Lutheran Church in Minneapolis. Now I remember almost nothing of those years, but I know and thank God that they are part of me. To Simpson Memorial Methodist Church and the youth movement to which it introduced me, I owe a tremendous conversion to the social implications of the gospel, to a conviction that God's reign of justice and peace begins with conversion and faith (with baptism's symbolic death) rather than with one's departure from this mortal coil (as so many Christians seem to believe and so much preaching seems to imply). And there was launched my literary career, with the editorship of a mimeographed Oxford League paper.

The Methodist youth movement of my high school and early

college years opened a world of excitement and exploration to me and in me. Critical opinions about militarism, racism, capitalism and developing pacifist and socialist convictions which remain with me to this day had their genesis and foundation in that experience of gospel as political and economic love. Mahatma Ghandi, A. J. Muste and the Fellowship of Reconciliation, Dorothy Day and the Catholic Worker movement, Norman Thomas and the Socialist Party, Bayard Rustin and the Congress on Racial Equality were among the influences of the time. In the same period, I met (through his books) P. G. Wodehouse, who kept me laughing and contributed substantially to my love of the English language and of the art of writing. High school journalism and the *Central High News* furnished a laboratory.

A scholarship at Hamline University, the decision to become a ministerial student, a Methodist Uniting Conference in Kansas City, and the presidency of the Minneapolis Council of Methodist Youth (I think the only presidency to which I have been elected) — all conspired in 1939 to open up some new areas of awareness: public worship, the nature of church, ecumenism. These led to a group of writers in the Church of England, A. G. Hebert among them, who proved to my not entirely unprejudiced satisfaction the congruency of a radical social critique with catholic tradition.

I had to quit college after two and one-half years to work full-time and help out at home. Selective Service claimed me in '42, classified me as a conscientious objector (on appeal), sent me to a Civilian Public Service (C.P.S.) unit in New Hampshire about which Gordon Zahn has written a book called *Another Part of the War: The Camp Simon Story*. During my last year at Hamline, I had become an Episcopalian, drawn to an historic Christian heritage that elevated liturgy and church unity to primary status, and without surrendering any of my Methodist-gained social conscience. Anglican sobriety, sense of tradition, discernment of essentials, humanity and love of the arts — all made an indelible impression on me. (It seems to me now that I was biting off more in those days than I could possibly digest, but it was an expansive time.)

Antipacifist animus forced like-minded folk close together in that decade. The new friends — several to be lifelong — whom I met in C.P.S. (ours was probably the only camp with a sizable Catholic contingent) brought another frontier into my life. *Catholic*

Worker people there made Dorothy Day and the movement an even greater influence, and other new friends revealed a variety and depth in Roman Catholic life that I had not suspected. One of them, an artist committed to church work, converted an old camp shed into a chapel in which a group prayed compline at night. Another, in my second C.P.S. unit, had attended St John's University in Collegeville, Minnesota, and told me about something called the liturgical movement and its prospects in the Roman scene.

War-related issues, of course, dominated that period, and I joined a further protest walk out from the system. The War Resisters' League supplied our bail, each of us drew a different judge, and we waited in Chicago for our trials. With the clear prospect of a three-to-five-year sentence, I thought seriously about many things. What had been taking shape in my reading, conversations, feelings, friendly pressures of Anglophile Romans and Romanizing Anglicans, together with a book called *Spirit of Catholicism* — all had a part in my decision in 1943 to become a Roman Catholic. Received into that communion the night before my trial, I had an opportunity during four unexpected trial postponements to pursue the new idea of a possible alternative of study in that formidable establishment. After much rejection, I was directed by a letter of rare kindness (from the then-rector of Theological College in Washington, D.C.) to St John's Abbey in my home state. When my case was transferred eventually to the courtroom of a retiring judge (who had nothing to fear from government pressure), I was granted probation. St John's accepted me without money or diocesan affiliation.

I felt at home almost at once, finished college, stayed for seminary under the aegis of Aloysius (later cardinal, I'll have you know!) Muench, then bishop of Fargo. I marvel more now at all the happy circumstances involved than I did then. I can't imagine another place where I could have *survived*, with all my snotty opinions and brashness, much less where I could have been initiated into the savingly ancient Benedictine tradition, an orthodoxy untainted by Counter Reformation hysteria, the writers and speakers and visitors who gravitated to such an oasis, patristics with Godfrey Diekmann and dogma with Paschal Botz, prayerful and serious (if not yet sensitive to the demands of communication) liturgy, The Liturgical Conference and its Liturgical Weeks, H. A.

Reinhold, *Commonweal* magazine, *Liturgical Arts* quarterly, the Catholic Interracial Council, more of Dorothy Day, ''The Baroness'' and Friendship House, the Jocist movement, and writers like Evelyn Underhill, Guardini, Bernanos, Bloy, Chesterton, and especially Eric Gill with whom I felt a special kinship.

Those St John's influences continued to increase even after I was ordained and in pastoral work in North Dakota: Aelred Tegels' sharp discernment, the bombshell genius of Frank Kacmarcik (who should have apprentices following him around), Michael Marx and *Worship*, former students who kept our abbey-formed interests and discussions going. I continued to write when I could. Five years at the cathedral, five as pastor of a country parish (gratifications and struggles tended to balance each other off), and I was ready when Gerard Sloyan invited me to teach in his department at Catholic University. I never felt like a good teacher, but it was rewarding to work with so perceptive, learned and eloquent a man, to take classes under Quasten and others, to prepare for courses which exposed me to masters like Jungmann, Congar, Vann, Bouyer, Tavard, Rahner, Newman, Chardin, Weigel, etc.

You must be sensing by now, with some relief, that we are approaching the modern era. And the Second Vatican Council, which gathered what had been scattered. And The Liturgical Conference, which gave me the job I loved most (probably through the benevolent machinations of Frederick McManus, invaluable guardian of the movement, and Gerard Sloyan). For thirteen years I was privileged to write and edit on its staff, attempting to popularize what the council had made the Church's agenda of recovery and reform. Trying to interpret. Trying to be popular. Although, as you can gather from this capsule history, the language that I knew from these experiences was not exactly what was needed to bowl over the masses. Virginia Sloyan, Carol Campbell, Gabe Huck became close friends during those years, as well as coworkers. Virginia and Carol held us together somehow. Gabe was there for a shorter time. Virginia and Gabe fed me so many ideas that I eventually could not tell which, if any, were my own. Although I owe many, many people a similar tribute, I have to name from those years Aidan Kavanagh, Thomas Talley, Joseph Sittler, Harvey Cox, Kevin Seasoltz, William Stringfellow, and, a bit later, Ralph Keifer and Nathan Mitchell, in addition to both Sloyans and all the other persons I have mentioned earlier, for conversations, papers and other work which I have pillaged shamelessly, and from which I got lots and lots of mileage. "I borrowed the shoes, but the holes are mine."

At the same time, Washington, D.C., and some old friends with whom I had new contact brought me to an appreciation that amounted to revelation: of what Black culture had to offer me — something that had not been in the forefront of my thinking or my efforts to "do good to 'them' "! Martin Luther King Jr helped me tremendously and remains an inspiration.

More than any other popular leader I can remember in this country, King embodied not only the ends or goals I had learned to seek, but also the insistence on nonviolent means as the only possible avenue. And, between a tavern on Capitol Hill called "Mr. Henry's," which for years featured gospel singers every Sunday night, and a parish named after St Benedict the Moor, my faith life was enriched with the beginnings of an acquaintance with a spiritual and gospel song tradition that eventually captivated me . . . and remains my favorite liturgical music.

A small non-territorial "parish," Nova Community, in northern Virginia, gave me — after work in Washington parishes was no longer possible because of a pastoral position a number of the clergy had taken with regard to *Humanae Vitae* — positive experience of potential alternatives to the formal parish structure.

Enough of the past. Here we are, in 1982, with the U.N. moving rapidly toward world government, with the democratic socialists (heirs of Eugene Debs and Norman Thomas, like Michael Harrington) in Washington and the state capitals, with pacifists converting the war (defense) department into an agency for the development of nonviolent strategies, with an economy of guaranteed employment with worker and cooperative ownership, with the young educated and rejected and handicapped and old people cared for, with the churches reunited and lapping up their reign-of-God countercultural witness with the enthusiasm of cats at the milk bowl — the energies of my age group are just about exhausted. The marvelous thing about the institution called church is that, even in this idyllic situation, it continues to hold up cultural, political, economic realities to the pure light of the new Jerusalem . . .

so that e'en now, we turn to the God who makes us free and makes us one in any and every social context.

At any rate, I want a few more minutes of your time to look quickly at the current scene, to walk out boldly from under all those umbrellas of gratitude, and to express a few opinions. If no strategies are indicated, it is because I know none. The high point of my political career was in the seminary in 1948, when a few of us managed to amass fifteen votes for Norman Thomas, out of the sixty students. My political clout declined rapidly thereafter and has not since revived.

OPINIONS

I think that liturgiology suffers with the rest of Western and European theology from an excess of one, particular, small talent. We are so good at dissecting, reducing, analyzing, abstracting, that we can create a whole world of our own, self-contained, independent of church, world, people. The reduction and the privatization of everything that seems to be related to this genius for the abstract are perhaps why so many of us regard the "liberation theologians" as freaks. Because they have tired of our fascination with the abstract and are doing what theologians of biblical faith should be doing: reflecting in the context of the current problems of human beings. Elie Wiesel says: "Literature today must be an act of conscience; words are no longer innocent."[2] Can we not, must we not, say the same of the symbolic action we call liturgy?

I think that we have to find more effective ways of pursuing the enterprise of liturgical studies and the direction of liturgical renewal in engagement with the life of the churches. Thanks to the communications phenomena I spoke of earlier, we have a counter-reform flourishing, retaining old positions and even assuming new ones, long before our lumbering reform gets off the ground. If we believe in a living tradition, we have to be more honest about the severe limits of our contemporary (and certainly welcome) reform of liturgical books. To admit those limits is tougher than the task of simply substituting one thing for another, or simply adding on. We have to help each other and all believers discern the contradictions in our centuries-old habits. We have to help free each other

---

[2] In a public lecture at Loyola University in Chicago.

from the burdens of mechanical, instinctive, counter-productive activity. We should each have to write a thousand times: "No gain without loss; no life without death; no growth without letting go." We simply must be less sanguine about the ability of the faith community to keep swallowing the recoveries and insights and progress of renewal without any corresponding elimination. We all know what that leaves us full of.

I think that we have to work even harder at listening to and learning from the world we live in and the signs of the times than we do at listening to and learning from our roots and past. We are good, excellent at the latter; not yet at the former. Is the liturgiologist, any more than another theologian, permitted to limit his or her efforts to the earlier part of our tradition? If an anthropologist like Turner can confuse the marvelous and rewarding concept of ritual liminality with the superficialities of antique rite, as I think he does in his comments on Christian worship, then perhaps it isn't surprising that we should regularly condemn "archeologism" while continuing to suggest, approve, or ignore pastoral practices whose merit seems to lie in their relevance to an extinct, if fascinating, culture.

Those are general opinions, which should be specified a bit. You have to remember that being specific, in my case, means being Roman Catholic. But the sicknesses indicated are generic, and any of you can find your own applications. Besides, we all need each other's help in tackling the problems of any of our churches. I've been on edge all my life, as you should know by now. So, if there is a certain edginess to these opinions, please keep in mind that it is there with my full knowledge and consent:

1. I think that the RCIA and all that it entails (there's the catch!) will fulfill its function to the degree that it gathers and integrates most of the activities now scattered in parish life. It is certainly close to the heart of all our hopes for a rediscovery of the meaning of the local church. Yesterday Ray Kemp gave us not only information but also a genuine feeling for what the RCIA entails. If it is simply added as another program to a schedule already crowded with unintegrated activities, meetings, committees, programs, it is hard to see how it can become the atmosphere in which old timers and newcomers live the life of a believing mission together. To do its job, the RCIA must be somehow the aegis

under which adult education, sacramental preparation programs, liturgy planning committees, social action projects, and so on find their community locus and as part of which they operate.

2. I think that joining the movement for the admission of qualified women to the diaconate, presbyterate and episcopate is not only a demand of the gospel, of justice, and of our time, but also one of the very important means of recovering a genuine feeling in the churches that the assembly is the primary ministry and that specialized ministries — all of them — depend on it, rather than vice versa. This means cultivating the appearance of a variety of ministers functioning in the Sunday assembly — a development which is already, like RCIA, one of the happiest signs of our movement's small success thus far — and making sure that within that variety we have the clear visibility and experience of talented and trained women exercising roles of liturgical leadership (assuming that this corresponds to roles of leadership they are already exercising in the daily life of the faith community). This means also recognizing our need for a drastic overhaul of our methods of recruitment and training of specialized ministers and of our thinking about ordination and commissioning. Qualification for these latter must be related to the job to be done, and ordination must again be at the behest of the community.

3. I think that von Allmen is profoundly correct when he suggests[3] that Protestants falsified the Sunday assembly by making the celebration of the eucharist only an occasional part of the service, and that Catholics falsified the Sunday assembly by making the celebration of the eucharist an ordinary, daily event. I am convinced that we cannot have the kind of Sunday eucharistic celebration we now envision — one in which, for example, the gathering of the community is a primary element in the symbolic action — as long as we do not face the incongruency and contradiction inherent in our habit of daily mass. The needless multiplication of Sunday masses is another problem in many parishes, militating as it does *against* the coming together of the believers. As is our refusal to support our clergy honestly and to rid ourselves once for all of the stipend-simony connection — facing the loss which our gain in the general intercessions demands.

[3] J.-J. von Allmen, *Worship: Its Theology and Practice* (New York: Oxford University Press 1965) 225–27.

4. I think that the service-station-for-individuals definition of and approach to the local church is still dominant in most places and that all of our heroic efforts to promote a faith-community definition and approach are vitiated by institutional patterns that try to oblige both. I think they are contrary, and that we have to make a great number of extremely difficult choices . . . or we have to say that the parish is irreformable and that some new form must be found. My feeling that they cannot co-survive is not at all an appeal for a closed church or a "believers' Church." The local covenant community must still be open and the passerby welcomed. But the passerby, or the inquirer, now comes into a community to taste its life, not into a building in which individual and private consumers are served by a class of clerics. And pastoral work becomes community building, climaxed in roles of leadership in the Sunday assembly's common prayer, rather than the supplying of an endless stream of ritual services.

5. I think a carefully promoted growth in our acknowledgment of and gratitude for our dependence on Judaism as our mother and our relation to contemporary Judaism as a sister community of faith is a most important item on our agenda. Gerard Sloyan has stimulated this concern, but my own experience and feelings corroborate his witness. We must stop speaking of "old" and "new" testaments in the glib fashion which has been our common Christian heritage. We must stop making all those easy contrasts which have such shaky (or polemical) foundations in reality.

6. I think our culture's insensitivity to symbol, and to the noncerebral and nonverbal in general, is so rampant in us all, no matter how sacramentally minded we fancy ourselves to be, that we must struggle against it all the time, and must rely on competent people in the arts not only for their professional work (which we need in any case), but also for our own formation, to make us capable of dealing with a liturgical reality that is not a bundle of texts but a symbolic action.

7. I think that those among us who share an ecclesiology in which bishop and eucharist and the communion of the churches are all joined (and that seems to be a good ecclesiology) and who therefore find it problematic to participate in eucharistic celebration without some clear connection with our bishop should ask our bishops to authorize the participation of members of their churches

in eucharistic celebrations with a presiding minister of another church, at least for special occasions and until we get off our asses and reunite.

8. I think that we have an obligation to each other — particularly in this ecumenical association — to bring the full weight of our grasp of our traditions to bear on the exaggeration of any of our specialized ministries, but especially on that of the papacy, the bishop of Rome. Our greatest service to reunion, I think, is not in theological conversations and dialogues (which everybody loves), but in all the work necessary for the recovery of a modest papacy — a modest and winsome papacy — a presidency among the conferences of the churches and their bishops, relieving the bishop of Rome of the burden of so many trappings and so much grandiosity once considered ornamental but now appearing as pretentious camouflage concealing a necessary pastoral ministry.

These are a few samples of what I think are problems that confront us in these early years of the best-equipped reform the churches have ever undertaken. Our tools are marvelous. Our courage and perseverance, naturally, are more fitful. We need each other. This place, this time are the only place and time we have. The aim, the desire, the love right now is what is important — for seekers, for believers. The means is as important as the end, for the means creates the end.

You can disagree with any or all of these opinions, and we can argue. And, if my arteries are still sufficiently flexible, I may learn something from the discussion. But if anybody responds to these opinions by saying, "What's it all got to do with liturgy?" I shall not be responsible for my actions.

Thanks again.

Don E. Saliers

The Berakah Award for 1982

To Robert W. Hovda

We are awed by his gifts. But the gifts are not what we honor with the bestowal of the Berakah Award — rather the steward, and the stewardship. None of God's blessings has he squandered: high intelligence, gracious pen, ironic wit, deft persuasion through speech — all put to use in serving two relentless taskmasters, integrity and truth.

He will not know the sweet taste of power because he cannot compromise or flatter or adapt the message to fit the hearer's ear. He is busy about other things, and has been for some forty years: witnessing to peace and social justice; urging a Church to be what it might be and should be; caring passionately about the Church at public prayer. All the languages of worship has he spoken and spoken to: sound, silence, sight, movement, gesture, space; and always toward one end — letting those languages, and the symbols of faith, speak . . . to transform us.

Dr Saliers is professor of theology and liturgics in the Candler School of Theology at Emory University in Atlanta, and served as president of the Academy in 1981.